© CyberStern.com

Colin Beavan
NO IMPACT MAN

Colin Beavan is the author of two previous books: *Fingerprints: The Origins of Crime Detection and the Murder Case That Launched Forensic Science* and *Operation Jedburgh: D-Day and America's First Shadow War.* His writing has appeared in *Esquire, The Atlantic,* and *The New York Times,* and he posts regularly at www.noimpactman.com. He lives in New York City.

ALSO BY COLIN BEAVAN

Operation Jedburgh: D-Day and America's First Shadow War

*Fingerprints: The Origins of Crime Detection and
the Murder Case That Launched Forensic Science*

NO IMPACT MAN

COLIN BEAVAN

PICADOR   FARRAR, STRAUS AND GIROUX   NEW YORK

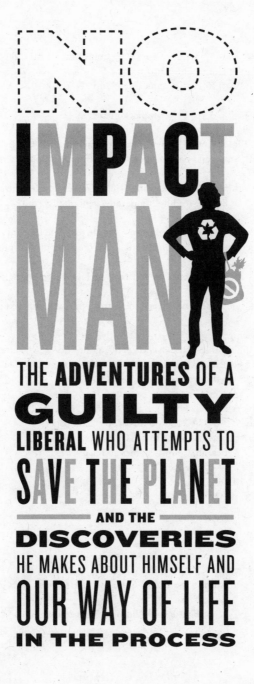

NO IMPACT MAN

THE **ADVENTURES** OF A **GUILTY** **LIBERAL** WHO ATTEMPTS TO SAVE THE PLANET ═ AND THE ═ **DISCOVERIES** HE MAKES ABOUT HIMSELF AND OUR WAY OF LIFE **IN THE PROCESS**

www.picadorusa.com

Picador® is a U.S. registered trademark and is used by Farrar, Straus and Giroux under license from Pan Books Limited.

For information on Picador Reading Group Guides, please contact Picador. E-mail: readinggroupguides@picadorusa.com

Grateful acknowledgment is made to Annie Leonard for permission to reprint material from the Story of Stuff project.

Designed by Jonathan D. Lippincott

The Library of Congress has catalogued the Farrar, Straus & Giroux edition as follows:

Beavan, Colin.
    No impact man : the adventures of a guilty liberal who attempts to save the planet, and the discoveries he makes about himself and our way of life in the process / Colin Beavan.—1st ed.
        p. cm.
    Includes index.
    ISBN 978-0-374-22288-8 (hardcover : alk. paper)
    1. Environmental protection—Citizen participation.   2. Sustainable living.   3. Beavan, Colin—Homes and haunts.   I. Title.

TD171.7.B43 2009
333.72—dc22
[B]
                                                    2009010188

Picador ISBN 978-0-312-42983-6

First published in the United States by Farrar, Straus and Giroux

First Picador Edition: June 2010

10   9   8   7   6   5   4   3   2   1

Printed on recycled paper

*To you, Michelle, with my deepest love
and the hope that you will always write on walls*

Our sages taught:

A man should not move stones from his ground to public ground.

A certain man was moving stones from his ground onto public ground when a pious man found him doing so and said to him,

"Fool, why do you move stones from ground which is not yours to ground which is yours?"

The man laughed at him.

Some days later, the man had to sell his field, and when he was walking on that public ground he stumbled over those stones.

He then said, "How well did that pious man say to me, 'Why do you move stones from ground which is not yours to ground which is yours?'"

—Talmud Bavli, Masekhet Bava Kama 50b

Contents

NO IMPACT MAN

How a Schlub Like Me Gets Mixed Up in a Stunt Like This

For one year, my wife, baby daughter, and I, while residing in the middle of New York City, attempted to live without making any net impact on the environment. Ultimately, this meant we did our best to create no trash (so no take-out food), cause no carbon dioxide emissions (so no driving or flying), pour no toxins in the water (so no laundry detergent), buy no produce from distant lands (so no New Zealand fruit). Not to mention: no elevators, no subway, no products in packaging, no plastics, no air conditioning, no TV, no buying anything new . . .

But before we get into all that, I should explain what drove me to become No Impact Man. To start, I'm going to tell a story that is more a confession, a pre-changing-of-my-ways stocktaking, a prodigal-son, mea-culpa sort of thing.

The story starts with a deal I made with my wife, Michelle.

By way of background: Michelle grew up all Daddy's gold Amex and taxi company charge account and huge boats and three country clubs and pledge allegiance to the flag. I, on the other hand, grew up all long hair to my shoulders, designer labels are silly, wish I was old enough to be a draft dodger and take LSD, alternative schooling, short on cash, save the whales, and we don't want to be rich anyway because we hate materialism.

Once, during a visit to my mother's house in Westport, Massachusetts, Michelle lay on the bed in my former bedroom and stared up at the ugly foam ceiling tiles. "You know, I grew up with much nicer ceilings than you did," she said. That, her facial expression seemed to say, explained everything.

My best friend, Tanner, meanwhile, once called me to tell me that his therapist had said that he "despairs of Michelle and Colin's differences." Why Tanner's therapist analyzed *my* marriage was a question best left for Tanner to explore in his next session, but the point was that Michelle and I had a lot to negotiate. And the story I'm telling here has to do with one of our negotiations.

For my part, I agreed to put up with the cacophony that comes with Michelle watching back-to-back episodes of *Bridezilla*, *The Bachelor*, and all the other trash-talk TV. I *hate* reality shows. Michelle conceded, on her shopping sprees, not to purchase anything made of or even trimmed with fur. That was the compromise.

Michelle liked a little fur. Not long fur coats per se, but fur hats and fur linings and stuff like that. Michelle was a *Daily Candy* girl, a Marc Jacobs white Stella handbag girl, a kind of *Sex and the City*'s Carrie Bradshaw grows up, gets married, and has a baby girl.

On the other hand, call me a pussy, but I felt bad every time I saw one of those raccoons or possums with their guts spilled out on the Palisades Parkway. I also felt bad for little animals getting killed for nothing but their skins.

Yet I managed to exempt, back then, my leather shoes from my concern that humanity puts vanity before kindness to animals. In the cold glare of my own I Want To Buy, my disdain for designer labels and all things consumerist became a little, shall we say, mushy. I was the type of guy who shopped for the fifty-two-inch television, then thought he was a rebel against consumerism because he bought the discounted floor model.

I don't mean to imply that I was a *total* do-nothing liberal. I did go to Pennsylvania to canvass voters in the 2000 and 2004 elections. I made get-out-the-vote phone calls for MoveOn.org when they asked me to. I tried to adopt some sort of an attitude of service in my daily encounters and to generally avoid doing harm. I volunteered at the World Trade Center site after 9/11. I even prayed for George Bush, on the premise that hating him just created a hateful world.

The question was, given the state of world affairs, whether I shouldn't have been asking more of myself.

A few months after our TV-fur negotiation, Michelle got offered a brand-new, thousand-dollar, white-fox shawl by a friend whose father is a furrier in Michelle's hometown, Minneapolis.

It's free and the fox is already dead, went Michelle's reasoning.

It's not one fox, it's *ten*, went mine. I've already suffered your freebasing bad television, and we have a deal about this, I said.

But those are *your* standards, replied Michelle. Then came her trump card: I want to discuss it at couple's therapy.

Not that what we actually went to was couple's therapy. What really happened was, I would drop by sometimes during one of Michelle's sessions with her own therapist. Anyway, I trundled along to the Upper East Side office, and Michelle explained the situation. Free fox shawl, on the one hand. No fur, on the other—which is Colin's standard. Why, Michelle asked, should I have to adhere to his ethic?

When the therapist turned to me and said, "Colin?" I surprised both of them by saying that Michelle could buy all the fur she wants. Except, I said, there's one condition to my releasing her from our deal—and here's the part where I look like a jerk—namely, that Michelle read out loud certain passages of a PETA brochure about the fur trade that I'd highlighted in green.

"I can read them when I get home," Michelle said.

"Nope," I said. "The deal is, if you want to renege on our fur deal, you read it out loud, here."

Sport that she is, Michelle grabbed the papers, cleared her throat, and began to read. Two results came of all this: First, Michelle decided that she didn't want to buy fur anymore because she actually has the biggest heart known to humankind and because we are nowhere near so different on the inside as we seem on the outside. Second—and here's the point of the story—I showed myself to be a smug little jerk. I had mobilized my intellectual and persuasive resources to get someone else to change her behavior, and remained, I saw, utterly complacent about my own.

It's true that I had occasionally tried to make a difference in the world, but I was coming to think my political views had too often been about changing other people, like Michelle, and too seldom about changing myself.

I made the mistake of thinking that condemning other people's misdeeds somehow made me virtuous. I'd become, I realized, a member of that class of liberals who allowed themselves to glide by on way too few political gestures and lifestyle concessions and then spent the rest of their energy feeling superior to other people who supposedly don't do as much.

A year or so later, news about global warming started coming out. I mean, it's been out for twenty years, but somehow it hadn't entered my liberal consciousness. We can't maintain this way of life, the scientists said, the world can't sustain it. The ice caps will melt, the sea levels will rise, there will be droughts—or, in short, the planet will be done for and millions of people will suffer.

> **I made the mistake of thinking that condemning other people's misdeeds somehow made me virtuous.**

The countries of the world had negotiated the Kyoto Protocol to the United Nations Framework on Climate Change, assigning mandatory targets for the reduction of greenhouse gases to signatory nations. But the United States, a signatory to the protocol, as well as the world's largest producer of greenhouse gases, refused to ratify it.

What had I done in light of our country's deaf ear to environmental concerns? Well, if it rained torrentially, I would say gloomily to whoever was listening, "I blame George Bush for this strange weather." If in conversation someone said global warming was just a theory, I'd say, "Actually, the scientists say it's a fact," and I'd also get a really angry look on my face to show just how adamant I was. And if it was so hot out that I felt the need to turn on both air conditioners, I'd sometimes even feel despondent for a moment or two about the fact that I was contributing to the problem.

Cut to 2006. At the age of forty-two, I have a little girl, Isabella, who is nearly one. We live on lower Fifth Avenue in Greenwich Village. It is January but seventy degrees outside. The middle of winter, and joggers run past in shorts. Young women from the nearby NYU dorm saunter by my building in tank tops.

I'm on the street. I'm walking our dog, Frankie. People around me are happy but I am not. Instead, I'm worried. I put the key in the front door of my building. I walk through the granite-floored lobby. I step into the elevator. The operator, Tommy, an older gray-haired man from Greece, says, "It's too warm, no?"

"Yeah, well, imagine how warm it would be if there was such a thing as global warming," I say.

I was being sarcastic, of course. People back then still argued about whether global warming existed. Not me. This was around the time when I had begun to feel really ill at ease. What I read in the news only confirmed, I believed, what I could already feel in my bones.

Summer seemed to toggle straight into winter, and then back to summer—the long fall and spring seasons of my childhood had disappeared. I'd witnessed, that December, a winter storm in which thunder clapped violently and lightning flashed the white blanket of snow into eerie green. Never in my recollection of northeastern winters had there ever been thunder and lightning in a snowstorm.

Tommy chuckled at my sarcastic remark. He threw the lever forward and the elevator lurched upward. After all, what could we do?

For the last few months I had traveled around, discussing a book I wrote about a secret Allied operation in France during World War II. For the last few months, in other words, I'd spent my time talking about sixty years' worth of yesterdays when I was really scared to death of what was happening today.

Here's what was on my mind when I rode the elevator that day:

I'd read that the Arctic ice was melting so fast that polar bears were drowning as they tried to swim what had become hundreds of miles between ice floes in search of food. Researchers knew this because they found their limp white bodies bobbing on the waves in the middle of the sea.

Worse: sometimes, too, desperate in their starvation, the polar bears cannibalized each other's young. We burn too many fossil fuels, the sky gets blanketed with carbon dioxide and other greenhouse gases, the planet warms up, the ice caps melt, the polar bears can't get to their food, they eat each other's babies.

You've heard it all before. But back then, in 2006, this was news, at least to me.

What really filled me with despair, though, was that I didn't believe that the way of life that was steadily wrecking the planet even made us happy. It would be one thing if we woke up the morning after a big blowout party, saw that we'd trashed our home, but could at least say we had had a rip-roaring good time. But if I had to generalize, I would say that, on average, the 6.5 billion people who share this globe are nowhere near as happy as they could be.

Leaving aside the people who have severely limited access to food and clean drinking water, so many people I knew, both in New York and elsewhere in the world's go-fast consumer culture, were dissatisfied with the lives they had worked to get—the lives they were supposed to want.

Many of us work so hard that we don't get to spend enough time with the people we love, and so we feel isolated. We don't really believe in our work, and so we feel prostituted. The boss has no need of our most creative talents, and so we feel unfulfilled. We have too little connection with something bigger, and so we have no sense of meaning.

Those of us lucky enough to be well compensated for these sacrifices get to distract ourselves with expensive toys and adventures—

big cars and boats and plasma TVs and world travel in airplanes. But while the consolation prizes temporarily divert us from our dissatisfaction, they never actually take it away.

And, to top it all off, I thought in the elevator on that unseasonably warm day, not only have so many of us discovered that we've been working our years away to

> **Back on that summery day in the middle of winter, I seemed to be hitting bottom.**

maintain a way of life that we don't really like, but we are waking up to the fact—I hope—that this same way of life is killing the planet. Thanks to global warming, we hear, the planet is facing, among other things, plagues of malaria, monsoons and hurricanes with unprecedented power and frequency, and a rise in sea level that will cause widespread destruction of people's homelands.

What things to have to think about.

Back on that summery day in the middle of winter, I seemed to be hitting bottom. At first I thought it was about the state of the world. Yet I had an inkling, as I rode in the elevator, that that wasn't it.

I'd been complaining to anyone who would listen, telling people that we lived in an emergency. Yet, as much as I complained, I lived and acted as though everything was normal. I just led my usual workaday life. Wake up, take my daughter, Isabella, to the babysitter, spend the day writing, pick her up, watch TV, start all over. I didn't feel I could do anything about world problems. After all, if the government wasn't doing anything, what could I do? Write another history book?

But is that what I wanted from myself? Is that what I was willing to accept? That I could be in a state of despair and do absolutely nothing about it? Was I really hitting bottom with the state of the world? Or was I hitting bottom with my state of self-imposed helplessness?

For some reason, that warm winter day in the elevator, I suddenly realized that my problem might not actually be the state of the world. My problem was my inaction. I was worried sick about something and doing nothing about it. I wasn't sick of the world. I was sick of myself. I was sick of my comfortable and easy pretension of helplessness.

Tommy brought the elevator to a stop at the ninth floor, where I live. It was just an elevator ride. It was just a couple of seconds. It was just a day when it is seventy degrees when it should be thirty. But I suddenly had these questions:

Am I really helpless? Is it true that a guy like me can't make a difference? Or am I just too lazy or frightened to try?

Winter leapfrogged into summer—another missing spring—and I had lunch with my literary agent, Eric Simonoff. We went to Beacon in midtown Manhattan, where lots of publishing types meet. Glasses clinked. Colleagues nodded. We were there to discuss my next book project.

"I can't write history anymore," I tell him.

"Don't tell me you want to write novels," he says.

Eric is accustomed to helping people like me to eke out a living from our writing.

"No, I don't want to write novels," I say, and then I launch into my dinner-party rant about global warming.

I inform poor Eric, who was simply trying to enjoy his lunch, that while reports pour in exclaiming the urgency of our environmental problems, government and big business move only at a snail's pace, if at all. We need, say the urgent reports, to reduce greenhouse gas emissions by 80 percent at the very least by 2050 in order to prevent global warming from spiraling out of control. Instead of acting, companies like Exxon use stealth PR tactics to discredit the organizations that try to warn us. Meanwhile, politicians try to "reposition global warming as a theory, rather than fact."

> **A sailboat ride west from Hawaii would soon have you crashing through a gigantic patch of floating plastic garbage, twice the size of the continental United States.**

I doubted, back then, that a Democrat in the White House would move a whole hell of a lot faster on the environment. In the voting booth, whether you pull the red handle or the blue handle, you always pull a big-business handle. And big business wasn't exactly filling the politicians' war chests with millions of do-something-about-global-warming dollars.

"What are we doing to our planet, Eric?" I cried, and continued my rant.

A sailboat ride west from Hawaii would soon have you crashing through a gigantic patch of floating plastic garbage, twice the size of the continental United States, that swirls around itself in the middle of the Pacific Ocean. Or you could go fishing and come up empty-handed in one of 14,000 Canadian lakes that no longer support marine life, thanks to acid rain. Or try going for a walk in the forest, hoping to see some birds but instead coming face-to-face with a big yellow bulldozer in the 32 million acres of woodland we chop down around the world every year to make toilet paper and disposable coffee cups.

Then there's what we're doing to ourselves. Here in New York City, for example, one in four kids who live in the South Bronx suffers from asthma, resulting largely from the exhaust fumes of trucks that haul away New Yorkers' trash. Meanwhile, experts find that an array of health problems, including lung disease, infertility, Parkinson's disease, breast cancer, prostate cancer, and childhood autism, to name just a few, are related to the unwholesome amounts of toxic chemicals we spew into our air, water, and soil.

So it's not that while trashing the planet the human race is having a party. Quite the opposite. We feel a malaise and a guilt that at another time in history might have motivated action, but that this time seems instead to be coupled with a terrible sense of helplessness.

My point, I told Eric, is that I want my work to align with my values. I want to write about what's important. I want to help change minds. I want, I told Eric, to find a way to encourage a society that emphasizes a little less self-indulgence and a little more kindness to one another and to the planet.

Here's what Eric had to say:

"The way you talk about it is a bummer. It's a drag. It's not that you're wrong, but how will I be able to convince a publisher that people will spend twenty-four ninety-five on a book that tells them how screwed up they are? And even if anybody wanted to hear it, why would they want to hear it from you, a history writer with no credentials in this area?

"Have you considered writing novels?" Erik joked.

As I opened the door to my apartment that afternoon, I felt an unnatural rush of cool air. I knew Eric was right. If I was the type of person who left his air conditioners on when no one was home, not only did I not have the professional authority to talk about the environment, I didn't have the moral authority, either. It was the whole Michelle-and-the-fur scenario all over again. It was as though I wanted to change other people but was unwilling or unable to look in the mirror.

If I was still a student, I'd have marched against myself.

There is a Zen koan that captures the fix I was in. As the koan goes, long ago in China, a stray cat wandered into Zen master Nam Cheon's monastery. Sometimes the cat would cuddle up in the laps of the monks who lived in the east residence and sometimes in the laps of the monks who lived in the west residence. Instead of taking care of the cat together, the monks from the east and west halls became jealous of each other.

"We love the cat more than you, so it should live with us."

"No, we know how to take care of the cat better. It should stay with us!"

One day, the argument broke out in the middle of the dharma room, where the monks were supposed to be meditating. Finally, Zen master Nam Cheon stormed into the room. He picked up the cat, held a knife to its throat, and said, "You monks. Give me one true word of love for this cat and I'll save it. If you cannot, I will kill it."

Nam Cheon was testing the monks. Did any of them really love the cat, or did they just want to win the argument? Were they willing to demonstrate real responsibility for its life, or had they become too distracted by their fight for control of it? As the story goes, none of the monks said or did anything. They were all still trying to figure out how to prove the other side wrong. So Nam Cheon slit the cat's throat.

What began to worry me was that I and the political system I participated in were a lot like those monks in the dharma room when it came to the health of the planet. Never exerting much energy toward anything but winning the argument. Too rarely taking any real action. Forgetting that the proverbial cat's life was at stake while we argued over who owned it.

This brings me back to the question I asked regarding my own progress in the arena of kindness and restraint: Am I self-evolved or just self-righteous?

I had begun with the idea of trying to encourage a little less self-indulgence and a little more kindness in our society. Now, I realized, maybe I ought not to be writing a book about changing other people. Maybe I ought first to worry about changing myself. I called Eric and made a date for another lunch.

"I have a new idea for a book about the environment that has nothing at all to do with trying to get everyone else to change," I told him.

"No polemic?"

"No. I'll only try to change myself. As a lifestyle experiment, I'll try, with my family, to live as environmentally as possible."

"One guy tries to save the world? Like Superman or Spider-Man?"

"Or," I said, "how about No Impact Man?"

Comic allusions to superheroes aside, what if, when it came to our environmental crisis, I tried to lead by example? Perhaps I had no power to change things from the top down, but what if, in my own limited way, I began trying to change things from the bottom up?

I planned to write a book about what I was doing, and in the meantime I'd keep a blog on the Internet. I would breach the norms of our normally consumptive society inside a transparent bubble, into which, I imagined, a small number of blog readers and, later, a larger number of book readers would eventually get to look.

I wouldn't preach (or at least I'd try not to). As an experiment, I'd simply dedicate a year of my life to researching, developing, and adopting a way of life for me and my small family—one wife, one toddler, one dog—to live in the heart of New York City while causing as little harm to the environment as possible. What would that feel like? Was it possible to live environmentally in our modern culture? Would it seem so unappealing that no one would follow my lead? Would I be making myself into a freak? Or would what I was doing have some real value?

> **I didn't just want to have no carbon impact.**
> **I wanted to have no environmental impact.**

I was not talking about taking easy environmental half-measures, by the way. I was not talking about just using energy-saving fluorescent lightbulbs or being a diligent recycler. My idea was to go as far as possible and try to maintain as close to no net environmental impact as I could. I aimed to go zero carbon—yes—but also zero waste in the ground, zero pollution in the air, zero resources sucked from the earth, zero toxins in the water. I didn't just want to have no carbon impact. I wanted to have no environmental impact.

I realized it would be hard. I decided that—if I didn't want my wife and family to move out—I should ease us in by stages.

Stage one was trying to figure out how to live without making garbage: no disposable products, no packaging, and so on. Stage two involved traveling only in ways that emitted no carbon. In stage three, we would figure out how to cause the least environmental impact with our food choices. Then we'd proceed through stages involving making as little environmental impact as possible in the areas of consumer purchases, household operations like heat and electricity, and water use and pollution. The whole thing would get harder and harder, or so I imagined, as we made each new adaptation.

I also decided I'd have to balance what negative impact we couldn't eliminate with some sort of positive impact. We would do this by cleaning up garbage in the Hudson River, helping care for newly planted trees, giving money to charity—environmental activism, maybe.

In blunt mathematical terms, in case you are an engineer or just a geek who likes math, we would try to achieve an equilibrium that looked something like this:

$$\text{Negative Impact} + \text{Positive Impact} = \text{No Net Impact}$$

This wasn't meant to be scientific so much as philosophical. Could we decrease our negative impact and increase our positive impact enough so that they would balance out? Could I, at least for one year, live my life doing more good than harm?

So this book, in short, is about my attempt with my little family to live for a year causing as little negative environmental impact as possible. If what I've described so far sounds extreme, that's because it's meant to be. My intention with this book is not to advocate that, as a culture, we should all give up elevators, washing machines, and toilet paper. This is a book about a lifestyle experiment. It chronicles a year of inquiry: How truly necessary are many of the conveniences we take for granted but that, in their manufacture and use, hurt our habitat? How much of our consumption of the planet's resources actually makes us happier and how much just keeps us chained up as wage slaves?

What would it be like to try to live a no-impact lifestyle? Is it possible? Could it catch on? Would living this way be more fun or

> **It was to be an experiment in putting the habitat first and seeing how that affected us.**

less fun? More satisfying or less satisfying? Harder or easier? Worthwhile or senseless? Are we all doomed or is there hope? Is individual action lived out loud really just individual action? Would the environmental costs of producing this very book undo all the good, or would the message it purveyed outweigh the damage and add to the good?

But perhaps most important, at least when it came to addressing my own despair, was I as helpless to help change the imperiled world we live in as I'd thought?

These are the questions at the heart of this whole crazy-ass endeavor. Answering them for myself required extreme measures. How could I figure it all out if I didn't put myself in the crucible of going all the way? This was not intended to be an experiment in seeing if we could preserve the habitat we live in and still stay comfortable. It was to be an experiment in putting the habitat first and seeing how that affected us.

As it would turn out, my environmental exercise would wind up drawing the attention of both some independent filmmakers, who wanted to make a documentary about the No Impact project, and *The New York Times*, which halfway through the year would stumble upon my blog and write a profile of my family. The result of that profile was as much a surprise to me as anyone. The world media was fascinated by my experiment, and I found myself in the middle of a press storm, sometimes centering, to my chagrin, on the somewhat trivial fact that, as part of the project, I'd chosen to find a more environment-friendly approach to bathroom hygiene than toilet paper.

I was thrust into a debate about collective versus individual action and unwittingly became something of an environmental spokesman. I got thousands of e-mails from people asking what they should do, how they should live their lives. I suddenly found that I was, though I hesitate to say it, an accidental leader.

So much has changed since I began this project. My thinking. My career. My friendships. My fatherhood. My marriage.

But on the eve of the start of the No Impact project, I simply thought that by taking a personal approach to the problem of the health, safety, and happiness of our species, maybe I had found a non-finger-wagging way to change some minds after all. But if I couldn't, when all was said and done, at least I would have been able to change myself. At least if I couldn't solve the problems, I'd be able to say that I had tried.

TWO

Day One and the Whole Thing Is a Big Mistake

On what does one blow one's nose?

That's the big question on the first day. For all my grand ideas about saving the world and figuring out a happier way of life and changing people's minds and living according to my principles and—let's face it—being way overearnest, it turns out that becoming No Impact Man does not mean running into a phone booth and coming out transformed into some sort of eco-hero with my underwear stretched over my trousers. It doesn't, in fact, feel heroic at all.

What it feels like, waking up at 6:00 a.m. and hoping to get just a little more shut-eye before your eighteen-month-old greets the day by jumping up and down on your head, is enforced martyrdom of the most trivial and ridiculous kind. Because day one starts with me standing in my skivvies, looking through the purple dawn light and into the bathroom closet at a roll of paper towel (which I've always preferred to flimsy tissues), really needing to blow my nose, and suddenly realizing I'm not supposed to use the paper towel.

Today is the first day of my environmental lifestyle experiment. The one that is supposed to make me feel like I'm not contributing to the planet's destruction. The one that I have decided to ease myself into by starting with the seemingly simple first step of not making trash. The one, in other words, that means that I should not use a paper towel to blow my nose.

So what do I do now that I am officially No Impact Man? Now that I have chosen a nom de guerre that makes me sound like an environmental superhero? Now that I have begun living in a self-blog, book, and documentary bubble where for the next 364 days, 23 hours, and 50 frigging minutes anyone can look and judge how well I'm living up to my public declaration about making no negative environmental impact?

What would anybody do?

I blew my nose on a dead tree.

I reach for the paper towel. I tear off a piece, blow my nose, realize what an awful mess I've gotten myself into with this project, start feeling depressed before I even wake up, turn around, and shuffle back to the bedroom. I discover Isabella standing in the crib, opening and closing her hands and saying, "Uppie, Daddy, uppie."

Instantly my self-recrimination begins: I'm selfish. I blew my nose on a dead tree. And now God has punished me by making the sound of my honking wake up Isabella so that she can jump up and down on my head.

Ten minutes into this project and I already realized there was a big reason why I had never changed my life to live in accord with my values.

This was going to be hard. I'd be bound to fail at times. It's a lot easier to *say* that you shouldn't use disposable paper products than it is to actually not use them. There's a wider lesson in there somewhere. Like, it's a lot easier to say that our culture should be more ainable than to actually make it that way. It might be easier, too, to rstand the challenges for our culture in solving our environmental gency if I didn't repudiate the culture. Both those lessons would long time to sink in.

t I'm getting ahead of myself. On that first day, I still held taken belief that I was about to spend a year, at least in part, g with my desires and trying to figure out how to suppress rder to be moral.

shed up Isabella, carried her to our bed, and lay down, hoping diap do the same. But no. Isabella, as predicted, planted her red butt on my face, giggled, and began bouncing up and down as though her body were a jackhammer and my head was a rock that, for some unknown reason, urgently needed to be cracked.

"Paper bag or plastic?" A few days earlier, before the project proper began, I was next in line at the cash register in the crowded little organic grocery store run by the Integral Yoga Center on West Thirteenth Street. I got to the front, put my groceries on the counter, and a young woman in dreadlocks now waited for my answer.

I'd been haunted by this paper-or-plastic question ever since my mother sent me, as a child, on my first errand. I turned the question back on her. "What's better?" I asked.

"Well, I find that paper rips," the dreadlocked woman said.

"Not that," I said. "What's better for the environment?"

She shrugged. "Everybody says it works out the same, but I like plastic better for the handles."

That wasn't exactly the answer I was looking for.

Earlier that same week, I had called a press officer at one of the big environmental organizations. I told her I was trying to figure out how to live a no-impact life in New York City and that all the information seemed confusing. "Yeah," she said, "we're good at scaring people, but we haven't gotten good yet at telling them what to do." She promised to e-mail me some guidance but never did.

I'd gone on the "living simply" websites, thinking their reduced-consumption philosophy might help the environment. I found ways to save soap scraps and compress them into whole new bars. I found directions for making cookie cutters out of tuna cans. But everyor knows that tuna fishing kills dolphins, and, besides, who needs a coo cutter?

Back in the grocery store, not yet realizing that the answer carry a *reusable* bag, I accepted, for then, the cashier's recomm tion and walked away feeling vaguely dismayed. Whatever th answer to the paper-or-plastic question was, the vegans did to know it. The world seemed truly screwed.

•

No one can live without making *some* environmental impact. Even breathing creates carbon dioxide. You can turn your own lights out, but residing in a culture that provides street lighting means you still have an impact.

The very fact that I had chosen to call this project No Impact went to the underlying point: I was naïve and idealistic. I was not an environmentalist or an activist. I had no credentials. All I had was the knowledge that world events were freaking me out and the faith that we could do better.

I knew nothing, at that stage, about environmental living or environmental choices or carbon offsets or green spin or the relative worth of individual versus political action or, for that matter, anything else relevant to the question of maintaining a safe habitat for humanity. Hell, I still didn't know the answer to the paper-or-plastic question.

But that was the point.

The idea was not to become an environmental expert and then apply what I'd learned. The idea was to start from scratch—with not a clue about how to deal with our planetary emergency—and stumble forward. To see what I could find out. To see how I evolved.

What I learned in that moment in the yoga grocery store was that 'd find no well-blazed path to follow. I would have to figure out me eco-lifestyle for myself.

f well-sourced information mixed with a surfeit of corporate ed only in confusion. I'd hear of one study saying that the d washing ceramic cups damages the environment as much f disposable plastic cups that won't degrade for a thousand r of another that said using hot water and detergent to wash rms the planet more than cutting down trees to make pa- f I listened to the promulgated wisdom, it seemed that is as bad as everything else.

erchants seemed to want to convince me that trying to

make any difference was futile. I might as well give up. Toss away another plastic cup. Forget about electric cars because of the deleterious effects of disposing of their worn-out batteries. Go on, guzzle, the spurious wisdom seemed to say. There *is* no right way to live lightly on the land.

Consider the reusable-cloth-versus-plastic-diaper debate.

Only about thirty cloth diapers are needed to raise a child if you wash them twice a week. Admittedly, laundering diapers impacts the planet (the heating of the water and the water use itself, for example). On the other hand, that same child, by age two, would go through some 4,000 plastic diapers. How could pumping oil out of fields in the Middle East, shipping it to factories in, say, China to manufacture plastic diapers, delivering those diapers back to the United States, and then burying those poop-filled 4,000 diapers not be worse than washing the thirty pieces of cloth 104 times?

My point here is that there didn't seem to be any reliable environmental-living road map to follow. The "science" did not seem to be so much about making things clear, but more about confusing us and wearing us down so that we just carried on the way things were. "Stasis through obfuscation," my wife, Michelle, called it.

I read an article in *The New York Times* about the corporate rush to label products "green." Companies were slapping environmentally friendly labels on everything from tree-killing chainsaws that used less gas to highly toxic bug sprays. "Greenwashing" abounded, and to obsessively try to figure out which products truly harmed the planet less seemed like a fast path to an ulcer.

Then I began to wonder: Instead of driving ourselves nuts trying to

> **A child, by age two, goes through some 4,000 plastic diapers.**

find a way through the maze of product spin, might it not be simpler just to climb out of the maze? The trick to environmental living might not be in choosing *different* products. Instead—at least for profligate citizens of the United States and Western Europe—it might partly be about choosing *fewer* products. It might not just be about using different resources. It might be about using *fewer* resources.

As the ancient Chinese *Tao Te Ching* says, "The man who knows that enough is enough will always have enough."

What about a handkerchief?

I was lying in bed, playing with Isabella, and my sinuses were filling up. I was realizing I was going to have to tear off another evil sheet of paper towel, another desiccated strip of dead tree, when suddenly I remembered a drawer full of cloth towels and napkins in the kitchen. Wedding gifts. Birthday gifts from acquaintances. Things we never used but couldn't bring ourselves to get rid of. I could use one of these cloths as a handkerchief and throw it in the laundry with everything else.

I threw back the covers, went into the kitchen, found the red-print rag that would henceforth be known as my "cloth," and blew my nose. What a relief! And not just in a physical way but also in a philosophical one.

Let's assume that I can say with confidence that wanting to blow one's nose is not, in fact, a sign of extreme self-centeredness, as I had somehow imagined when I first woke up. Let's assume that I was not, as I thought, faced with a conflict between my "selfish" need to blow my nose and an "altruistic" impulse to save the planet. Let's assume that framing the No Impact experiment in terms of the conflict between the self and the whole would get the whole thing off to a wrong start.

Selfishness versus altruism frames the discussion of environmental or any other kind of social change in a dangerous way. People argue, maybe correctly, that if you pit the survival of the planet against human selfishness, the planet will lose every time. More important, casting the discussion as a conflict between human selfishness and altruism doesn't even have the benefit of being entirely true. The problem does not pit selfishness against altruism. It simply pits old habits and methods that no longer work for us as a species against new habits and methods that will work.

The coming year of my No Impact experiment, I realized, should have nothing to do with asceticism. Asceticism has to do with renouncing worldly pleasures. It means not eating when you're hungry. It means not blowing your nose when you need to. It means denying your human needs and longings. To some people, it means accepting an implication that human desire and passion are bad.

That's not me. I'm an optimist about human nature. Our desires are fundamental to who we are and therefore essentially good (even if we should not necessarily allow ourselves to be ruled by them). I was not interested in the question of how to quash human passion and desire. But I was interested in the question of whether our passion and desire point our lives in a direction that actually makes us happy, something I'd come to doubt.

My plan was to get off what "positive psychologists," I discovered, called the *hedonic treadmill*.

Just at the time I started the No Impact project, a magazine editor assigned me a seemingly unrelated story about the psychology of human happiness. It turned out, I learned, that most early psychologists—Jung and Freud, for example—had conducted studies into what made neurotics happier, or at least less neurotic, and assumed that what they found would apply to the rest of us.

In the past ten years, however, a group of academics—the so-called positive psychologists—began to study happy people rather than the mentally ill. They doubted that observations made about neurotics were applicable to the rest of us. Instead of working on the precept of curing us of illness to make us "normal," positive psychologists sought to improve on that "normal" to make us happy. They wanted us to go from, say, 0 to +5 instead of −5 to 0.

What the positive psychologists had learned was that, while get-

ting a new cell phone or a new car or a new house did give us a burst
of pleasure, the pleasure did not last. If we wanted to feel the same
spike of happiness, we would have to get another fix—yet another
phone, yet another car. They called that mode of pleasure-seeking the
"hedonic treadmill."

The happiest people, the shrinks discovered, did not live their
lives on this perpetual loop. Rather, these folks had raised their base-
line mood in ways that did not require repeated doses of new stuff.
The people most satisfied with life, it turned out, had strong social
connections, found meaning in their work, got to exercise what they
considered to be their highest talents, and had a sense of some higher
purpose.

The positive psychologists confirmed scientifically, in other words,
what simple-living advocates have been asserting for so long anec-
dotally: a life lived with less emphasis on acquisition might have the
effect of leaving more time for richer, less resource-intensive life re-
wards, making both the planet and the people happier.

That's why, as I started the project, I became excited about the
possibility of breaking through our societally endemic isolation and
connecting to our community and to some larger sense of purpose as
a replacement for the material things
we'd be giving up. The challenge
was that my family and I were your

> **The happiest people did not live
> their lives on the hedonic treadmill.**

typical media-addicted take-out slaves. Asceticism or any variation
on it was not a realistic way forward for my family any more than it
was for the rest of the world.

I would have to find, over the coming year, some sort of middle
path that involved neither the self-indulgence of the unconscious
consumer nor the self-denial of the ascetic. I wanted to find a way to
thoroughly enjoy the fruit without killing the tree. I wanted to find
a way of living on the planet's dividends instead of its capital.

Take, for example, something I discovered about the Menominee
tribe of Wisconsin. According to William McDonough and Michael

Braungart, authors of *Cradle to Cradle*, the Menominee have harvested wood for sale from their forested land for many generations. In 1870, the Menominee inventoried 1.3 billion standing board feet of timber on their 235,000 acres. Since then, they have harvested nearly twice that amount: 2.25 billion board feet.

Employing the "clear-cutting" method of some corporate lumber merchants, which completely strips land of its trees, the Menominee would have barely a single tree left, not to mention any forest wildlife. In fact, they currently have 1.7 billion standing board feet, more than they had in 1870, along with a thriving forest ecosystem.

This is because the Menominee tend to cut only the weaker trees, leaving behind the strong mother trees and enough of the upper canopy for the arboreal animals to continue to live there. As McDonough and Braungart write: "One might say they have figured out what the forest can productively offer them instead of considering only what they want."

That is the philosophy I hoped to embody during the No Impact experiment. Like the Menominee, I wanted to figure out, with my family, what the world could productively offer us rather than considering only what we wanted. Deprivation was not the order of the day. I simply wanted to see if we could learn to behave like good guests while enjoying a good life.

In the coming weeks, as I went about my garbageless life, I tried to be subtle about steering social outings away from restaurants that use throwaway utensils but ended up being more overt about environmental living than I'd hoped. "If you're sincere about this, why don't you leave New York and go back to the land?" asked one bemused acquaintance.

I mentioned to a very liberal friend—a sort of comrade in arms, someone I thought would be in line with my values—that I was trying to figure out how to live an environmentally sound lifestyle while staying in New York.

"Forget it. It's impossible," he said, completely dismissing me. "It's one thing to try it in the countryside, maybe in the woods, like Henry David Thoreau, or on a farm, where you grow your own food. But in New York? No way."

Could he be right, I wondered? Did the very fact that I lived in a big urban center undermine my whole idea?

I hope not. More than half the world's population now lives in cities. According to the UN, 180,000 more people move into urban centers every day. Meanwhile, city dwellers tend to set the consumption patterns for the rest of the world. People buy what metropolitan people buy. The entire agricultural and consumer product distribution system is designed to cater to our urban needs. If city dwellers can't learn to reduce their ecological imprints, we're all in deep trouble.

The good news is that in cities, especially one like New York, a lot of people cram into a small area, which gives us efficiency of scale. People need not drive so often. Not every home needs its own boiler. Products come to one central depot instead of being distributed over miles and miles. Outlying landscapes are left undisturbed. We share transportation, dwellings, and resources. It is a remarkable fact that, here in New York, the average citizen's per capita carbon emissions is 29 percent of the average American's.

> **New Yorkers make nearly 9 billion pounds of garbage every year.**

On the other hand, because there are so many of us, city people produce pollutants in huge concentrations. Thanks to car and truck exhausts alone, which make up 80 percent of Manhattan's air pollution, the island's residents face the highest risk in the country of developing cancer from chemicals in the air. New Yorkers make nearly 9 billion pounds of garbage every year and dump 27 billion gallons of raw sewage into our waterways. We even, in spite of our efficiency, produce nearly an entire 1 percent of the world's greenhouse gases.

"How can a person like you, who lives in one of the dirtiest cities in the world, even dare to use the word 'environment'?" I'd get asked during the course of the No Impact experiment. If the questioner lived in a rural area near New York City—say, on Long Island, or in upstate New York—I'd say, "Well, how about if all eight million of us moved to your neighborhood to try living off the land? Would you consider that a more environmentally sound way forward?"

The planet is much safer if we city people stay where we are. In fact, many environmentalists would be happier if more people—especially suburbanites, who drive around and heat their separate homes—moved to the cities. On the other hand, as energy- and resource-efficient as cities around the world might be, we need to do much better.

To what extent doing better is a matter for each of us as citizens to take up, and not the sole responsibility of the governments and municipalities that regulate our resource use and waste disposal, remains a question I intend to explore. But concerning my planned No Impact experiment, I remain confident that it makes much more sense to try to see what can be done in one of the world's great cities than to attempt some sort of back-to-the-land act.

With these few ideas in mind—staying in the city, living with enough, eschewing asceticism—I have a sort of philosophy to underpin my seven-stage plan.

Coming up with philosophies is one thing. Coming up with practicalities that wouldn't end up dissolving my marriage is entirely another.

Back on that day when I'd ignobly blown my nose on a paper towel and been rewarded with the predawn waking of my child, I discovered that the two good things about your eighteen-month-old jumping on your head are, first, you quickly become aware that her diaper needs changing and, second, the fact that the wet diaper is slamming into your face reduces your inclination to put it off.

I threw off the covers and went back to the same bathroom closet where I'd retrieved my paper towel. I found myself in my second environmental crisis in only ten minutes.

Once more standing in a moral quandary before the bathroom closet, I was forced to consider not what I'd thought would be the

most extreme and difficult parts of this experiment, like not using
elevators, electricity, or hot water, but a baby's wet bottom and a
package of throwaway plastic diapers. Diapers, according to the Real
Diaper Association, make up 4 percent of our trash.

Not making garbage. This was the first phase of the experiment,
presumably the easiest part of the whole thing.

I had thought I'd be easing my family in. Yet I'd failed on the paper towel.

Strike one.

And, at this moment, I had no more sustainable way to prevent
Isabella's feces from ending up all over the apartment. I reached for
the plastic diaper.

Strike two.

Things were going to have to change radically. For a moment,
I thought about the major lifestyle changes I had yet to face. Then I
realized that was the easy part. I looked at the lump under the covers
on the far side of the bed: my wife, Michelle. How on earth was she
going to deal with all this?

This whole thing could only get much harder.

Michelle was thirty-nine. She had married me under a tent at Wood-
hill Country Club, outside Minneapolis. She, like me, earned her
keep by writing.

Dr. John Pacuik had pulled Isabella out of her mommy's tummy
a year and half earlier. Frankie, our four-year-old dog, whom Isabella
calls "my sister," came to live with us after being saved from a kill
shelter in North Carolina when she was a puppy. The dog looked like
a mix of some sort of hound and a border collie.

Ten legs and a tail, I liked to call our family. Michelle agitated constantly to make it twelve legs. One
morning, around the time I first brought
up the idea of the No Impact project, I
opened my eyes to hear Michelle sing-

> Ten legs and a tail, I liked to call
> our family. Michelle agitated
> constantly to make it twelve legs.

ing a baby song she had made up for Isabella. "My last egg is dying but my husband doesn't care," sang Michelle. Isabella took to the tune and danced around the living room in the style of an Oompa Loompa.

Our first conversation about the No Impact project, which took place when Michelle was half asleep on the couch reading a book, went something like this:

"Honey," I said, "I have this idea for a project where we would live environmentally for a year."

"Uh-huh," she said, turning a page.

"It might be really hard," I said, "but I think it would be worthwhile."

"Uh-huh," she said.

"Will you do it with me?"

She didn't register the question.

"Will you do it with me?" I repeated.

"What? Sure, honey, no problem. Sounds good."

And that, by the way, is how you get your spouse to do almost anything. You ask them when they aren't really listening so that, later, when they want to change their minds, you're both in way too deep to back out.

There would be one caveat, Michelle said the next morning. In our ongoing negotiations about a possible second child, she didn't want to hear anything about whether or not it would be bad for the environment. She was in, but only on the condition that it would not be a factor in our decision whether or not to have more children.

"Deal?" Michelle said.

"Deal," I said.

•

Looking over at her in bed on the day of the paper towel and diaper failures, I knew that she hadn't really been listening to a thing I'd said about how hard it might be.

Isabella stood by Michelle's side of the bed, trying to wedge her mother's eyelids open with her toddler claws. "Lake up, Mommy, I want nilk," she said. When you're a year and half old, one consonant is as good as another.

Michelle looked at me from the dizzy eye wedged open by Isabella's first two talons. "Can you get it?" she asked.

I shuffled into the kitchen and opened the fridge. I grabbed the Tiny Monster's sippy-cup, poured it full of organic milk, killed the carton, and opened the cupboard under the kitchen sink to get to the trashcan. I was poised to chuck the cardboard milk carton in when suddenly the No Impact Man side of my brain exploded. *The trashcan!* Oh God. I froze with the milk carton in mid-throw.

I had woken up when it was still dark, I now stood in my underwear, and, so far, between blowing my nose, changing Isabella's diaper, and getting her milk, I'd already been assaulted three times by the travails of the human race—before even having a cup of coffee.

"This project is a big mistake," I say, shuffling gloomily into the bathroom.

Michelle is brushing her teeth.

"I've really gotten us into a mess this time."

"Don't be silly," Michelle says. "This will be the most important thing we've ever done."

"I don't want to do it," I say.

She spits, rinses, and pushes past me out of the bathroom. "We're doing it," she says over her shoulder. I follow her.

"Then we're going to have to start by cutting out the trash," I say. "It's going to be hard."

"I know," Michelle says.

The previous week, Michelle and I had made a mission of saving all of our trash in order to sort and count it. No throwing away coffee cups in the corner trashcan. No chucking a plastic bottle. We brought all of it home, where it fermented in our front hallway in three large black bags, which we were ashamed to discover amounted to a total of ninety gallons in only four days. The plan now, over the coming couple of weeks, was to figure out how to completely cut out trash.

"And we should stop watching the TV straightaway," Michelle adds, "if only because I'm addicted to it. I'm also going to stop all shopping. I'll start walking to work, and we should start taking the stairs instead of the elevator."

Oh God. The whole idea was to ease ourselves into this thing. Why is she interfering? Why is she pushing into the transportation and electricity phases when I could see that the trash phase would be challenging enough.

"I'll also get my bike fixed," I said. What the hell.

There is a beat of silence.

"Let me warn you now," Michelle says, "that if you think you are going to get me or Isabella on a bike in this city, you are dead wrong."

"Okay," I say, trying to cover the fact that I don't mean "okay" at all.

That was about it when it came to negotiating. It was clear what our roles would be throughout the coming twelve months. I would be captain and leader. Michelle would be second-guesser.

We're all dressed and ready now to venture out into the world on which we are learning how to make no impact. I put Isabella in a sort of backpack contraption instead of the stroller because it will be easier to deal with on the stairs. We say goodbye to a dejected-looking Frankie—who every morning seems to think that this is the one when we won't come back. Without giving it a second thought, the three of us pile into the elevator. We get down to the ground floor before we remember we're supposed to be taking the stairs.

THREE

What You Think When You Find Your Life in the Trash

A quick and partial inventory of the crap I found collected in our three large garbage bags in only four days: fourteen plastic coffee cups, two cardboard coffee cups, four Styrofoam coffee cups, twelve plastic straws, six plastic straw wrappers, nineteen paper napkins, fourteen small paper bags, nine sets of plastic cutlery (unused), five receipts (never even looked at), three balls of used paper towel, fourteen plastic bags, three plastic and four aluminum take-out containers and their lids, two sets of wooden chopsticks, one cardboard french-fry container, three crumpled balls of tinfoil, and two cardboard boxes that had contained a new pair of desk lamps, along with the Styrofoam packing materials.

I call this a "partial" inventory because I dissected my way through the insides of only two out of the three bags. To the third, we had added the contents of the bathroom garbage pail, the last resting place of Isabella's dirty diapers. Some of them had burst open, and I couldn't bring myself to paw through the result without a gas mask. Suffice it to say that the third bag added to our trash a total of about eighteen dirty diapers, a further twenty-five gallons or so of poop-covered take-out containers, some greasy chow fun noodles, pizza crusts, and a head of lettuce gone bad in the fridge before we ever used it.

Surrounded by all this debris, sitting there on my hallway floor with a pen and paper in my hand, I felt like I'd just stepped on the scale and the news was much worse than I'd thought. It was not trash per se that got me. It was the throwing away of things used for less than five minutes without so much as a thought before reaching for the exact same product to use for another five minutes before throwing that away, too. The truth was that every coffee cup and every water bottle in the corner trashcan gave me a tiny micro-twinge of guilt. For years, I had been giving myself a daily pass with the intention of eventually doing better.

If you had asked me if I tried not to make trash, not to waste, I would have told you that I certainly didn't produce the average American's 4.6 pounds of trash per day, or roughly 1,700 pounds per year. I would have probably told you I didn't try as hard as I

> The truth was that every coffee cup and every water bottle in the corner trashcan gave me a tiny micro-twinge of guilt.

should but that I tried. I made an effort, I would have said. I'm not all talk. I care about the world.

What had the crumbled-up, grease-covered dross around me demonstrated? That I had a long way to go.

I grew up in Westport, Massachusetts, a little seaside town, just up the road from my grandparents. I'd walk down their gravel lane and sit with my grandfather, watching television. He always held in his hand a switch attached by a long wire to the "box," as he called it. The switch he called the "clicker." When ads came on he snapped the clicker and the volume went off. When the show started again, with a snap he'd turn the volume back on.

My grandmother, meanwhile, carefully folded up her brown paper bags to return to the store or use for garbage. They insisted I climb back up the stairs to the bathroom to turn the light off if I'd left it on. They taught me to take only what food I would eat and never to throw trash on the ground. They wore sweaters and kept the heat down low.

My grandfather, before he retired, had been a very senior assistant deputy director in the CIA. My grandmother had been a model. In other words, they weren't exactly hippie environmentalists. But they didn't believe in wasting. And when I was young, they had tried to teach me, too, not to waste.

What would my grandparents think of me now? I'd come to associate the conservation values my grandparents taught me with the Depression, which they had lived through. Thinking about it, though, I felt pretty sure that their idea that we should hold our resources precious came not just from a "waste not, want not" point of view. Something deeper imbued their exhortations not to waste.

They held dear the simple idea that we ought not to take for granted what we had been blessed with. For my grandparents and all my adoptive uncles and aunts who were their friends the belief that we shouldn't waste seemed to come not from environmental ideas but arose simply as an outgrowth of the idea that we should act with gratitude for this life we've been granted and all that comes with it.

My grandmother's best friend once busted me after, as a teenager, I left a cigarette butt on her land. "Look, chum," she said, "I don't care if you smoke, but don't litter."

And so, sitting on the hallway floor, I looked at the volume of stuff I had used for less than five minutes, and I felt ungrateful. I took things for granted in a way my grandparents had tried to teach me not to.

That was the result of considering the volume. There were still the contents to consider.

Archaeologists often find out most about an ancient civilization from its trash, and if I were an archaeologist, I figured, what I would notice first about this pile of trash at my feet, besides its volume, was the lack of any carrot peelings. Not just carrot peelings but potato peelings and melon rinds and apple cores and broccoli stalks and eggshells and bean pods and avocado pits. If I were an archaeologist, in other words, I would ask: Where is the detritus of even a little fresh produce?

Not to put too fine a point on it, but given that, as an archaeologist, I would be studying trash from one of the richest civilizations ever known, I would want to know: Where was the evidence of a good and healthful life? Where was the evidence of a family who had more than enough resources to take care of themselves and their health? Why, as the trash seemed to suggest, didn't moderately well-off cosmopolitan families like this one take the time to cook a decent meal?

Or even, sadly, to sit down over good home-cooked food, eaten leisurely off plates, instead of hastily, out of plastic tubs, for family-bonding time around the dinner table?

For Michelle and me, a typical workday, before the No Impact project started, went like this:

We'd wake up, tickle and joke with Isabella for half an hour, get her a bottle of milk, quick-change her out of one plastic butt wrapper and into another, pop her into an outfit from Lucky Wang, brush out the tangles in her hair, race Frankie around the block (scooping up her poop in a plastic bag provided by last night's delivery boy), stop at Thé Adoré around the corner on Thirteenth Street to throw back a quick coffee and croissant (if we hadn't already had them delivered), wheel Isabella to Peggy, who took care of her, rush to work, toil away for ten hours, pick Isabella up, get her home for another bottle of milk, sing, read, and roughhouse on the bed, lower her into her crib, beg her to cuddle her "pink blankie" and go to sleep, cave in to her protests and pick her up and put her down for another twenty minutes, flop down in front of the TV for an hour, argue about whether Michelle or I would put our shoes on to take Frankie out, fall into bed, sleep, wake up, and start all over.

Who, in other words, had time to peel a carrot, or even go to the grocery store to buy one? Who had time to sit around the kitchen table to enjoy a leisurely family meal?

Instead, Michelle and I Googled the phone number for the Big Enchilada for rice and beans, Japonica for sushi, Bagel Bob's for breakfast (when we needed a break from Thé Adoré), Souen Macrobiotic if we felt guilty about all the crap we'd been eating, or Two Boots Pizza when we got realistic and asked ourselves who we thought we were kidding by trying to eat healthily.

I'm not complaining, because, if you take out the hamster-wheel quality, what I'm describing definitely had elements of a nice life—a "high standard of living." The question is, if you factor the hamster-wheel quality back in, is this "high standard of living" the same as a good quality of life?

But who was asking questions? By the standards of the set of New York working parents we belonged to, our rush through the day seemed pretty typical. We'd stand around our local playground in Washington Square Park and ask our friends when

> **Food packaging makes up 20 percent of our solid waste nationwide.**

they had last cooked for the kids and we'd all laugh guiltily. And, as the joke goes among us, once your two-year-old has learned to ask for calamari or duck and mango salad, you've passed the point of no return.

It turns out that my family's plastic take-out-tub trash is part of a huge societal garlic-sauce-covered slop of molded hydrocarbons and other petrochemicals that, after perhaps twenty minutes of use, will end up in landfills and incinerators, to leach chemicals into the water we drink or vaporize into the air we breathe.

According to the Environmental Protection Agency, food packaging makes up 20 percent of our solid waste nationwide. The archaeologist studying our nation's trash, it seems, would see that it's not just the city folks who don't have time to cook. A lot of suburbanites aren't exactly finding the time to peel a carrot, either. It's just that instead of getting their throwaway packaging from takeout, they're getting it from the frozen-food section.

Think of the grocery store. If you're lucky, in the aisles around the edges you'll find some fresh produce—some food you can actually cook. But every other aisle—the aisles in the store's heart—has shelves crammed with cereal in boxes and vegetables in cans and frozen food in plastic trays. That's the stuff that is destined to become, after a couple of minutes in a microwave and a couple more on a table, or a lap, a full 20 percent of our nation's trash.

However much my grandparents' ghosts might cluck their tongues at my way of life, it is not that my family alone had turned into some sort of monstrous, garbage-making machine. It's not that I'm a marred human being who took a wrong turn, or that I've turned bad in the twenty-five years since my grandparents wielded their influence over me. It's not that I'm the lazy ingrate I thought I was. But it may be that, as a member of the crew of the huge steamship that is our culture, I had acquiesced to some decisions that caused the whole boat to take a wrong turn, and possibly sink.

All this trash we threw away so unconsciously would quickly disappear as the project unfolded. I'd even manage to persuade Michelle to let me keep a special bin in the apartment containing a species of earthworm that would digest—quickly and without the smell of rotting—thrown-away food scraps into compost, which could then be returned to the soil. With this measure and others, we'd reduce our trash to less than 5 percent of what it had been. But that's all in the future.

For now, as I hold my nose and pick up the trash from my hallway floor and put it back in the bags, what I want to do is console myself with the fact that all these plastic tubs make life more convenient. They make life more efficient. They make it easy to live.

I try to push away from myself the irony that something supposedly intended to make life more efficient creates so much polluting waste. But so far, picking up the trash, not only am I not doing a good job keeping the goop off my clothes, I'm not consoling myself too well, either.

As the argument goes, all this food packaging helps cut down on the time I have to spend taking care of myself and my family so that

I can have more leisure time. But that's not what happens. In my family's life, the convenience doesn't mean more time for hanging out together. It means more time for work. After all, so many of us shuttle between two jobs and break our backs twelve hours a day and more to pay for all this "convenience."

Take the case of my wife, Michelle, during her midtown workweek. Every lunchtime, she joined hundreds of thousands of people who, like ants from anthills, poured out of their skyscrapers to buy themselves their fifteen-dollar takeout.

Michelle, like the other working minions, then whooshed in elevators back to her desk to eat as she worked because she couldn't waste time. She needed to keep working to get a raise. She needed the raise to afford the $5,000 a year in lunches she had to buy so she could get back to her desk so she could get a raise so she could afford her lunches so she could get back to her desk . . .

Thirty years earlier, dinner at my grandparents' house was the opposite of a rush. My grandmother would call us all into the dining room to sit in slat-backed wicker chairs around the polished mahogany table. She would not bring in the food. Instead, we would look west out the dining-room window, down the hill, across the field to Westport's salt-marsh harbor.

Grannie made us all sit quietly for a while. The red sun would settle from orb to half orb to sliver behind the hills across the water. Scales of salmon swam through the clouds. The harbor flamed orange and violet, and I would fidget, because I was young. I would want to talk, and if I did I'd get hushed.

During quiet days at my grandparents' house, I would sit on the couch and read. My grandmother sketched line drawings—of my grandfather's fishing hat hanging on a hook, of a lamp—and I would wonder why. My grandfather penned funny little poems, which he would read on holidays. At dinner, we sat till the orange and red had gone and the sky and water faded into quiet purple. Swans might fly overhead. Or honking geese.

We watched the sunset. Then we ate.

When my grandmother washed the dishes, I would stand beside her and we'd look out the window together at the New England stone wall in her backyard. Chipmunks had burrowed there. "That's the father," my grandmother would say. "Those are the babies." The birds would come. A red-winged blackbird, Grannie would tell me. A goldfinch.

While it was hard to appreciate when I was young, I wonder if it's Grannie's world I crave now. You might think that hers were only country pleasures, but there are things to watch for in the city. The sunset is reflected in the top floors of Manhattan windows. Instead of turning west to watch the sun, you can turn east. It's like watching the audience instead of the play.

> There is a reason why trash bags aren't made of transparent plastic.

The problem is, to enjoy it, to savor it, I'd have to take the time to stop and watch.

With my trash all packed back up and hidden in the black bags, I realized there was a reason I didn't want to look at it. There is a reason why trash bags aren't made of transparent plastic that would allow us to see inside. It is the same reason I and my kind keep bodily remains in closed coffins. We're uncomfortable with what we might see.

It is because, having to look at our garbage on a daily basis, people like me would be faced—again, daily—with hard questions about how we live. We'd have to ask ourselves questions like the one I was faced with as I humped my trash bags to the bins down the hall: Do we work for and pay for all this convenience in order to live our lives, or do we live our lives in order to work for and pay for all this convenience?

Here's what happened when, sitting on the floor with the remains of my life spread around me, I looked into the black plastic bags: I thought about how I found it hard to spend enough time with my little girl, or my wife, or my friends, and I realized that I had been scratching out a living doing work that didn't truly motivate me, and it occurred to me that what I was paying for with my time and money is stuff that I would be throwing away in ten minutes.

My grandparents' no-waste rules seemed pointless when I was young. You shouldn't this. You shouldn't that. And for the sake of . . . what? Piety? Sanctimony? But something about their intention not to waste and their emphasis on cultivating gratitude—Depression-era thoughts or not—seems connected to making time to watch the sunset and the chipmunks.

You sit down with your trash and you see your life laid before you on the floor, you see what an archaeologist would see when he studies your life a thousand years from now, and you wonder: If life begets life and death begets death, does waste beget waste? If my life begets waste, what does that say about my life? Is a waste of resources a sign of a waste of life?

Half an hour on the floor with my trash and I'd gotten myself stuck in an existential morass. My grandparents' experience aside, was there some larger wisdom I could apply to my life that addressed itself to all this waste? Although I'm not Jewish, I thought I'd e-mail the man I call my rabbi.

I met Rabbi Steven Greenberg on an Amtrak train from New York to Washington, D.C. I went to the bathroom and, when I came back, I saw that my father, who was traveling with me, had handed a copy of my most recent book, *Operation Jedburgh*, to the stranger across the aisle.

"So you're a writer," the stranger said.

I was horrified. I didn't want to talk to strangers about being a writer, but then the stranger said, "I am, too." Steven, it turned out, had written *Wrestling with God and Men*, a book about homosexuality in the Jewish tradition.

"Are you gay?" I asked him.

"Yes."

"Are you a rabbi?"

"Yes."

I couldn't restrain myself: "What does your mother think?"

Steven laughed, told me great stories, and ever since then, Steven has been my good friend—and my rabbi.

What I asked Steven, in my e-mail, was whether there were any religious prohibitions against the kind of waste I had just spread on the floor around my feet. Was there anything that confirmed the values of my grandparents? I have no interest, as I've said, in piety for its own sake, but I did wonder if ancient wisdom could answer my question about waste begetting waste, and if, by making so much waste, I was also somehow wasting my life.

Steven e-mailed me back, and it turns out that, as part of the law that must be obeyed in order to live in the Promised Land, Moses said that "you must not destroy" fruit-bearing trees during war. Now, I'm no religious scholar, but applying my own metaphorical terms, it struck me that this could well mean that to have a peaceful spirit (to live in the Promised Land) one must not, while living life (fighting war), waste life-giving resources (fruit-bearing trees).

That's my thinking, not Rabbi Steve's, but he did tell me, also, that the second-century rabbis whose discussions are collected in the Talmud interpreted this passage from Moses' sermons as a more general exhortation not to needlessly destroy. "This is the law not only for trees," they wrote, "but anyone who breaks containers, tears clothes, destroys a building, stops up a well, or wastes food violates the prohibition of 'do not destroy.'"

Based on the crap on my floor, my life of waste and the Promised Land did not exactly coincide in time and space. In my crazy mind—and also, I guessed, in the minds of my grandparents, if they could have read Steve's e-mail—the passage suggested that living a life of waste might make me less happy. Doing less of it might make me more happy. The idea gave me hope that finding an alternative to blowing my nose on a paper towel made from dead trees and generally making less trash might turn out to be more fulfilling than I thought.

There's another religious story that my pile of trash brought to mind. It has to do with the five Buddhist precepts, which are akin to the Ten Commandments of Judaism and Christianity. The precepts, as I see them, suggest an attitude toward life, or a spirit of living, that brings peace, both for me and those around me.

The first of the precepts, like the biblical "Thou shalt not murder," can also be thought of simply as "Don't kill."

So . . . as this little story goes, a Zen master is sitting outside, meditating under a tree, when one of his monks walks past with a big pot on the way to get water from the well. Once the monk fills his pot, he returns down the path, hurrying past the Zen master and slopping water as he goes. "Hey, you!" the Zen master shouts from under the tree. "Why are you killing that water?"

The choice of words is important. What the Zen master means is that the monk is disobeying the spirit of the first precept, which, like Moses' exhortation not to kill trees, extends beyond killing to wasting and destroying. The needless wasting and destroying implies that the monk is not attending to life as it is right now. The waste is a sign of something more profound about how the monk lives his life. Perhaps, like mine, it is short on the joys of chipmunks and sunsets.

Why are you more concerned with where you're going than where you are, the Zen master might just as well have asked? Why are you more concerned with what you're going to do than what you're doing? Why aren't you paying attention to how you live your life right this very moment? Why are you wasting this moment? Why, indeed, are you wasting your life?

So much of my trash-making and waste is about making convenient the taking care of myself and my family. It's about getting our needs out of the way. But is this so? When did taking care of ourselves become something so unimportant that it should be got out of the way rather than savored and enjoyed? When did cooking and nourishing my family become an untenable chore? What is more important that I'm supposed to do instead?

For every task I need to accomplish there seemed to be some throwaway item I could buy to help get it out of the way. My whole life appeared to have turned into a moneymaking machine intended to buy more convenience, with the seeming purpose of getting my life out of my way. I'm like a snake eating my own tail. It's as if I'm just trying to get the whole thing over with . . .

At times like this, when I feel like I've lost my way, I turn to the religions, though not out of a sense of piety. Rather, I look to them as a way of reminding myself of what I already hold to be true. Sometimes I get too busy or distracted to hear the gentle voice of my own wisdom. The great religions have the benefit of codifying that wisdom and reminding us of it, the way guardrails help keep us on the road.

We have a natural compass inside us—our innate human wisdom—that tells us where true north is, but the rush I live in seems to point me somewhere else. My grandparents always told me to live with gratitude and not to waste. I understood the importance of what they said because

> **My whole life appeared to have turned into a moneymaking machine intended to buy more convenience.**

they told me, and because when they told me it resonated with something inside. The big question I'm asking is: What has going against my compass achieved? Has it helped me or hindered me?

I'm not saying that I want to go back to the years when my grandparents lived. I'm simply asking, have I somehow lost something that, through good economic times and bad, through high resources and low, they always managed to hold on to?

•

Even modern replacements for priests, rabbis, and Zen masters—the positive psychologists—have something to say on this point. That new breed of shrinks has discovered that happy people spend a lot of time being grateful for what they have and savoring their experience. They don't rush through "now" to get to later. They don't make taking care of themselves or taking care of their families something they have to get over with so they can get to the good stuff. Instead, they insist that this moment, whatever it is, *is* the good stuff.

So while I'm humping my three heavy black bags down the hallway to the building's trash bins, while I'm getting all the undone chores out of the way, what I can't help thinking is that all this wasting somehow contradicts the very possibility of savoring my short life. Is it not implicit in wasting for the sake of convenience that what I'm doing right now, in this moment, has no value—that the life that produces such waste is itself being wasted?

So I wonder. Just a thought. But if I treated the resources that pass through my hands as though they were precious, might I also begin to feel that this very life—the one right under my feet right now and right this very moment—might be precious, too? And excuse me for generalizing—I don't mean to preach—but what if instead of just me, it were *we*? By this I mean if we, as a culture, treated resources as precious, might we not begin to act and feel as though this life we lead together—the one we live when we look in each other's eyes—might be precious, too? And might this planet be precious, too?

I say this because now that I've put the trash in the hall, now that the trash is out of my house, it is no longer an "I" problem. It's a "we" problem. Something we get to deal with together.

We will together injure our lungs as we inhale the diesel particulates produced as American trucks drive literally millions of miles to move our waste. We will together drink the water laced with battery acid that has leaked from landfills. We will together suffer the greater chance of cancer as we breathe in the dioxins produced by incinerators.

Now that I've disposed of my throwaway products, you see, my convenience has become the entire race's inconvenience.

•

Given all that waste, did it really matter that I blew my nose on a paper towel? Wasn't there a planet that needed saving?

Sure, it was just one piece of tissue, but the problem is, as Heather Rogers points out in *Gone Tomorrow: The Hidden Life of Garbage*, some 80 percent of our products are made to be used only once. As trivial as that paper towel might seem, it points up a multitude of individual and cultural choices we make every day, choices that mean we are sucking resources out of the planet and sending them to the landfill or incinerator, having barely used them.

As long as we're talking about waste, it's worth noting that, according to the Environmental Protection Agency, 4.8 million tons—nearly 10 billion pounds—of disposable paper napkins, towels, cups, and plates is what the United States sends to landfills every year. I don't know why it never occurred to me before, but what we're talking about when we talk about 10 billion pounds of trashed paper products is 10 billion pounds of dead trees.

Dead trees. Like where my grandmother's beloved birds might live. Like where her chipmunks might make their home. And, most important for those of us who aren't chipmunks or birds, like where the planet stores a whole bunch of the greenhouse gas carbon dioxide, which we really don't want released into the atmosphere right now.

Because, it turns out, where our trash comes from is sometimes more important than where our trash goes. And how we made it is more important than where we toss it—especially if it's for a throwaway, single-use product like my snot-covered paper towel.

According to the Natural Resources Defense Council, Kimberly-Clark, just one of the many companies that make disposable paper products, mows down half a million tons of trees a year from Canada's ancient boreal forests. Meanwhile, the world is consuming paper tablecloths and party hats—and, yes, office and printing paper—at such a rate that we are mowing down some nine football fields of trees in the Amazon rain forest every minute.

The two biggest contributors to climate change are, first, the burning of fossil fuels and, second, the destruction of forests. The forests are the planet's lungs,

> **We are mowing down some nine football fields of trees in the Amazon rain forest every minute.**

except that instead of breathing in oxygen as we do, they take that problematic carbon dioxide out of the atmosphere. Trees could help save us from ourselves. We just have to stop killing them all in order to wrap up our bagels.

According to the U.S. Forest Service, forests in the United States alone sequester some 827 million tons of carbon dioxide annually, nearly 10 percent of the country's CO_2 emissions. So, if you're trying to be No Impact Man, blowing your nose on trees that were cut down especially for that purpose may not be entirely in line with your larger goals. Not to mention that forests provide numerous other ecological services, such as wildlife habitat, preventing soil erosion, and assisting the water supply cycle.

Once I knew the facts, what I blew my nose on in the morning didn't feel so trivial to me anymore. To me, the paper towel began to represent my throwaway lifestyle. It represented the fact that we are trashing the planet's resources for conveniences that turn out not even to be convenient. It represented the fact that I had been, for years, using throwaway products that I'm not sure have really made me happier and certainly haven't been making the planet happier.

These are the things you think about when you see your life in the trash.

FOUR

If Only Pizza Didn't Come on Paper Plates

Early on, when we were dating, Michelle made me her "signature" dish, spaghetti carbonara. Candles cast a warm glow. She set the table beautifully. She placed before me a dish of undercooked, nearly crunchy pasta, piled on top of a runny puddle of heavy cream.

"Delicious," I said dutifully.

"I think I forgot to put something in," Michelle said.

"The eggs?" I ventured.

Michelle blushed. "I don't actually cook," she said.

"It's delicious," I insisted.

When the No Impact project started, as a matter of simple self-preservation, we never even discussed the possibility of Michelle taking charge of grocery shopping and cooking. What I would have to come to terms with, if we were to eliminate our appalling twenty-gallon-a-day waste habit, was an end to takeout and its assortment of disposable plastic tubs. I would have to make a new habit of—God help me—grocery shopping and cooking. Me. Myself. I. By which I mean: not Michelle.

"Besides, it's your project," Michelle would, fairly, point out. Or, as she liked to note to friends: "One fun thing about No Impact has been watching my husband transform himself into a 1950s housewife."

A Provençal housewife. For my initiatory jaunt into the world of fresh-food shopping, as an ideal I had in mind what I'd seen in the

markets of the little villages of rural France, and even in the small
shops that line the high streets of the residential neighborhoods
of Paris. Fresh goods laid out on
wooden tables. Not a morsel packed
in containers, cardboard boxes, or
aluminum foil wrappers. At worst, a baker in a red-and-white apron
might twist a fresh little quiche into a piece of waxed paper with a
flourish.

> In Paris, I once saw a woman make a carrier out of the hem of her dress.

Baguettes stick out of chic ladies' reusable shopping bags protected
by not so much as a piece of cling film. Heads of lettuce, salamis, and
peaches balance precariously in bicycle baskets. There is no plastic or
paper to peel off the food once it's home. There is no packaging. And if
you don't have your own reusable shopping bag, if you should suggest
that a throwaway plastic bag might be supplied, the clerk scowls and
tsks and offers to let you reuse a cardboard box from that morning's
deliveries.

In Paris, I once saw a woman, who had purchased some food items
during an obviously unplanned shopping trip, make a carrier out of
the hem of her dress, carefully calculating, as she walked home, the
balance between dropping her vegetables and showing everyone her
underwear. I'd seen Parisians carrying their groceries in canvas bags,
backpacks, wicker baskets, or those bags made from netting—*les filets*,
as the French call them—that scrunch into a ball in your pocket but
then, voilà, can carry home your family's dinner.

So as I was preparing to venture into the world of grocery shopping and cooking in order to stop making trash, expunging disposable bags from my world became my first obsession. I should be like
the French, I thought, which was fine with me, because the French
are cool.

And for starters, what I needed to be truly environmental, I decided, was to buy myself a French net bag.

●

Wasn't anybody who cared about the planet at all already carrying canvas shopping bags? Not if they were anything like I was. Certainly, in periodic blusters of goodwill toward all creatures, I had *bought* canvas bags, but they now lay crumpled and completely forgotten at the back of some closet.

My goal now was not just to own an alternative to the throwaway bag, but to actually use one—all the time, no exceptions. As Environmentalism 101 as this sounds, it's a good benchmark for how far behind the touchdown line I had started, and, symbolically, how far behind the United States lags when it comes to cleaning up its environmental act. China, South Africa, Ireland, Bangladesh, Taiwan, Uganda, and Tanzania had already taxed or restricted plastic bags into virtual extinction.

This was an easy entrée for a neophyte like me just making his first steps into environmental living. It was merely the opening salvo in my brewing jihad against the disposable plastic crap that filled my trash bags.

And it was a simple test, like the cloths I'd been carrying around as handkerchiefs, of my hypothesis that eliminating the colossal waste from our lives, responsible for so much of the damage we do to our planetary habitat, does not entail depriving ourselves but just changing some no-longer-functional habits. After all, who would suggest that to do without plastic bags is to be deprived? Who could possibly argue that using plastic bags makes us happier?

Every year, we junk some 4 to 5 trillion plastic bags worldwide, according to the Worldwatch Institute. Around the globe, plastic bags, used for a matter of minutes and then thrown away, leave stores and markets in quantities hundreds of times greater than any other piece of merchandise. They are the world's most ubiquitous consumer item and, not coincidentally, its most pervasive throwaway product.

We recycle plastic bags at a rate of less than 1 percent, and thrown-away bags formed some 4 million tons of municiple waste in the United

States in 2006. They poison our air when burned in incinerators, or
leach nasty chemicals in our landfills for hundreds of year. And thanks
to their lightweight aerodynamics, the wind carries an estimated 1 percent of plastic bags out of trash depositories. These renegade bags end
up billowing from trees, hanging from fences, or, worst of all, floating
in the ocean.

In 1988, across a span of just two weeks, fifteen leatherback turtles,
an endangered species, washed up dead on the beaches of Long Island.
Alarmed by the deaths, marine biologists performed autopsies. They
discovered that eleven of the fifteen dead turtles had ingested plastic
bags that blocked their stomach openings. Leatherback turtles, you see,
have the unfortunate twin qualities of a taste for jellyfish and bad eye-
sight. To these nearly blind turtles, it seems, a submerged plastic bag
looks simply delicious.

The crazy thing is that the bags, which are designed to be thrown
away, are made out of a material that is designed to last forever. They
are far from the only plastic-containing disposables: think of razors,
eating utensils, toothbrushes, water bottles, coffee cups, pens, combs,
and on and on. Because plastic is so durable, all these things persist
for hundreds of years. As a result, there are 46,000 pieces of plastic
floating in every square mile of ocean, according to the United Nations
Environment Program.

A thousand miles off the coast of California, in the middle of the
Pacific Ocean, there is a swirling soup of floating trash twice the size of
the continental United States. The "garbage patch," as it's called, contains six times as much plastic, by weight, as bio-matter. Way out there
in the Pacific Ocean, a thousand miles from the nearest human, plank-
ton, jellyfish, and fish are outnumbered (by weight) six to one by
plastic bags, water bottles, and other throwaway plastic tchotchkes.

In the North Pacific alone, an estimated 100,000 sea turtles and
sea mammals, a million seabirds, and countless fish starve to death each
year after plastic blocks their digestive tracks. A recent study on Sand
Island, in the northwestern Hawaiian chain, showed that 97 percent

of Laysan albatross chicks had ingested plastic picked up by their parents from the ocean surface and mistakenly fed to them as food.

Meanwhile, those floating plastic discards that don't choke marine animals slowly break down in the salt and sunlight until they are suspended in the water like microscopic Christmas-tree bobbles. The plankton-eaters devour them, then the big fish eat the little fish, and then guess who eats the big fish? The sushi restaurants that make dinners for us grown-ups and the fish-stick factories that make school lunches for our kids. What starts at the bottom of the food chain inevitably ends up at the top.

It turns out that each of us has, in our body, detectable amounts of up to one hundred industrial chemicals nobody had even heard of fifty years ago. Many of these chemicals come from the production and use of the same disposable plastic crap that fills my garbage bags. Bisphenol-A, for example, a compound used in the liners of food cans and to make disposable water

> To these nearly blind turtles, it seems, a submerged plastic bag looks simply delicious.

bottles and other hard plastics, is a known hormone disrupter that raises the risk of certain cancers, hampers fertility, and may contribute to childhood behavioral problems such as hyperactivity.

You are what you eat, they say, and it's not just the turtles who are ingesting the plastic crap we throw away. What happens to the wildlife on this planet is an early warning sign of what's happening to us.

The way my culture lives its life, I can't help wondering: Really? Are plastic bags (and paper bags, which aren't any better for the environment) something for which we are willing to threaten the planetary habitat we all depend upon for our health, happiness, and security?

On balance, if we have to choose—and I think we kind of do— would we rather have a planet overflowing with plastic bags and all the rest of the disposable plastic crap, or would we rather have sea turtles and chemical-free children?

•

It is with a fixation not so much on saving turtles, I have to admit, as on getting myself a couple of those cool French net shopping bags that, in the middle of a late-November afternoon, with what I think is plenty of time to spare, I venture out into the world to gather food for our first non-trash-generating meal.

I call Michelle and give her the choice between omelettes and tofu scramble for dinner. In the spirit of a true eco-wannabe, she chooses tofu scramble. I head, first, to the nearby Whole Foods on Union Square.

Down in the store's lower level, I explain very carefully to a shop clerk what I am looking for—and it's not tofu. "You know," I say, "those bags that kind of look like fishing net but they have handles."

The clerk doesn't follow.

I start to explain again.

The clerk stops me.

No, he says. Whatever it is I'm after, Whole Foods doesn't have it. They carry black, canvas-type bags made out of recycled plastic. "But, no, nothing made out of, um, fishnets."

I go to Bed, Bath & Beyond. Nope. I go to the Container Store. Nope. I try Home Depot. Nope. I walk up Sixth Avenue and down Broadway, explaining to every shopkeeper who will listen all about the net bags they use in France. But, no.

Suddenly it's 5:00 p.m. I have to pick up Isabella from Peggy, our child-carer. The ample couple of hours I'd allowed for shopping is up. Once home, I look out of my ninth-floor window, down at the trees, and see three plastic bags tangled in the branches. I look around the apartment and see that it is virtually littered with bags I could have used to go shopping—including the ones at the back of the closet I'd bought in my last blush of eco-consciousness.

Michelle gets home from work. "Is dinner almost ready?"

I give her a dejected look. I have no tofu, and there will be no tofu scramble. Yet again we Google the number for the Big Enchilada. Yet again we order takeout. Yet again our trash is filled with plastic tubs.

Since the tubs will persist for a thousand years, I realize, I could put a note in one in the hope that it might be found by my grandchildren's grandchildren's grandhildren's grandchildren. Here's what the note would say: "Dear kids. Sorry about the turtles."

If the goal is to keep empty the garbage bags that used to be filled with take-out containers, filling a grocery cart with plastic-wrapped veggies, cardboard-boxed pasta, yogurt in tubs, and eggs in cartons won't do the trick. Prepackaged grocery-store food is out. By the time I wake up first thing the next morning and make shopping for food—and only shopping for food—the priority of the day, I've realized that loose produce and unpackaged food sold from bulk bins are my holy grail.

So I grabbed my long-neglected reusable bags and walked over to the Integral Yoga grocery store, where I'd had my plastic-or-paper-bag ordeal. Integral Yoga Natural Foods, as it is called in full, is run by the acolytes of someone called Sri Swami Satchidananda. They sell an extensive selection of unpackaged food that you scoop into containers with little shovels. The Swami, I suppose, preached the importance of bulk bins.

The problem, though, when you're faced with bins full of everything from pasta and rice to seaweed and raisins, is that you still have to find a way to carry the food home. You can't just stuff your pockets with brown rice. Normal people—those who aren't making their life's work out of not making trash—tear off plastic bags from rolls hanging by the bins. But with last night's take-out enchilada slip, I'd hit a bottom with my turtle choking, and starting today I had very proudly thought of a better solution.

Back at home, I had gathered a bunch of empty glass jars out of our cupboards and stuffed them in the canvas bags I'd finally rescued from the back of the closet. I lugged the jars with me to Integral Yoga with the intention of putting my pasta and my rice and coffee and freshly ground-up peanut butter in them. I had even weighed the jars, so I knew how much the cashier should subtract after I'd filled them with commodities.

So, I arrive at Integral Yoga, scoop various grocery needs into jars, and am feeling very proud of myself. I'd found my place. I'd arrived at my new eco-home. I'd discovered my family's new nutritional center of gravity.

With filled-up jars, I get in line to pay. My turn comes and I put my jars on the counter and smile at the young woman behind the cash register. I look forward expectantly to her recognition of my eco-effort and her smile of encouragement.

"What's all this?" she asks, looking at the jars.

I explain about the jars and not using plastic bags and I point to the weights I'd written on masking tape stuck to the lids and she calls the manager to figure out how to do the subtraction. I'm growing anxious about the line of customers behind me yet looking forward to the cashier telling me how great I am for not using plastic bags.

But she doesn't.

You know what she does instead?

She sighs.

Then she looks at me. Then she looks at the jars. Then she looks at me again. Then, you know what she does? She rolls her eyes.

Since deciding to loosely model my life, for a year, on the smidgeon I'd heard about the wood-harvesting philosophy of the Menominee tribe, I've idealized them in my mind. They've become my symbol of good living, of living happily, taking from the planet what it can sustainably offer and not taking what it can't.

> **Do the Menominee suffer crises of confidence? Because I am hitting my first.**

Today, though, I want to know: Do the Menominee suffer crises of confidence? Because I am hitting my first.

The Menominee's philosophy, as McDonough and Braungart put it in *Cradle to Cradle*, demanded that they never took more lumber than the forest could sustainably offer them. But what about years of hunger or drought? What about years when wood prices fell so low that they couldn't meet the needs of their children? What about years when they were just overwhelmed by wanting and desire and craving?

I mean, it's been a couple of weeks now since the Integral Yoga cashier scowled at me; and, in truth, I've made a lot of progress.

We've stopped eating takeout in plastic tubs. Canceled our newspaper subscriptions. Avoided buying anything in packaging. Put our names on the do-not-send-me-catalogs-and-junk-mail lists. Begun taking clothes to the tailor for repair instead of throwing them out. Taken our own reusable containers to take-out places when we just couldn't get ourselves to cook. Replaced paper towels with rags made from discarded clothes. Collected used printer paper from my publisher and used the other side to write on. Kept a cloth handy to wrap things in, use as a napkin, and dry our hands on when we're out of the house.

Further: We've carried reusable cups everywhere. Accepted that we can't have coffee if we forget our cups. Turned a nose up at bottled water by using our cups for tap water, too. Replaced throwaway products, like Bic pens and Gillette razors, with reusable versions (think straight razor and fountain pen). Celebrated the diminishing of our waistlines, since we're pretty much off packaged cans of Pringles, not to mention Ben & Jerry's Chubby Hubby.

I'd even proved my environmental bona fides by having an argument with Michelle about whether she would make the switch from throwaway tampons to those reusable menstrual cups made from medical-grade silicon. I lost (but I'd wear her down eventually).

None of these steps was too unpleasant at all. I'd even found little pull-string organic muslin bags so light that you don't have to subtract their weight when you fill them with pasta from the bulk bin and put them on the scale at Integral Yoga. Even my old nemesis, the cashier, is secretly starting to like me. My family's trashcan and even our recycling bin is yawningly empty. I've come to think I can do this. I've hit my stride. Or so I thought.

Although today, walking past a pizza place on Fourteenth Street, I find myself looking longingly in the window. Not hungrily. Longingly. It's just a hankering, really. And before this no-impact thing started, such a hankering would have had me marching straight through the door and up to the counter to chow down a slice on a now-prohibited paper plate. Same if I wanted soda in a now-prohibited plastic bottle. Same, really, if I wanted just about anything.

But today I'm thinking maybe I'll cheat.

Living in New York City, I'd long felt that I could gratify my wants pretty much the moment I had them. No more. To avoid making trash, I've had to say no more than a few times in the last couple of weeks.

No to an everything bagel with scallion tofu wrapped in waxed paper from Bagel Bob's. No to a bottle of seltzer water. No to herbal tea in a paper cup from News Bar. No even to a tinfoil-wrapped Hershey's Kiss from the snack area at the Writers Room, where I go to work. No peanuts. No potato chips. No popcorn at the movies. Our entire universe, apparently, is individually wrapped. Unless you're willing to toss out that handful of barely used packaging within five minutes of getting it, without ever even using it, you're screwed.

"Good Lord, man," National Public Radio presenter Scott Simon would say to me during an interview for *Talk of the Nation*, "isn't the whole point of living in New York to enjoy the good life?"

"God, yes!" I would have shouted if he asked me today. I felt like I was making sacrifices for the sake of environmentally poor decisions that other people had made. There was no reason that pizza needed to be on a plate made from a dead tree. Couldn't the geniuses of our culture find an ecologically sensitive way to do these things? For now, I felt like I was the one paying for their bad systems.

It's true that I discovered Ronnybrook Farm, a dairy with a stand at the farmer's market that sells its milk in glass bottles that I can return for reuse. I love that I've found blocks of unpackaged tofu I can put in my own container, and egg farmers who take back and re-use their egg cartons. There are some small-scale systems that can be found that don't require resources to be wasted, and I feel really good about getting our groceries home and making our meals without making trash. And I dig the childishly naughty feeling I get that by doing all this I'm somehow being subversive and giving a finger to the Matrix.

But there comes a time when, hell, you just want a slice of pizza, even if "the man" hasn't thought to provide it in a sustainable way. What I've accomplished until now mostly has to do with investigating and planning—where to shop, what unpackaged product to buy. Passing up a slice of pizza (and the paper plate) would have more to do with accepting that, if I want to live sustainably, I can no longer have exactly what I want exactly when I want it. Because our systems are not designed to be sustainable, I had to swim against the cultural tide, and sometimes I got tired.

Self-restraint. Crap!

That's how I imagine the Menominee must have felt on so many occasions over their hundreds of years of managing their forests. There must have been many times when they wanted more but could not take it, many times when enough did not seem like enough. But how would they keep their lumber business if they cut too many trees down? How will I make discoveries in this experiment if every time I have a craving I cave in?

Today, again, since I have no way to avoid using a paper plate and napkin, I say no to the pizza. But I'm not happy.

I walk away down Fourteenth Street. Stopped at the red light on the corner of Third Avenue is a guy in a BMW. Anger washes over me. And self-righteousness. This idiot is guzzling oil and pumping carbon into the air in the middle of a city that has wonderful public transportation, my mind tells me. But I'm not mad so much as I'm envious. This guy gets to sit in his fancy car, listening to his Bose in-car stereo while pretty girls crossing the street turn to look at him, and I'm stuck in my self-imposed year of not having a piece of pizza when I want one.

How do the Menominee-in-my-mind feel when they are exercising self-restraint but they see a company like Kimberly-Clark raking in millions by clear-cutting every tree in sight to make paper plates to put pizza on? Do the Menominee feel sorry for themselves? Do they have the feeling I do today—that everyone can have what they want but me? I doubt it. By now, I'm sure, they've learned that there is a strong payoff to living the way they do.

The Menominee know that in a hundred years they will have still more trees to cut down. With the Amazon rain forest losing 2,000 trees a minute, Kimberly-Clark and the rest of us very well may not. That's the sustainability payoff for the Menominee. My question is: Where's the sustainability payoff for me?

Michelle comes bursting through the door, carrying a big plastic cup filled with nuclear-purple goop.

"I have great news," she says, all smiles.

"What?" I ask, eyeing her disallowed plastic cup.

"I've discovered the No Impact weight-loss diet."

The thing is, Michelle is one of those New York media-industry glam-girl fashionistas. It's who she is. For her, a great carefree night out consists of ten friends at Pastis, shouting over the din about clothes, then men, then diets, probably in that order. Michelle and her friends are like the spymasters of undiscovered designer-sample sales and the mad scientists of weight-loss schemes that will get them to fit into those clothes.

In the week before the No Impact project, in a panic about the coming year, she went on a clothes-shopping bender that reaped her two really nice pairs of leather boots and cost us the cashing-in of one small, unserviced 401(k). The No Impact project, in other words, doesn't come easily to her. But she's a sport. And she has an open mind about how it might turn out.

Anyway, her last high-tech weight-loss scheme involved payment of huge amounts of cash to a nutritionist and then a month spent eating space meals from little tinfoil packets to which you add water. As of to-day, apparently, it's juice fasting. She has just come home from a place on Third Avenue called Juiceteria. Her friend Tara told her about it.

"I know, I know. I got a disposable cup," Michelle says, "but I talked to the lady behind the counter and she supports our project. She says I can bring my own reusable bottle or cup."

I force a smile.

The thing is, while my grandparents had their nice little retire-ment home in Westport, Massachusetts, Michelle's maternal grand-parents did everything they could to get their children a better life than they themselves had on a farm in the Midwest. Their families had lived through the hardship of the Dust Bowl. They had eeked a living off the land. To Michelle's family, therefore, who had moved off the land and become rich, to buy what they wanted when they wanted it—like the juice—had become a sign of their overcoming dif-ficulty. It was, in their way, even an expression of gratitude for their good fortune. This purchasing freedom was evidence of the family's hard work.

Is this expression of identity any less true or valuable or under-standable than my own grandparents' insistence on thrift? No.

But the question remains: How do we reconcile such a way of life with the fact that the planet we depend upon for our health, happi-ness, and security is so depleted? The trick, in part, will be to make living sustainably as easy as falling off a log. We must find produc-tion processes, ways to generate energy, and manufacturing materials that do not damage our planet so substantially. Then Michelle can have her juice and affirm her family's success, too.

Meanwhile, our culture's whole way of operating is one huge jug-gernaut heading in a consume-every-resource direction. Somehow I'm supposed to persuade poor Michelle to live differently, to reject, in a way, the culture of her family. Is this right?

Besides which, I wonder: What's so great about trying to be right if it keeps you separate? What's so great about trying to be right if it makes you lonely?

The juice is Michelle's version of the French net bag. You try to go to the end of the consumerist universe but keep finding yourself back at its center, back in the old buy-something-to-fix-something, eat-to-lose-weight, consume-to-conserve trance that we're all stuck in. But, today, I just don't have the heart to say anything.

My thought process around this discouraging time:

1. I worried that the whole pizza episode pointed to the larger fact that the human species may be called upon to exercise superhuman restraint when it comes to not using resources the planet cannot afford for us to use. "The problem with people like you is that you don't accept that people are basically selfish and they're never going to change," I'd get told more than a few times during the No Impact project. At this low point, when I still felt bitter about the things I could not have, and awful for denying Michelle the things she wanted, I thought maybe they were right. I began to worry again that people were just too selfish.

2. But, for starters, the idea that people, including me, are driven first by selfishness goes against my whole world-view and my gut instinct. Most of us love our children and want to be polite to our neighbors. Most of us, unless we are hobbled by terrible living conditions or alcohol or drugs, would rather help than harm. Most of us, in our hearts, want peace and harmony for ourselves and for everyone else. Most of us believe that we should take good care of the planet. None of us actually *likes* trashing our resources.

3. Besides, it's not an issue of whether we want things, it's an issue of how the system delivers the things we want.

My desire for the pizza was not the problem. The fact that it came on a disposable paper plate was the problem. Our system makes it virtually impossible to get the things we want and need without leaving behind a trail of trash and pollution and greenhouse gases. Sit down at a fast-food restaurant, for example, and within moments the garbage surges at you. First comes the paper placemat and the paper napkin, then the straw, the straw wrapper, a throwaway glass bottle with your drink, a paper doily, a Styrofoam box, a little plastic cup for ketchup. "You're going to think this is weird," I must have said to a hundred servers, "but I'm on this don't-make-trash kick. I brought my own cloth napkin. Would you mind terribly much putting this paper one back where you got it?"

4. Just because trash crashes like a tidal wave through my life doesn't mean I made the tidal wave. Trash and pollution and greenhouse gases, therefore, are not a result of some total flaw in human nature.

5. But when I started reading a little history, I learned that there were reasons why I felt so guilty and selfish. "People start pollution. People can stop it." Remember that message? It came from the Keep America Beautiful (KAB) campaign's public-service announcement, the one with the Native American who cries because of

> My desire for the pizza was not the problem. The fact that it came on a disposable paper plate was the problem.

all the litter. Well, guess what? It turns out that KAB was established by the American Can Company and the Owens-Illinois Glass Company, the inventors of the throwaway, nonreturnable beverage can and bottle, respectively. They recruited fellow industrial polluters, from paper-cup manufacturers to oil companies, to help fund KAB and then use it to promote the idea that individuals rather than companies are responsible for litter and pollution. As Heather Rogers writes in her book about garbage, *Gone Tomorrow*, "KAB wanted to turn any stirrings of environmental awareness away from industry's massive and supertoxic destruction of the natural world . . . singling out the real villain: the notorious 'litterbug.'" No wonder I feel so guilty.

6. History also taught me that the United States has already proved that it's perfectly possible for a culture to operate without sending so much to landfills and incinerators, selfishness and altruism notwithstanding. Before 1900, most households didn't even have a trashcan. The rag-and-bone man came to your door and paid you to give him, among other things, your old clothes for paper-making, your meat bones for button-making, and your cooking grease for soap-making. What was left, you burned in your stove for heat. But this cultural ethic of reuse changed when, by way of example, button factories discovered it was cheaper and more efficient to get their bone from the conveyor-belt slaughterhouses, and paper producers discovered a way to make paper from trees instead of from cloth. With industrialization, our materials economy stopped working in a circle that went from producer to consumer and back again, and instead became unidirectional—from producer to consumer to landfill and incinerator.

7. To me, this proves again that making so much trash and pollution and greenhouses gases is not the result of our natures—selfish or otherwise—but simply of corporate habits our culture can no longer sustain. And if we changed once, from closed to open loop, I figured, we can just as easily change from open to closed loop. Germany, I discovered, already has a system called "extended producer

responsibility," a policy that requires producers to be phys-
ically or financially responsible for their products, including the packaging, after their useful life. This take-back
obligation gives producers an incentive to think of ways
to make their products more reusable or recyclable so that
fewer resources end up making a beeline for the landfill
or incinerator.

8. But after thinking all this through, my mood took a turn
   for the worse. I thought, Oh great, the problem is not selfish human nature; it's just our whole manufacturing and
   distribution system. Like that's going to be easier to fix. If
   I'm hoping for change, I might as well blow my head off.

9. What was the point of this stupid No Impact project?

10. Then, a regular reader of my blog, a woman who lives in
    India named Uma Padmanabhan, left behind this quote
    from the *Bhagavad Gita*, the epic Hindu poem: "To action
    alone hast thou a right and never at all to its fruits; let not
    the fruits of action be thy motive; neither let there be in
    thee any attachment to inaction." In other words, just do it!

11. And a woman calling herself Jen from Brooklyn left on
    the blog the story of Nachshon, who was the first of the
    Israelites to enter the Red Sea when fleeing from Egypt.
    Nachshon, she wrote, was an ordinary guy, not a leader or
    anything like that. Nachshon didn't have the slightest
    idea how he was going to get across the Red Sea, but he
    marched on in just the same. All he had was courage and
    determination and maybe faith, and so he just did the
    only thing he could, which was to take each step as it came.
    He didn't know what would happen. The good news is,
    and maybe it will be the good news for all of us who try,
    that just as he got to the point where the water came up
    to his nose, the Red Sea parted.

12. I find myself reminded that the whole project is about

not waiting around to see what might help. It is about
stumbling forward and beginning to try to make a difference, rather than sitting around wondering if I can make
a difference.

13. So whether it's human nature or industrial systems that
need to change, when it comes to saving the world, the
real question is not whether I can make a difference.
The real question is whether I am willing to try.

14. Am I willing to try?

Here's a little thought experiment that keeps obsessing me.

We know that for all the material that ends up in our products,
the manufacturing process has already trashed seventy times that much
material. Do the math and that means that, of all the raw material
taken from the earth to make consumer products, only 1.5 percent of
it actually ends up in our hands. Meanwhile, 98.5 percent of what we
suck out of the ground, the rivers, and the forests ends up being trucked
straight to the landfill or the incinerator without it ever even being
used by us.

Now, I'm no economist or production analyst, so I'm sure the situation isn't as perfectly straightforward as I'm about to make it sound,
but from where I'm sitting, this means that of the water and air the
manufacturing sector pollutes, of the forests it cuts down, of the natural habitats it destroys, of the greenhouse gases it creates, of the total
environmental damage created by manufacturing, 98.5 percent results
in nothing but industrial waste, producer trash that consumers never
even see.

So here's my little thought experiment:

Suppose we, as a culture, ask the manufacturing people to reduce
their waste by just 1.5 percent. "Hey, you guys," we could say, "just
tone it down a little. Tell you what, though, you can still waste 97 percent of what you dig out of the planet. We just want you to reduce your

waste by 1.5 percent." Personally, I don't feel that asking this of them would be too terribly harsh.

But here's the thing: if they wasted just that little bit less, then the amount of raw materials available to actually end up in products would jump from 1.5 percent (what's left behind by 98.5 percent waste) to 3 percent (what's left behind after reducing waste to 97 percent). That's huge. Because that's a doubling of the resources available to go in products, this would mean that, for manufacturing to get what it needs, it could chop down half as many trees, blow the tops off half as many mountains, pollute half as many rivers, and pump out half the greenhouse gases. And what would it take? Reducing their waste from 98.5 percent to 97 percent.

That doesn't sound like too much to ask, does it?

As I walked away from the pizza, I was feeling angry, as if everybody else were allowed to have what they want but not me. I suddenly felt like I was transported back to being the ten-year-old "have-not" of my seaside childhood town, where the motorboat and minibike of my classmate Skippy Manchester were mysteriously denied me.

But to suggest that that feeling derived from being the quasi-poor kid doesn't explain it, either.

Because Michelle, who grew up the child of millionaires, lived in the then-biggest house in Bismarck, North Dakota. She was, in fact, the Skippy Manchester of her town. But she tells me she spent half her time wishing she lived in a one-story ranch house like "normal" people, and the other half wishing she could drive around a family estate in a golf cart like her even richer, billionaire friends.

Michelle and I talk about this because the No Impact project forces us to come face-to-face with daily desires we're so unaccustomed to confronting. We talk about how the poor kid and the rich kid—me and her—both suffered the same amount of want and envy. We talk about how everybody, in any life situation, in any circumstances, at any time, seems to want something. We talk about how wanting is a kind of perpetual-motion machine that lives in our minds.

My attention now drawn to the fact, I see that when I get what I want, my want does not go away, it just turns to the next thing. In some ways, it's incorrect to say, "I want this" or "I want that." It's more correct to just say, "I want," in the same way as we say, "I ache." If I got the net bag, I would have just gone on to want something else. I wonder if, understanding that wanting is at the base of human experience and that it is not alleviated by fulfilling the capricious desire of the day, I might perhaps allow myself to get off the hamster wheel.

At the same time, Michelle and I noticed that what we wanted on the surface—the minibike or the "normal" ranch house—were just proxies for what we really wanted: to fit in. We wanted to be loved. We wanted not to feel what we imagined that everyone else didn't feel—insecurity. We wanted to feel accepted.

So, here's the big question: If we want to demonstrate our membership in the human race, if we want to fit in, where on earth did the idea come from that we have to do it by having or aspiring to have exactly what everyone else has, by eating what everyone else eats, by drinking what everyone else drinks? People are such social animals, so much more than we realize. We'll do, or can be tricked into doing, almost anything for the promise of love.

"We're getting rid of the TV," Michelle announced when I came home one night. It had been a few weeks now that, by Michelle's original insistence, the TV had been unplugged. Our television, by the way, was this forty-six-inch-screen, rear-projection giant that took up much more living-room space than we could spare.

"Hold your horses," I said. "We may want it when the project is over."

"It's evil," Michelle said. "It's never caused us anything but problems and I want it out of here."

What she was saying was true. Michelle had developed, by her own admission, a little bit of an addiction to reality television. We had fought about it. I felt it got in the way of our relationship— something to do with her preferring to watch *The Bachelor* than to talk to me. And Isabella, in the week or two before the project began, had actually said, in her squeaky going-on-two-year-old voice, "I want *Bridezilla*, Mommy."

"When your kid asks for *Bridezilla*," Michelle said, "you know you're putting your viewing pleasure before your parenthood. Get rid of it. This is non-negotiable."

For the woman who had spent a small retirement fund on boots a few weeks earlier, this was quite the turnaround.

I thought about it. I thought about the 2,000 to 5,000 advertisements people like Michelle and me see every day, depending on where you're getting your stats. I thought about how the consumption activist Annie Leonard said, in her video *Story of Stuff*, that "three thousand times a day, we're told that our hair is wrong, skin is

> **Four weeks after the project began, we weren't just changing the way we lived; changing the way we lived was changing us.**

wrong, clothes are wrong, our furniture is wrong, our cars are wrong, we are wrong but that it can all be made right if we just go shopping." And I thought, No wonder I feel like a loser for no longer buying exactly what I want the moment I want it.

I'm trying to become a nonconsumer of planetary resources, and here in the middle of my house was this box whose purpose was to pump messages at me, telling me that unless I used more resources I was a loser. To be No Impact Man, it told me, was to be a loser. It told me that to put not making trash before having more stuff was to be a loser. Waking up to the fact that the TV was making me feel bad about my life—and making the project harder—was like discovering that the enemy was encamped in my living room.

Which clinched it. By Michelle's decree, we would be a no-TV family from here on in. Four weeks after the project began, we weren't

just changing the way we lived; changing the way we lived was
changing us. Michelle made arrangements to give the TV to a family
who might otherwise buy a new one. Two huge 250-pound men
marched into our living room, lifted up our forty-six-inch television,
and carried it away.

FIVE

How to Reduce Your Carbon Footprint and Anger Your Mom at the Same Time

A dilemma: Suppose you have the choice, on the one hand, of not contributing to the extinction of just about everything, the raging of gigantic storms, the rising levels of the oceans, tropical disease spreading as far north and south as the poles. Suppose, on the other, by making an extreme effort not to create greenhouse gases, you could really piss off parents on both sides of the family.

Wrath of parents? Wrath of the planet? Which would you choose?

Between November and February, my little family had planned four road or rail trips from New York to New England, where I'm from, and one air trip to see Michelle's parents at their winter home in Palm Springs, in sunny Southern California.

Looking at it from an aggregate perspective—the faraway view through the telescope—airline flights account for only 3 percent of the worldwide carbon dioxide gas emissions, though they also spew other gases into the atmosphere that may double their warming effect. Six percent. No biggie, right? Ah, but that's not because air travel isn't carbon intense. It's because most of the world's population can't afford to fly.

Taking the microscopic view, looking at it from the perspective of individual contributions to greenhouse gases by a privileged citizen of the affluent Northern Hemisphere (i.e., me), a single long-haul round-trip billows three tons of carbon dioxide into the atmosphere, as much as an entire average year of driving. Short of setting up an oil refinery in my bathroom, flying—movie stars who drive a Prius but still fly in private jets, please take note—is about the most carbon-intensive thing my family and I can do.

Palm Springs and the trip to see Michelle's parents, in other words, was out.

Goodbye, O excellent trip to Southern California in the middle of winter. Goodbye, swimming pool. Goodbye, sunbathing when there might be snow on the ground back home. Goodbye, walks in the mountains, holding hands with my wife. Goodbye, hot tubs. Goodbye, grandparents on babysitting duty. Hello, difficult conversation with Michelle.

> A single long-haul round-trip billows three tons of carbon dioxide into the atmosphere, as much as an entire average year of driving.

Meanwhile, on the subject of visits to *my* neck of the woods, the four planned New England trips by car or rail, there was, first, the trek to Westport, Massachusetts, my hometown, for Thanksgiving dinner at my mother's and my sister Susan's baby shower (her first). Second, to Cumberland, Rhode Island, to the Kwan Um Zen Temple, to sit a retreat led by a friend and favorite Zen teacher, Zen Master Soeng Hwang (Bobby Rhodes). Third, back to Westport, for Christmas. And, fourth, back to Westport yet again, for the birth of Susan's baby, who would pop out in mid-February.

Conversations with my mother and sister about canceling these trips weren't going to go much smoother than talking to Michelle. So I came up with a plan. I performed some quick, back-of-the-envelope calculations showing just how much less environmental damage short trips by rail cause than flying. Using them as ammunition, rather than face my mother and sister, I would persuade Michelle that we should cancel the air travel (the trip to her family), but that the impact of the rail travel (the trips to my family) was relatively insignificant.

"We can't in good conscience go on all these trips," I said.

"You're right," Michelle said.

"The thing is, though, the flight to Palm Springs causes more impact than all the other trips combined, so I was thinking . . ."

"No way," Michelle said.

"No way *what?*" I said.

"No way am I going to be the only one to cancel. I'll cancel the trip to my parents, yes, but not if you're not canceling your trips." Michelle saw straight through me.

It was only fair. Besides which, the whole point was not to make a bunch of calculated exceptions. Else I would never see how trying to live no-impact affected lifestyle. I wasn't calling myself A Little Bit Less Impact Man, after all.

I stalled calling my mother. Michelle, on the other hand, felt no apprehension whatsoever about calling hers.

"If you tell my parents it has to do with your work or career, they automatically accept that as a priority," she said. "Watch this."

She matter-of-factly picked up the phone. Just like that. And just like that she told her mother, Sorry, but we have to cancel our planned visit to Palm Springs. They talked for a minute and a half and hung up.

I was amazed. "What did she say?"

Michelle just looked at me.

"Well?"

"She said that my life is being subsumed by yours and that it's as though I've joined some sort of eco-cult and you are the cult leader."

"The one that brainwashed you into not visiting your elderly parents in their twilight years?" I asked.

"Exactly."

"Do you think she's right?"

Michelle shrugged.

What could I say? It's not like I didn't see her mother's point of view.

Michelle pointed to the phone. My turn.

Not yet.

So began phase two: no carbon-producing transportation. Back in November, at the onset of the project, mistakenly thinking that getting rid of trash was easy, I'd decided we might as well get started on the transportation phase from the very beginning, too.

As a result, true to the obsessive-compulsive-seeming standards I'd set myself, no carbon-producing transportation meant not only no planes, trains, or car rides to the beach, it also meant, from the start of the no-impact year, no taxis, subways, buses, or even elevators (Michelle's forty-third-floor office—because security refused stairwell access—and necessary work trips excepted). For the entire year, we would pretty much not be going anywhere except under our own steam; horses and sailboats would be allowed, except that they run a little short in Manhattan. For all intents and purposes, Michelle, Isabella, Frankie, and I, each in our own fashion, would be self-propelled.

> Does being able to jump on a movement machine, so that you never have to walk across town or climb up stairs, necessarily improve quality of life?

Even when it rained. Even when it snowed. Even when it froze.

Why no elevators? Why no public transportation, incredulous friends would ask? Isn't public transportation part of the solution to climate change? Yes, it is. But when you go around calling yourself No Impact Man, you have to acknowledge that even riding the subway involves the carbon emissions generated at the electric plant (though about a fifth, on average, of what the same trip by car would cause).

Plus, I had, to me, a more interesting reason: I wanted to know what would happen if, living in a huge metropolis, we decided to forgo, as much as possible, the mechanized, automated, fossil-fuel-dependent infrastructure. Does being able to jump on a movement machine, so that you never have to walk across town or climb up stairs, necessarily improve quality of life? Was there a possibility that there might be some benefits to a life without mechanized transportation?

Prepared by my experience with the project to date, I anticipated and sidestepped the buy-something impulse that found me nearly drooling before a shiny new fifteen-speed, carbon-frame bike hanging in the window of a shop on Sixth Avenue. Instead, I dusted off my old, heavy, red mountain bike, stored for years, except for the annual burst of exercise-and-get-rid-of-my-gut intention, in the basement of our building. I took the bike—true to the ethos of the No Impact project— to a nonprofit shop in the East Village that trains inner-city youth to fix up old bikes from recycled parts, called Recycle-A-Bicycle.

A really skinny—sign of things to come for me, I hoped—guy named Joe, the manager, took my bike into triage and, with a tire pump, some grease, and a couple of cables, brought it back to life. He added to it a secondhand "handlebar extender" (so I could sit up straight for comfort and visibility in traffic) and some fenders (so I didn't get sprayed with greasy rainwater and garbage juice). What had once been a red bike was now red, black, and chrome.

"Now you've got a great commuter bike," Joe told me.

I thought it was looking a little like a patchwork quilt.

But as I infiltrated the New York City bike culture and found my way to the activists of commuter biking in New York City, the staff and volunteers of an organization called Transportation Alternatives, I'd learn that the chances of keeping a shiny new bike from getting stolen were close to nil. The trick to commuting by bike in Manhattan, I'd be told, is to make sure that your bike costs less than your lock. In other words, kudos to me for not getting a new one.

As for Michelle's carbon-free transportation initiative, she dug out of the closet an old pair of silver Prada sneakers and sent them to the cobbler for a spiff-up. She also bought a new pair of Converse. She planned to walk the daily forty blocks to work, proud that her feet were sufficiently dressed to greet their public. Michelle wanted to save the planet, yes, but she wanted to do it wearing the right lipstick, sunglasses, and shoes.

"You should probably get a bike," I told her. "It would be much quicker."

"I warned you about that when we started," Michelle said.

Because of a past incident involving me, a bike, the streets of New York, a broken bone, and an ambulance, Michelle wasn't altogether pleased that I'd be riding bikes, either. We'll come to that later. For now, suffice it to say that Michelle made me promise that I wouldn't ride in midtown traffic, a promise I planned to keep only until I could persuade her to let me retract it.

Without the alternative of public transportation to turn to, the midtown no-go zone wasn't practical. Nor, I knew, was Michelle's intransigence about getting her own bike. The daily forty-minute-each-way walk to work she planned would get old for her pretty fast. I saw fights on the horizon. But this was now, and that was later. I'd figure that out when the time came.

By the way, greenhouse gases, for all the bad press they've been getting lately, keep us alive. Well, not so much keep us alive as allow us to be born in the first place. Because the greenhouse effect, as it's called, is what keeps the earth at livable temperatures. The moon, for example, which has no atmosphere, and therefore no greenhouse effect, bakes away at inhuman temperatures during the day and becomes an icicle's icicle at night. On Earth, however, greenhouse gases in the atmosphere help keep us cozy.

"We'd all be dead if it weren't for the greenhouse effect," the climate change naysayers like to say, "so what are you worried about?" But the problem is not the greenhouse effect, per se. The problem is that the greenhouse effect is getting, as the climate scientists say, "enhanced."

I'm finding this stuff out, by the way, because while I'm sneaking around, riding my bike in midtown traffic, hoping my wife doesn't find out, and figuring out how to cancel visits to my poor mom, I ought to know what I'm talking about.

As one story goes, certain naturally occurring gases in the earth's atmosphere have little or no effect when it comes to warming up the planet—like oxygen and nitrogen. The sun's rays pass through the atmosphere and warm the earth's surface. The earth, in turn, radiates some of that warmth, unencumbered by oxygen and nitrogen, back out into space. Certain other natural components of the atmosphere—like water vapor, carbon dioxide, methane, nitrous oxide, and high-altitude ozone—have the effect of trapping the heat absorbed from the sun and warming the place up—the greenhouse effect. This, as I've said, used to be an entirely good thing.

It turns out, though, that since the beginning of the Industrial Revolution, human activities—especially burning fossil fuels, cutting down forests, and raising cattle—have begun increasing levels of those naturally occurring greenhouse gases. We've also added to the atmosphere a cocktail of other greenhouse gases that would not normally be there—among them low-altitude ozone and substances known as halocarbons.

The more we fill our atmosphere with these gases, the more we "enhance" the greenhouse effect, the more of the sun's radiation gets absorbed and trapped, the warmer the earth's surface becomes. Think of throwing on a heavier blanket or putting double-glazing on the greenhouse or adding insulation to a building. Except that in the case of a planet warming, things get a lot more complicated and difficult to understand and predict.

For one thing, there is a tipping point, a level of greenhouse gases beyond which the associated temperature rise will cause damage—such as massive species extinction and the complete melting of polar ice—that cannot be undone. For another, as we continue to produce greenhouse gases, we'll reach this tipping point much faster than simple analysis might predict, because it turns out that the more we warm the planet, the more the planet warms itself. The scientists call this a "positive-feedback loop." The rest of us might call it a frighteningly vicious circle, one that goes something like this:

Warm the planet by adding greenhouse gases, and next thing you know, you get water evaporating from the oceans and entering the atmosphere as water vapor at an accelerated rate, which warms the planet more. Warm the planet enough to melt some sea ice, and what used to be a highly reflective white surface that sent sunshine back into space is now the dark blue surface of ocean water, which absorbs it. Again, more warming, which causes more water to evaporate, more ice to melt, and on and on.

The bad news is that the list of positive-feedback effects goes on and is more extensive and complicated then anyone understands. Warming causes a domino effect that begets more warming. In fact, in a late 2007 study of the earth's geological history, the U.S. government's most senior climate scientist, James Hansen, discovered that feedback effects increase the warming potential of carbon dioxide, the most important greenhouse gas, by a factor of three.

> For every million pounds of atmospheric gas, no more than 350 may be composed of carbon dioxide. The problem is, we're already at 387 parts per million.

To put it another way, theoretically, when the warming contributions of feedback effects are left out, a doubling of the carbon dioxide in the earth's atmosphere from preindustrial levels would cause a temperature rise of 2 degrees Celsius (3.6 degrees Fahrenheit). But in real life, in the actual recorded history of our planet, thanks to the contributions of the positive-feedback effects, a doubling of the carbon dioxide in the atmosphere has actually caused temperature to rise by 6 degrees Centigrade (10.8 degrees Fahrenheit).

Which brings me back to this question of the tipping point.

Climate scientists around the globe agree that there is an atmospheric concentration of carbon dioxide beyond which, if it stays at that level too long, the temperature will rise too much and the planet will irreversibly change. According to Hansen's analysis of climate history, that level is 350 parts per million (ppm), measured by weight. For every million pounds of atmospheric gas, no more than 350 may be composed of carbon dioxide. We must reduce carbon dioxide concentration to this level, Hansen believes, if, in his words, "humanity wishes to preserve a planet similar to that on which civilization developed and to which life on Earth is adapted."

The problem is, we're already at 387 ppm. And it's rising by 2 ppm a year.

So, tying it all together, here is why the No Impact project has a no-carbon-producing transportation phase:

The United States, with just 5 percent of the world's population, is the largest producer of greenhouse gases, accounting for nearly 25 percent of these emissions. Meanwhile, about one-third of our carbon footprint comes from transportation. And, overall, our driving produces *nearly a full half* of the entire planet's automotive greenhouse gases.

That's it. I'm calling my mom.

The good news is that in my desperation to keep everyone happy, and not get shouted at, I've come up with a plan that will, well, keep everyone—meaning, my mother and sister—happy. In fact, I think it's so brilliant that it's something I start recommending to anyone who asks about cutting emissions caused by travel. Here it is: cut your emissions by going half as often but staying twice as long.

By this I mean that Michelle and I have decided to cancel two out of the four trips to New England, but, eco-lifestyle or no, it would be too cruel to my mother and sister to cancel them all. Yet at the same time I feel like I've stumbled onto a great eco-tip.

Instead of two three-day trips at Thanksgiving and Christmas, for example, take one weeklong trip for one holiday and stay home and relax for the other. The great news is that you get to save half your travel money, too. And half the stress—who likes packing up and driving or flying?

Not only that, but my mom's always complaining we never stay long enough. So, she's going to love this. I'm brilliant. I sit at the kitchen table, pick up the phone, and punch in her number. My mom answers. I explain about the travel moratorium of the No Impact project but say that although I've canceled the baby-shower and the Thanksgiving trips, we're going to come at Christmas and when my sister Susan's baby is born.

"And listen," I say, throwing down my don't-get-mad-at-me trump card, "you won't see less of us because we're going to stay twice as long!"

The long silence at the other end of the phone suggests my sales pitch may not have been successful.

"I don't get it," my mother says. "The train will run whether you're on it or not. What extra emission would it cause if you just climb on?"

"You missed the part where I said we're going to stay twice as long," I say.

There's another long pause. You can't hear lips tightening over a phone line, but if it's your mother, even from two hundred miles away, you can sense it.

"Your sister is going to be mighty upset about your missing the shower. I wouldn't call her at work. You better wait until tonight to tell her."

I agree.

"I just don't see the point of this No Impact thing if it's everybody else who makes the sacrifices instead of you," my mother says.

"But I'm the one who can't travel . . ."

"And I'm the one it hurts."

•

A fifteen-minute bike ride up Madison Avenue to Fifty-first Street and I'm in the dentist's chair, getting my teeth cleaned. My cell phone rings. It rings again. It rings again. And, yes, it rings again. The hygienist takes the polish machine out of my mouth.

"Do you want to check who's trying to get you? It might be important."

I look at the caller ID. My sister. I sigh. The phone starts ringing in my hands.

"You can take it," the hygienist says.

Thanks a lot, I think.

"Hello."

"I hope you know you ruined my baby shower."

I open my mouth to say something.

Click.

So much for waiting until tonight to tell my sister.

It's easy to make the story sound funny, but hurting my family's feelings in order not to hurt the planet brings up important questions. Much later, when I began making friends with people who worked in the movement to do something about climate change, one of them said, apropos of pretty much nothing, "You know, I just think it's really important that we don't

> "You should worry less about your carbon footprint and more about your family footprint."

forget to put love and kindness at the center of what we're doing."

Later, when I spoke with my friend about what she'd said, she wrote to me privately, "If we don't spread the love, we're not going to make it."

After an argument I had with my dad, he wrote to me, "You should worry less about your carbon footprint and more about your family footprint."

Before this project started, when the only thing I did to try to change the world was complain about politicians to anyone who would listen, Michelle would say to me, "You're creating missiles in your head." I was spreading hatred. I hesitate to repeat this Gandhi quote because it's invoked so often that it's becoming a saccharine cliché, but here goes: "Be the change you want to see in the world."

Way back, when I first discussed this project with my agent, Eric, I said that I wanted to convince people to treat each other with a little more love and kindness. But how can anyone bring more love and kindness into the world if they can't find more love and kindness in themselves? It's not that I thought I did the wrong thing by not going to Thanksgiving this one year, but I did think I needed to be careful that I didn't allow this project to blind me to my propensity for self-righteousness.

What we need is not to draw lines between people. We need to draw lines around them.

A couple of weeks into this no-propulsion thing and, much to my surprise, the only member of my household who's complaining is Frankie, our little dog. Climbing up and down the nine flights of stairs as the cost of bathroom privileges has made her legs sore. She whines a little before she jumps on the bed. I'm hoping that her muscles get used to it before someone tips off the American Society for the Prevention of Cruelty to Animals.

As for me, the day starts by going down and up the nine flights with Frankie. Then, assuming it's my turn to take Isabella to Peggy the babysitter's, down the nine flights again with Isabella riding on my shoulders (which is why, by the way, Isabella considers the stairs a vast improvement on the previous routine). Next, six blocks over to Peggy's and up her six flights of stairs—again, carrying the girl. Now comes a nine-block walk and a twelve-flight climb to the Writers Room, a collective working space where I tap away on my keyboard.

It's 9:23 a.m. I've already climbed up 27 flights (6 of them carrying the twenty-five-pound Isabella) and down 24. My record for a day would ultimately be 124 flights—nine more than the Empire State

Building. "Buns of steel," I say, and grab my butt whenever anybody makes a remark about what they consider the hardship of taking the stairs. Besides, I've discovered that step power is actually faster if you include the time spent waiting for the elevator to come. My longest contiguous trip, 20 flights, took only five minutes, at a very easy pace.

Not that I don't enjoy the respite when, for security reasons, I find myself in a building that does not allow visitors into the stairwell and I have no choice but to take a ride in the box. There are many buildings in New York, I'd discover, where you can't use the stairs even if you must frequently shuttle between, say, the twenty-third floor and the twenty-fourth. "People with elevator phobias like you have to phone ahead if you want to take the stairs," one security guard told me.

While I do get occasionally jealous of passengers zoning out in their taxis, between the walking, the bike riding and the stairs, I'm really enjoying using my body. I feel less like a neck-mounted head that needs to be moved around by machine. Exercise is part of my life without trying, and I feel a certain sense of independence, like maybe I can transport myself and possibly even survive without being entirely dependent upon the Matrix.

But here's the more surprising thing: Michelle is digging it, too. "It's the only time I get alone," she says of her walk to and from work. She sees on the corner of Fourteenth Street, through a window, a bunch of people running on treadmills in a gym and thinks of them rushing there in taxis from work. How crazy, Michelle thinks, when, by walking, they could just kill two birds with one stone—getting themselves to work and getting exercise all at once.

She sends me this e-mail:

I just heard two women talking about real estate. One was bemoaning how she'd never lived in a building with an elevator. The other, who was quite overweight, was talking about how "there is no way I'm going to buy a fourth-floor walkup because my body is too decrepit."

I felt so sad.

A fat young girl not wanting to walk up four flights?

A 70-degree day in New York City in December?

People at the Rockefeller Center Christmas Tree Lighting Ceremony the other night in sleeveless tops?

A pizza man who refuses to touch my pizza with his hands when I say I don't want him to use paper or plastic?

Every Starbucks in town not knowing how much to charge me for my coffee because nobody ever brings Starbucks' own re-usable cups into their stores?

How did we ever get ourselves into this upside-down situation? We're only a few weeks into the No Impact project and I already feel as if normality is actually totally insane.

I pick up Isabella from Peggy's, climb down the six flights carrying her, get outside, and it starts to rain. Isabella rides on my shoulders and I have an umbrella, so I can keep her from drowning in the downpour, but we will both be soaked by the time we get home. There are, surprisingly, plenty of available taxis on Sixth Avenue, but no-impact means no taxis, so I do my best with the umbrella and commence the trudge home.

Before long, Isabella begins crying. Of course she does. A no-impact dad gets his poor daughter cold and wet. A no-impact dad, I'm ashamed to think, is a bad dad.

I try tilting the umbrella so that it covers Isabella better, but she only cries harder. This goes on for a block or two. Then a gust of wind blows the umbrella over, rain pours over both of us, and Isabella quiets. I wrestle the umbrella back over us, and she starts crying again. I walk as fast as I can, and everywhere people run and hail cabs and hold newspapers over their heads, desperate not to get wet.

The wind blows the umbrella off us again. The rain wets our faces. Isabella again stops crying. I finally realize. Isabella isn't crying because she is getting wet; she is crying because the umbrella stops her from getting wet.

On another day that same week, I planned to take Isabella to the park. She waddled along beside me on the sidewalk. We hadn't traveled half a block when she stopped to play with a little chain hanging from a fire hydrant. She tapped the chain with her finger so that it swung back and forth. She patiently waited until it came to a standstill and tapped it again, fascinated. I tried to push her along so that we could hurry up and get to the park.

She started to cry.

I relented and she went back to the chain, patiently poking it and watching it swing back and forth until it stopped, and then poking it again. I wanted to rush to the park so we could start having fun. It took me forever to see that Isabella was already having fun.

At what age did I start to think that where I was going was more important that where I already was? When was it that I began to believe that the most important thing about what I was doing was getting it over with? Knowing how to live is not something we have to teach children. Knowing how to live is something we have to be careful not to take away from them.

On the day of the rain, I finally close the umbrella. Isabella's crying is over. This is what walking on a rainy day, instead of using mechanized transportation, is like: you get wet sometimes.

And on this rainy day, here is what happens when I treat my body as something more than a means to transport my head, when I finally learn to treat the landscape as something more than the space that stands between where I am now and where I want to be later:

I take Isabella down from my shoulders and let her jump in a puddle, soaking her shoes and her pants. For fun, I jump in the puddle, too. Isabella laughs. She stretches out her arms with her palms facing up to catch the rain. She opens her mouth, sticks her tongue out and leans her head back. I try it, too.

When did the child in me disappear?

People are running past. They look desperate, miserable, trying to get out of the rain. What has happened to us?

An invitation arrives for a birthday party for some friends with kids in Brooklyn. A pleasant, hour-long walk over the bridge. We plan to go. Then, on the day, it rains again, more intensely this time, and we don't. Sacrifice. That's what it feels like at first.

We hang out in the apartment, Frankie hides from the thunder in the bathtub, Isabella plays with blocks. The water streams down the windows and we read. This is no sacrifice. This is a relief. Without some sort of a mechanized box to whisk us through the rain to where our schedules say we're supposed to go, we can just relax. We have a good excuse. We can just stay home.

There are two rhythms playing out here in NYC. On the one hand, there is the fast street-level rhythm of elevators and subways and taxis and delivery boys and have a slice of pizza the moment you want it. Saturday breakfast with one group of friends, lunch with another, dinner and a movie with a third. Same on Sunday. By the time you're back at work on Monday, you're exhausted. That's the techno music beat.

Then there's the classical beat. The one where you get wet when it rains, or you stay in. The one where getting places takes a long time because you walk. The one that is linked to the natural movement of life, where you actually know in your body what season it is, even in the middle of Manhattan.

> **Without some sort of a mechanized box to whisk us through the rain to where our schedules say we're supposed to go, we can just relax.**

Isabella makes a lion with her blocks. Michelle falls asleep on the couch. How strange and wonderful for my little family, here in New York, to be living in the rhythm of the weather.

So here comes my theory:

Back before the days of mechanized transportation and personal telephonic communications and coffee in to-go cups, there would be down times between the times of stress. Maybe you had a presentation at the office or a great party to go to or a tense talk with your girlfriend. But between those things you'd get a break. You couldn't carry your coffee, talk on the phone, and ride a taxi to the next stressful event all at the same time.

Instead, with no to-go cups, you'd just sit in a café. With no phone, you'd just rest. Yes, there would be stressful times. But in between would come delicious periods of ho-hum where you could just decompress.

As my theory goes, the mechanized boxes that transport our brains from here to there and the portable electronics that keep us constantly connected have robbed us of the ho-hum. Those periods that interrupted the everyday rush, like a red light periodically bringing the quiet of stopped traffic, have been excised. Now peak moment follows peak moment, and they have all been accordioned together.

Is that good for us? Does that make us happy?

So many people are now taking Prozac that unmetabolized traces of the drug, excreted in their urine, show up in our drinking-water supplies. So many people are depressed that the Prozac in their pee is tainting our water! A psychiatrist friend tells me that our sky-high societal depression rates come from the combination of two factors: biological predisposition together with life circumstances that trigger that predisposition. Stress, he tells me, is among the triggers. The preponderance of stress in our culture contributes greatly to our depression rate.

So when it comes to Prozac and drinking water, I see two possible ways forward.

We could put back the time that used to be taken by walking or sitting in cafés or not having a gadget constantly beeping for our attention. We could turn down the techno and turn up the classical. We could put back the space in people's lives so coping didn't require medication and peeing didn't include Prozac. That might mean less efficiency.

Or we could just say screw it. You know how tooth decay is just a fact of life so we dump fluoride in the water to try to prevent it? Well, we could go the same way with depression. We could just accept that efficiency—and the stress caused by trying to achieve it—is more important than really enjoying ourselves. We could just accept that the modern way of life is as agonizing as hell and that depression in epidemic proportions goes with the territory. Instead of worrying about traces of Prozac in the water, we could go the other way and dump garbage trucks full of the stuff into water. Like fluoride.

At least that way, worriers like me would quit complaining and just get back to work.

About true efficiency, part 1:

The second wife of the famously melancholic Kurt Vonnegut once told him that he wouldn't have to stand in line at the post office every day if he would just get himself a fax machine (this was before e-mail). Vonnegut demured. He wrote—at least as I remember it—"The purpose of life is to futz around and don't let anyone tell you otherwise."

About true efficiency, part 2:

Kurt Vonnegut writes, "I asked [my son] Mark a while back what life was all about, since I didn't have a clue."

"He said, 'Dad, we are here to help each other get through this thing, whatever it is.'"

I've climbed the twelve flights to the Writers Room, where I work. I go into the kitchen to get a cup of coffee and two fellow writers are sitting around, kvetching. In particular, they're kvetching about the pressure of packing up their families and taking them to the grand-parents for Thanksgiving (I'm feeling pretty smug, I can tell you).

The guy writer says, "What I wonder is how our parents' genera-tion always dealt with this travel hassle, before there were so many planes and cars?"

The woman writer says, "I don't think they traveled so much. I think they just said, 'This is where I live and that's that.' "

Thanksgiving travel is stressful. In fact, just plain travel is stress-ful. You're packing, picking up the car, trying to figure out how to keep the kids quiet for four hours, dealing with holiday traffic, wait-ing around for delayed flights at the airport, trying to find Internet connections so you can keep up with your e-mail. Then you get there and you can't stay long, so everyone has to immediately start having enforced fun. You don't even get time for a nap. And then it's over and you turn around and go back.

In 2007, according to the American Automobile Association, 38.7 million Americans traveled more than fifty miles from home for Thanksgiving. During Thanksgiving month, according to the Federal Highway Administration, we lay down 243.3 billion vehicle miles. That adds up to the emission of 232.5 billion pounds—nearly 1 pound per mile—or 116 million tons of planet-killing carbon dioxide. Amer-icans' dragging our butts back to Mom and Dad's for Thanksgiving costs the planet more than the entire annual greenhouse-gas emissions of Finland and Ireland combined.

I'm not saying no one should go home for Thanksgiving. All I'm wondering is, who was actually happier during Thanksgiving week? Me and my family and the populations of Ireland and Finland, who got to stay home and didn't have to eat overcooked turkey, or the 38.7 million Americans who suffered the holiday traffic jams and the airport delays? All I'm asking here is how much carbon dioxide could we save if those of us who didn't want to go home for Thanksgiving told our parents we had a last-minute case of the stomach flu?

•

I'm kind of joking, but I'm kind of not. Because, for all our automotive-related polar bear drowning, we're not even having a gas (pun intended).

Listen:

- American adults average seventy-two minutes a day behind the wheel of a car, according to the Worldwatch Institute.
- That's more than twice as much time as the average American father spends with his kids, according to the U.S. Department of Labor.
- It's the equivalent, if you do the math, of just over one eight-hour workday a week or just under eleven forty-hour work-weeks a year.
- According to the Bureau of Labor Statistics, 17 percent of the average American's income goes toward the costs of owning and running a car.
- In other words, we spend, on average, eight weeks of every year working to pay for our cars.
- Putting it all together, we Americans spend the equivalent of nearly five work-months a year either driving our cars or working to pay for them.
- And a lot of the time, reports the Texas Transportation Institute, we aren't even getting anywhere, since we annually spend the equivalent of 105 million weeks of vacation time sitting in traffic jams.
- Every ten minutes we spend commuting, according to Robert Putnam's *Bowling Alone*, means 10 percent less connection with our friends and communities.
- Even if you don't own a car, research also shows that the more vehicular traffic there is on the street where we live, the fewer friends we have, because the traffic causes us to spend less time hanging out in our neighborhood.
- You don't need to own a car, either, to breathe the 70–80 percent of air pollution that automobiles and trucks

contribute in New York, Los Angeles, and Dallas, according to the Environmental Defense Fund.

- Meanwhile, studies show that the more a nation's citizens get to work by walking, biking, and public transportation, the less obese they are.

- To top it all off, people who ride bikes or walk to work are 24 percent more likely to be happy with their commute than those who drive their cars.

What if having to depend on mechanized boxes to zap us from point A to point B doesn't represent a life improvement? Because it seems to me that the real measure of waste, the real tragedy of waste, the real lack of efficiency, is if us-

> We spend, on average, eight weeks of every year working to pay for our cars.

ing all these planetary resources and working our butts off to pay for them doesn't even make us happy.

I'm not saying the entire United States should refuse to go anywhere except by bike. It's just that living, for the period of the No Impact project, outside the system of transportation that I've been part of all my life, I've come to wonder if we couldn't do better for ourselves.

I wonder if we couldn't find a safe and comfortable way for people to be able to walk or bike if they want to. Or a way that they could spend less unwanted time in their cars. I'm not talking about deprivation here. I'm talking about a public transit system that's so good and so comfortable and so pleasant that we don't want to drive cars. Instead, we could take the time we spend working to pay for them and spend it with our kids.

About true efficiency, part 3:

What's at the root of my argument, here, really, is the question of the efficiency of our economy when it comes to return on investment (when you define the "return" as quality of life) and "investment" as the planetary resources spent). And it turns out that there's a whole think tank, the New Economics Foundation (NEF), based in London, that attempts to put that question in scientific terms.

NEF has calculated, first of all, for the citizens of 178 countries, what it calls their "years of happy life." NEF defines the years of happy life of a country by multiplying the country's average life expectancy by a figure, arrived at through international studies, for the average life satisfaction of the country's citizens. In other words, "years of happy life" attempts to be a measure of the number of years the people live multiplied by how happy they are.

NEF then calculates what it calls the "Happy Planet Index" (HPI) by dividing the happy life years of each country's average citizen by that person's ecological footprint.

Thus, in my slightly simplified version of NEF's equation:

$$HPI = \frac{\text{Life Satisfaction} \times \text{Life Expectancy}}{\text{Ecological Footprint}}$$

HPI measures the efficiency, essentially, of a country's economy in terms of the health and happiness of its citizens experienced per ton of greenhouse gases emitted. HPI is a way of asking, therefore, how well a country delivers good lives to its citizens in return for the green-house gases it produces. Of the 178 countries for which an HPI has been calculated, guess where the United States falls?

> A total of 149 countries give its citizens more happy years per ton of greenhouse gas than the United States.

Here are some hints. China gives its citizens more happy years per ton of greenhouse gas than does the United States. So does India. So do Austria, Switzerland, Italy, Iran, Belgium, Germany, Spain, Hong Kong, Denmark, the United Kingdom, Canada, Ireland, France, and Australia. So, even, does Mexico. In fact, a total of 149 countries give its citizens more happy years per ton of greenhouse gas than the United States, because, sadly, we come in 150th.

The great news is that, looking at the better HPI scores of other countries, we can see that Americans' lives could be just as long and happy with a much smaller environmental impact. Germans, for example, have about the same satisfaction with their lives and the same life expectancy as Americans. Yet the average German's ecological footprint is about half the average American's. That means, taking Germany as an example, we could have the same happy, long lives using many fewer planetary resources.

And why are so many other countries able to deliver more health and happiness for their carbon buck? Because, among other factors, their cultures and economies depend less on cars.

But we have a free market system, and its indicators tell us that Americans have a love affair with their cars. Cars make Americans happy, as in any love affair does, right? If Americans wanted to give up their cars to keep the planet safe, they'd just quit buying them, right? Companies, so they tell us, only give us what we want.

But if we love cars so much, why did the automobile industry, according to, among other sources, a 1974 report by U.S. Senate Counsel Bradford Snell, feel the need to kill competition by buying up and dismantling nearly every electric trolley system in the country? Why, by 1950, had a coalition led by General Motors dismantled more than one hundred trolley lines?

Of course Americans buy cars. The automobile industry has ensured that it is the only way we can move around easily. But you have to wonder whether the United States' relationship with the automobile is a love affair or a forced marriage.

It's late at night and I'm in the bedroom with Michelle. Isabella is sleeping in her "big girl bed"—as in, not a crib. Michelle decides to tiptoe over to the scale and climb on. She looks. She gets off. She climbs on again as though she didn't believe it the first time. She looks. She gets off. She gets back on. She looks. She sighs.

"Guess what?" Michelle says. "All this walking, all these stairs, and I've still gained weight."

Michelle is already stressed. A source from one of her stories has decided to sue her. She has written two cover stories in two weeks. And now, well, the bathroom-scale slot machine has come up badly.

If I open my mouth, my foot's going to end up in it, but I can't help myself. I feel as though I'm expected to say something.

"Do you think there's something wrong with your diet?" I ask, grasping at straws.

"Yeah, like all the peanut butter and bread we keep eating."

Michelle is alluding to the fact that our dietary adjustment in the face of no take-out containers has still not reached great culinary heights. All the same, I'm thinking about the fact that I've lost ten pounds since the advent of stairs and biking, and about how many times I've been woken up lately by Michelle midnight-snacking on the peanut butter and bread that at the moment appears to offend her.

Long silence. I'm trying to think of how to change the subject. "It's your turn to walk Frankie," I say, which includes walking up and down the nine flights of stairs at ten o'clock at night. Wrong change of subject. What was I thinking?

"I don't think you appreciate that I walk an hour and a half every day to get to and from work for this project."

"But I do all the shopping and cooking."

"But it's your project," Michelle says.

I harrumph out of the house and walk the dog.

The next morning, while taking Isabella to Peggy's, I see a man on a cool, fold-up, foot-push scooter. I ask him where he got it. He tells me he commutes over the Brooklyn Bridge with it and that he feels fine riding it on the sidewalk. It's called a Xootr Scooter.

This is the answer to Michelle's commute, I think. Walking takes too long. Biking feels unsafe to her. Xootr Scooter to the rescue. I rush home, look it up on the Internet, and order one for next-day delivery. I'm really excited, so I call Michelle to tell her I have a surprise coming for her.

Michelle hates surprises.

So I tell her that she is getting a brand new Xootr Scooter!

Long silence.

"First, you don't have any money to spend on stuff like that, and, second, people who ride those scooters look like idiots."

"There is a thirty-day, hundred-percent satisfaction guarantee."

"Forget it," Michelle says.

I'm about to call Xootr Scooter to cancel the order when the phone rings. The caller ID says it is Xootr Scooter calling me. This is weird. I pick up the phone and a guy named Dave explains that they are out of stock of the model I ordered, the Ultra, but how about if they send me the better model, the MG, for the same price?

That figures. The first time in my life that I feel like I'm getting something for nothing and I have to cancel the order. I'm about to break the news to Dave when the call waiting beeps. It's Michelle. I click over.

"I'm sorry," she says, "I'll try the scooter. I was being a closed peduncle."

I tell her I've seen moms walking these scooters while their little kids stand on them.

"That's cute," Michelle admits.

I tell her that Dave is on the other line offering us the better model. "It was meant to be," I say.

Michelle laughs, but we both know there's a better than 50 percent chance the scooter's going to get sent back.

For all my maybe-we-could-be-happier-without-mechanized-transport musing, Michelle, I have to admit, is having a hard time. Plus, my sister is not speaking to me. My mother is still upset about the coming Thanksgiving. I feel like I've caused a fair amount of unhappiness over the last few days and I've done it simply by not using cars.

•

I was standing on the roof of a building on First Avenue and the sun was setting and there were pink clouds and the top of the Empire State Building was drifting in and out of mist and a plane was flying over Manhattan and I thought: How amazing! We build tall buildings in part because they are, after all, cool. There is something awe-inspiring and creative about them.

And when you think of the Wright brothers on the dunes in the Carolinas trying to fly, why not? What human hasn't looked at birds and wished he could fly? And how amazing to go to the moon? And isn't it awe-inspiring to live in a world where these things happen? There is something magical about these things. The same as transmitting moving pictures through the air. How amazing, too.

I suppose the thing is that when they are created and done they are magical, but once we become addicted to them, once we have to have these things in order to feel just barely satisfied, they aren't so magical after all. Maybe it's a matter of balance. Can we take the flying to the moon but leave the driving everywhere behind? Could we just drive less? Could we just figure out a way to do these cool things in relative moderation?

In conversations about this, friends have wondered if I'm against progress. But keeping things the way they are is not progress. More of the same isn't progress. Progress is about looking at where we are and striving to get someplace better. I don't want less progress. I want more progress, real progress.

It's just a question of how we define progress and whether, for instance, that means more cars on the street or fewer.

Worldwide, the big push in transportation has been in biofuels—growing crops to make either ethanol or biodiesel as a potential replacement for gasoline. But it turns out that the massive push has caused a massive transfer of farmland out of food production and into fuel production, contributing to the global food crisis. And some developing nations have begun tearing down forests to create land to grow fuel crops. Since we need those forests to absorb carbon dioxide, cutting them down for biofuel is borrowing from Peter to pay Paul.

On the other hand, we may be able to find sustainable ways to create biofuels from agricultural waste and other sources that

> **Suburbia, the great American experiment in the solitude of "a man's home is his castle," is pretty much a failure.**

would not cause the same problems. Although we clearly need a replacement for fossil fuels, biofuels and other gasoline replacements would do nothing about traffic jams, nothing about the four work-months we spend driving and working to pay for our cars each year, and nothing about the obesity problem that goes with so much driving.

Suburbia, the great American experiment in the solitude of "a man's home is his castle," is pretty much a failure. Not the live-outside-the-city part—that can be good. But the spread-the houses-far-apart-and-have-no-central-community part. And the build-to-make-the-place-good-for-cars-instead-of-good-for-people part. And the you-can't-walk-to-the-grocery-store-or-get-to-know-your-neighbors part.

Suburban living forces us out of our families and out of our communities, away from our jobs and into our cars. It also forces cars, carrying suburbanites to work, into our cities. We leave the cities to get away from traffic and air pollution; so we move to the suburbs, then climb into our cars and drive into the cities and *cause* the traffic and air pollution we meant to get away from in the first place.

What if we built villages we could walk in, and connected them with good, comfortable convenient public transportation, thus reducing the need for cars? And what if, by reducing the need for cars, fewer of them drove into the cities, so that the kids could play on the street, and in turn we didn't feel the need to move out of the cities—to places where we'd need cars?

What if, in other words, we could find a way to make what's good for the planet good for us, too?

•

The scooter comes, and I kiss Michelle goodbye as she starts her first zip up Sixth Avenue to work. I'm holding my breath.

The phone rings and it's my sister. She says, "I'm sorry I got so mad. I'm disappointed you're not coming, but I admire what you're doing."

Pretty much the same day, my mother calls and says how excited she is that we'll be coming for a whole week at Christmas.

And Michelle, by the way, has lost five pounds since our incident with the scale.

I'm sitting at the Writers Room checking my e-mail every five minutes to see whether I'll need to find a way to get the Scooter back to Xootr. Finally the email comes.

"It was wet and slippery," Michelle writes.

Oh *boy*, I think.

Then I scroll down: "It was so much fun! I love it! You were right!!!! The scooter is a real hit here at the office . . . everyone is zipping around the hallways on it!!! Thank you so much, honey. It is better than walking because I couldn't really get my heart rate up walking but on this thing I totally can. . . . Hoorah! I'm so excited!"

For the first time in my life, I find people wanting to talk relentlessly about what I'm writing about—the No Impact project. My previous two books would sustain a five-minute conversation. But about this book, about trying to live environmentally, about trying to live differently, everyone wants to talk.

When Michelle and I go to Angelica Kitchen, the busboy automatically knows not to bring us paper napkins. He brings us cloth rags from the kitchen instead, so we don't have to use our own. At French Roast, a restaurant on our corner, Bradley, the waiter, told us he was talking about us to some friends, and when I asked why, he said it was because he was proud of us. Friends tell me they've spent entire dinner parties talking about the project.

I've begun to carry a glass Mason jar around both to put tap water in, as a replacement for plastic water bottles, and to use as a to-go coffee cup, to replace throwaway cups. I like it better than something that you buy because it signals the reuse of resources. After all, my jar once had peanut butter in it. Anyway, very often, when I put the jar down on the counter at the coffee shop, the baristas like it so much they give me my coffee for free.

"Thank you so much for what you're doing and for letting us read about it," say e-mails I've received from blog readers. "I'm starting to change my life, too." All sorts of people are writing to ask my advice about what they can do.

I'm working on an op-ed, meanwhile, that *The New York Times* asked me to write about our attempt at genuinely clean living, and a reporter from its Home and Garden Section will soon begin to shadow us for a profile. What I didn't expect was that

> **Often, when I put the jar down on the counter at the coffee shop, the baristas like it so much they give me my coffee for free.**

this project that I started because I felt voiceless, helpless, and powerless is apparently giving me some sort of voice.

The final results of all the Thanksgiving Day mishigas:

We woke up on the morning with nothing pressing to do. We played with Isabella. We felt relief that we didn't have to rush or get mired in holiday traffic. With nothing particularly special to do, we embarked on a purging fest and started cleaning out the closets. We gave Isabella little jobs, like collecting all her trinkets in a bowl. She wanted to be at the center of it all.

At three in the afternoon, we walked around to our friends John and Debra's apartment and they made vegetarian Thanksgiving dinner.

I brought a delicious apple crumble that I made myself because I could not find an apple pie to buy—my normal strategy—that didn't come in a cardboard box, on a tin plate, or wrapped in plastic.

We got home around eight. We were tired from socializing and having fun, but not from traveling. We denied ourselves the trip and ended up having no stress. This was revolutionary for me, who, coming from divorced parents, normally has two holiday trips to make and twice the normally allotted travel.

Without the television, I find that I have time for my meditation practice at night. Michelle and I have time to talk. We are particularly pleased that, with Thanksgiving Day over, we now have the luxury of a three-day weekend to spend together as a family.

I'm not promoting enviro-rationalized misanthropy. We would see everyone at Christmas, but today, we got to relax. The way I saw it, between Thanksgiving and Christmas we managed to halve our carbon emissions, halve our stress, and double our fun.

By the way, here's the story that explains Michelle's antipathy toward bicycles. It happened a couple of months before the No Impact project started, back when I was still toying with the idea of doing it.

My best friend, Tanner, was visiting our apartment so he could play with Isabella, but the plan was to eventually meet our friend Bill uptown. Meanwhile, I'd been reading that bicycles move faster than cars in New York. I was wondering, though, how the speed of a bike compared to the subway, which usually doesn't suffer from traffic congestion. So Tanner and I were going to have a race. He would walk to the subway and take the train. I would ride my bike. We'd see which was faster.

So I zigged my way over to Third Avenue and rode casually uptown. I was meeting Tanner at Eighty-eighth Street, and I was anxious about not trying to go artificially fast. I wanted to get a realistic idea of which way was quicker. So far, I found the bike ride more comfortable than the subway. It wasn't hard on the legs and made for a cool breeze.

I rode in the lane nearest to the sidewalk, but around Fiftieth Street I veered toward the center of Third Avenue to skirt around a parked car. As I pulled back toward the curb I heard a loud screech from behind me. Then I had the surreal sensation of speeding up unaccountably, then flying through the air and . . . whack!

When I was on the asphalt, my first thought was that Michelle would kill me for hurting myself again—I had broken an ankle when I crashed on a toboggan earlier in the year. Next, this hugely tall man got out of the maroon BMW that just hit me and I was on my feet shouting my head off. It was pure vitriol coming out of my mouth and I had no control over it. What kind of an idiot are you? What on earth is so important that it's worth risking my life for?

Then he called me a jerk and then a lady on a bike with a basket with plastic flowers rode up and started shouting at the driver for shouting at me. "Can't you see he's bleeding," she says. I hadn't noticed. The guy pulled out his cell phone to dial 911 and I started shouting, "You were talking on your stupid cell phone when you hit me," and I was just beside myself with nuttiness. The blood dripped from my right knee and the palm of my right hand, which looked like hamburger. It hurt when I bent my left thumb.

BMW Man was calling an ambulance and I was thinking I don't need an ambulance, and suddenly I felt so terribly lonely. The ambulance siren screamed from about four blocks away, and I could see the lights flashing above the cars and there was something beautiful about that. I thought: Imagine if there were no cars. Then how would we all get to the hospital? And surely Michelle will never let me ride my bike again, so how will we do this No Impact experiment?

In the back of the ambulance, the paramedic wrapped gauze around my hand and the police officer explained that I could be arrested for riding my bike without carrying ID. I eyed the cell phones hanging from everyone's belts. I didn't bring mine. I needed to call Michelle.

Anyway, what I was wondering was, how do I, first, borrow a phone and, second, get out of earshot to begin a conversation that I knew was going to begin with me saying, "Honey, please don't be mad at me but . . ." Who wanted to say such a spineless thing in front of a cop with a shaved head and an ambulance man wearing those fingerless black leather gloves and a backward baseball cap?

I went up to the guy who hit me and reassured him that I would be all right. Why did I do that? Later, I realized that it was because I needed to connect with someone, because I didn't want to think that the experience of nearly getting killed was one I had entirely alone. I wanted to pretend that he was in it with me.

He didn't offer me and my broken bike a ride home. He wasn't in it with me at all.

Then I sat for a moment on the back bumper of the ambulance, and my heart broke for the world. Feeling so vulnerable, I understood how we all wanted to protect ourselves by being inside these big, tanklike SUVs.

Then I wished I had an SUV and that I had run this guy over instead of the other way around. Then I chastised myself for having had such a thought. Then I realized how trying to protect ourselves with SUVs is the whole problem.

Nothing can really protect you from life's uncertainties, after all. Sitting on the bumper, bleeding, I felt the insecurity of life with all my being. There was no escaping it. You never know when you're going to be hit. There is no point wrecking the world, trying to protect myself with an SUV, I thought. In this experience, I felt the two rhythms—the techno and the classical—collide.

I declined taking the ambulance to the hospital. Instead, I picked up my bike, which was unridable because the front wheel had buckled, and I carried it over my shoulder to the Lexington Avenue subway stop. To get home, I had no choice. I took the subway.

•

The doctor (I went the next day) tells me a bone in my wrist, the trapezium, is broken. It is a tiny bone, the size of a sugar cube, at the base of the thumb, but it is crucial. Lots of important ligaments attach to it. I have to wear a splint for six weeks. There is likely to be more physical therapy on top of what I already do for my ankle. I can't pick up Isabella with my left hand. I can't hold Frankie's leash in that hand. I can't swim this summer.

Michelle starts going on about how I didn't listen to her about the toboggan and I didn't listen to her about the bike. We're coming out of the movies and I say, "Let's just accept the fact that you married Evel Knievel all right? I'm Evel Knievel, okay? If you have anything else to say, start by calling me Evel!"

Believe or not, she stops her lecture, smiles, and says, "Okay, Evel."

We push through the glass doors of the cinema and out onto Thirteenth Street. Michelle says, "Say it again!"

"Say what again?"

"The bit about Evel Knievel."

"I'm Evel Knievel, all right? So just keep quiet and call me Evel."

She laughs. She pulls my head toward her and kisses me. "You are so hot, Evel."

Then we walk home holding hands, not forgetting, of course, to stop first and get money for the babysitter. He's Evel Knievel, Michelle tells her. I give the girl her money and go check on Isabella.

SIX

The Cabbage Diet Saves the World

It's hard to believe that we've negotiated only the first and second stages so far—no making trash and no carbon-producing transportation. I managed, unwittingly, to put what would be two of the most life-changing parts of the project right at the very beginning. Talk about culture shock: we've become Americans who don't make trash or drive.

It will soon be time to begin moving into the sustainable-eating phase, but there is still one glaring exception to the no-trash rule to take care of: Isabella's throwaway plastic diapers. I had been to Babies R Us on a cloth-diaper fact-finding mission, but faced with the choice among Velcro, snap, or pin fastenings, I got overwhelmed and ran out. I turned for advice to the head of—get this—the Real Diaper Association, Lori Taylor.

As a result, a brown box arrives via UPS. I open it and discover inside twenty-four reusable organic cotton diapers, corresponding to the number calculated from the formula Lori had given me: "Take the number of changes Isabella needs per day"—six—"and multiply by the number of days you want to go between washings"—four. That made twenty-four.

Don't ask me why, but I'd decided No Impact Man should go for the old-fashioned flat diapers instead of the new Velcro-closing, self-sealing fitted diapers with their own built-in rubber covers. Out of the box, therefore, also spill the safety pins and the wool diaper covers, which would need occasional hand-washing when the diapers leaked through. "One cover for Isabella to wear, one in the wash, and one drying," Lori had said, "so you'll need three."

I'm looking at my new baby-poop-containment system and really hoping that this world is worth saving.

Michelle is lying on the couch, reading a magazine.

I hold up what looks, thanks to the absence of bleach and dye, like a handful of slightly dirty rags. "The cloth diapers are here," I say.

"Uh-huh," Michelle says. "Have a party." She flips a page.

Isabella, on the other hand, is already digging in. I explain how she has new diapers and how we're going to try them on.

What I don't explain is that we would be exposing her sensitive buttocks and thighs to the dangerous combination of a clumsy dad and a stainless-steel, potentially flesh-puncturing pin. I don't explain that, from now on, every time her diapers are changed she will be risking a sharp poke to the most sensitive part of her body (it only happened once in the whole time she wore diapers—I swear).

And since I don't explain the danger, Isabella is excited, which, in turn, makes me think I've stumbled upon a great ploy for getting Michelle interested. Her commonsense reticence to take part in the Great Cloth Diaper Experiment will be overwhelmed by the maternal pull of her daughter's enthusiasm.

Isabella waves a diaper in the air like a flag. She points at the box. "Those Bella's new diapers!" She runs up to her mother. "Mommy, Bella's new diapers!"

Michelle doesn't even lower her magazine. From behind it comes her voice. "That's something you get to play with with your daddy, sweetheart," she says. For the time being, anyway, I have made the transition from half-time to full-time diaper-changer.

> **I'm looking at my new baby-poop-containment system and really hoping that this world is worth saving.**

I spread a diaper on the floor and consider the directions. In attaching this diaper to my child's body, I discover I have some choices to make. I have to choose between the "angel twist," the "newspaper fold," the "reverse newspaper fold," the "thigh fold," and on and on. All I want to do is contain my child's poop, but apparently I'm learning origami.

I decide on the "basic fold" and lay Isabella down on the diaper. The trick is to get the diaper tightly sealed around her little legs. The challenge is that the pictures I've printed out feature a doll that doesn't squirm. Isabella does. Everything tickles. This is a diaper change cum wrestling match. I think of temporarily duct-taping my child to the floor. But finally I'm done.

Isabella stands up and beams. She looks a little more like she is wearing a toga or a skirt than a diaper. I figure I'll get the hang of it in time. I'll have to, at least if I'm hoping not to send all our furniture to the landfill. Because twenty minutes after I've attached the diaper, there is a puddle of pee the size of Lake Michigan on the floor.

Time passes. It's mid-January and we're nearly three months into the project now. We've taken the train to my mother's and back for our Christmas visit. I've learned an important lesson. Turning your life over to cloth diapers is one thing, when it comes to being environmental. Agreeing to spend an entire week at your mother's in order to limit the back-and-forth travel of several shorter visits is another.

For reasons that will become clear, I do believe we can convince people to use cloth diapers. But one thing I've learned from my own experience—and I'm not saying more—is that if the planet depends on all of us adult children agreeing to spend weeks at a time with our parents, we may just be doomed.

Maybe what really got to me was this:

Christmas Day in my mom's living room and everyone is opening presents. Perfectly good paper is getting torn off the gifts, crumpled into balls, and stuffed in a big black plastic bag. I keep surreptitiously taking the least damaged pieces of paper and smoothing out the crumples, as though someone would actually save it and use it again. What has happened to me? I'm not taking this in my stride.

My sister, instead of carefully removing the tape from one end of a gift to preserve the paper, rips it haphazardly. I'm sitting on the floor with, literally, a knot in my stomach. I want to grab gifts from everyone to try to save the paper. My sister sees what is going on and laughs at me. For my part, with the idea of reducing resource use, I've given for presents nothing but experiences: two massages for my mom, a fancy meal for my dad and his wife, money for baby supplies to my sister.

I don't like what the project is doing to me lately. I feel I have to control everything. I started out saying it was all about "keeping my side of the street clean," which simply means I keep my mouth shut when I want desperately to wade into everybody else's business. I'm not judging everyone. Really, I'm only judging myself. Why can't I do more? God help me. Is there a way to do this and have peace at the same time?

"We're becoming freaks," I say to Michelle.

"No, *you're* becoming a freak."

What's hard for me about this project so far is, yes, the incidentals: I sometimes wish I could have a candy bar, I wish I could hop on a plane to Bermuda, I wish I could veg out in front of the TV. But what's harder, I think, is so often coming face-to-face with myself. My judgment. My weakness. My obsessiveness.

The question morphs.

It's like pulling at a ball of string that starts to unwind. Instead of just thinking, How do I live without harming the environment? I find myself asking: How shall I live?

Michelle has wanted a second child forever. Around this time she asks me: "Would you be willing to play Russian roulette? I'm not saying we have to actually *try* to have a baby. What if we just see what happens?"

I'm not comfortable. I'm scared. I am so worried about our ability to afford and care for another baby. Where would we find the money and the time? But we've been through those discussions and Michelle still persists.

"Okay," I say. "We'll play Russian roulette."

But somehow, in some unspoken way, my acquiescence is a quid pro quo for her participation in the project. Is that a reason to agree to something like this?

I'm faced with myself again.

You see what I mean? How shall I live?

If no one takes anything else from this story—if by the end we haven't figured out how to preserve our habitat—perhaps I could at least consider this whole thing a lesson in how to talk a poor, unsuspecting, I-used-to-have-a-good-life-till-my-husband-went-bonkers wife into doing almost anything.

Because the good news about the Christmas trip is that, in order to avoid car use as much as possible while we are in my countryside hometown of Westport, Massachusetts, Michelle has agreed that we could rent bikes, mine with a child seat for Isabella, since we would be on country roads.

"I want to go on a bike ride," Isabella cries, looking at the bikes, but we don't ride on the first day because it rains. To calm Bella down I put her in the child seat on my bike, on my mom's covered porch. The bike's balance shifts a little before I get a good grip on it. Isabella changes her tune immediately: "Bella scared of bikes!" I take her out.

Until the rain stops the next day, Michelle and I talk a lot about whether we'll force Isabella to ride. Michelle is on the safety side. I am on the daredevil side, and that's the way our marriage is. All the same, we agree we will urge Isabella beyond a little bit of resistance but not if she is truly terrified.

The next day is cloudy but dry and we take the bikes outside. Michelle holds my bike still, and I say to Bella, "We're just going to try it. If you don't like it we'll take you out."

Isabella looks intent and apprehensive but not scared. I put her in the seat and click her in and the helmets go on and all that. I roll my bike to the end of the driveway and Isabella is already smiling. We ride out and turn left up Cornell Road and past the little restaurant called Ellie's Place, then turn right onto Main Road, down into a valley of pastureland. Michelle is shouting, "I've got your back!" with the idea that if a car plows into us, she will protect us as a human shield.

Bella begins screaming. "Mommy! Mommy! Mommy!"

"You better ride up beside us and see what the matter is," I shout over my shoulder.

Michelle pulls up. "Yes, Isabella?"

"I like it!" Isabella says.

So we ride. Over the days of our week we see cows, and the first time Isabella says, "Don't want cows, don't want cows." But as we ride past them again and again, she begins to moo instead, and the same with the horses, and so on.

We see—and smell—the farms and the old white clapboard and black-shuttered captains' houses, with their widow's walks, from Westport's whaling days. We ride down to the part of town where I grew up, known as the "Point," where the harbor wharf is, and I show my family where I used to fish. We look out over the winter harbor and I point to the bridge I used to dive off in the summers, then we ride back past the captains' houses and our wheels crunch down a gravel lane to what had been my late grandparents' home.

We look up at the small Cape Cod from the bottom of the hill it perches on. There is a loft above the garage where my uncle used to stay when he visited. To our left is the west branch of the harbor, where the sun would set and my grandmother would teach me to watch quietly. But the memories aren't all treating me kindly. Emotion presses like stuffy air on a muggy day.

"This is the house where your uncle killed himself?" Michelle asks. And I say yes. I point to the stone foundations of the house. When I was twelve and my favorite uncle was twenty-nine, he put a shotgun in his mouth and pulled the trigger. In the basement.

"It's also the house where my brother David died," I tell her. That was on the second floor. We look up at the bedroom window. He was eight months old. I was four. He had a congenital heart defect. My mother found him in his crib.

Later we ride our bikes to the cemetery. Uncle Bing, my aunt Dossie, and my grandparents are there. And my brother David. My father sometimes tells a story of how, at David's funeral, I apparently shouted out, "God, thanks for letting David visit us."

"Is that why it says 'Beloved Visitor' on his gravestone?" Michelle asks.

Yes, I tell her.

We sit on the grass by the graves for a little while. Just quietly. Michelle weeps a little. Isabella pulls grass up by the roots, cute in her bright yellow bike helmet.

Faced with the old house where wonderful and terrible memories linger together, I think that my motivation for embarking on what I called the No Impact Man experiment probably has a lot less to do with polar bears and corrupt politicians than I thought. The truth, for me, may have more to do with the eight-month-old baby who died of a heart defect and the twenty-nine-year-old man who died when he stuck a shotgun in his mouth and pulled the trigger.

A lot of life hasn't made real sense to me since then.

I don't mean that nothing makes sense. But certainly not a lot of the things that our culture keeps telling us are supposed to—like that we should

> My motivation for embarking on what I called the No Impact Man experiment probably has a lot less to do with polar bears and corrupt politicians than I thought.

spend our lives trying to get rich or struggling to acquire a really big house.

It's not, sadly for me, that I never *want* to be rich or have a big house. It's that when I do want such things, my mind quickly reminds me that cash and homes, like brothers and uncles, can be lost as quickly as they're gained. I am, a person with a Ph.D. in psychology told me, "conditioned to be suspicious of material satisfactions." Before I have a chance to turn the juggernaut that is my life in the direction of money and mansions, I find myself asking: "What meaning will it all have when I'm gone?"

Not that I'm complaining.

After a few career U-turns, the Universe has bestowed on me the privilege of earning my living as a writer. I have a fistful of articles and, not counting this one, two books to my credit. I even get to live in a lovely prewar building in Greenwich Village, my favorite part of New York City. I have, in many ways, the life I dreamed of when I was six. What more could I want?

But the question still plagues me: What will it all count for when I'm gone?

We're at the cemetery still.

Transportation by bike means you are riding *in*, not driving *through* like a car. You are life-*experiencing*, not sight-*seeing*. You are in it and of it, and the beauty goes so deeply inside you that you could weep, and you just never want to get off the bike again.

Michelle, who has resisted bikes until today, asks me whether, when we get back to New York, we could get her a bike, and whether we could add a kid's seat to my bike for Isabella. For reasons of marital diplomacy, I don't dance with my arms in the air, waving my fingers in the V-sign and shouting "Victory."

Instead, I lean over, kiss Michelle on the cheek, and say, "Yes, we can."

Maybe that house, my grandparents' house, is where this project really started. Where the dead baby and my uncle were.

Is that macabre?

It's easier to figure out how to get another iPhone or a flat-screen TV or a trip to Bermuda or some other life distraction than to think about these questions. Like, How should I live? Like, What is my life really for?

It's easier to assume that the purpose of life is to get a good job and a good salary and a good box to live in and another good box to ride in and hope that the boxes will keep you safe from everything. Including these questions. We all, I think, want to hide from the questions. I know I do.

But sometimes they force themselves upon us, just like that humidity on a muggy day. Sometimes there is nowhere to go.

There was this Zen master from Korea's Chogye Order of Zen Buddhism. He's dead now. He founded a school of Zen Buddhism here in the United States, where I like to go to meditate. Dae Soen Sa Nim, his students called him, which means, in Korean, Great Honored Master.

Anyway, Dae Soen Sa Nim would say, "Everybody says I want this and I want that but nobody really understands this 'I.'" What is this "I" that wants everything? Where does it come from? Where does it go? Why does it live? Why does it die?

These questions are so important, because we live our lives on the assumption that the way to happiness is to fulfill our desires. The economists believe that our desires are limitless, and that the economy is one big machine intended to fill those limitless desires. The problem is that our planetary habitat's resources are not limitless.

Everybody says I want this and I want that. If our assumptions about happiness and the fulfillment of desire are true, well, then, so be it: the economy is rightfully predicated on the fulfillment of desires and it will burn along until there's nothing left to burn. But if that is so, why did Jesus say that a camel can fit through the eye of a needle more easily than a rich man can get into the kingdom of heaven?

If my understanding is correct, his meaning was not that no one should be rich. It was that if we attach ourselves to riches to the point that we exclude more pressing concerns, we may well cause ourselves a lot of difficulties.

What if we don't really understand this "I" and what its true purpose is? What if we kill the planet filling our desires and then discover that that's not what we were here for? Isn't this worth stopping to figure out?

There is a poem from the Chogye funeral ceremony. The congregation recites it together. It's called "The Human Route," and it goes:

> Coming empty-handed, going empty-handed—that is human.
> When you are born, where do you come from?
> When you die, where do you go?
> Life is like a floating cloud which appears.
> Death is like a floating cloud which disappears.
> The floating cloud itself originally does not exist.
> Life and death, coming and going, are also like that.
> But there is one thing which always remains clear.
> It is pure and clear, not depending on life and death.
>
> Then what is the one pure and clear thing?

One cold, cloudy day in mid-January, I'm standing at one end of the country's largest farmer's market, in New York City's Union Square. I'm looking at the throngs of people weaving from stand to stand. One stand sells apples, one sells eggs, one sells vegetables the likes of which I've never seen before. Lots of stands sell the same thing as the stand right next to them.

Which vendor is better? How are you supposed to work your way through this crazy maze? I ponder a vegetable called a rutabaga, which looks vaguely like a brain tumor and wonder: Even if you buy this stuff, what on earth do you do with it?

Since the project began, I've avoided take-out containers and food packaging by buying from Integral Yoga's bulk bins, but essentially the grocery-store experience is just the same. You decide what you want; you go buy it (the only change being that you take your own containers and muslin bags). In this way, I can get peanut butter, bread, pasta, rice, tropical fruits and vegetables, and just about anything else I want.

Standing in the cold at the farmer's market, being jostled by the crowd, I'm thinking about how I barely know how to cook anything that requires more than plunging something into boiling water. I'm mourning the coming end of our regimen of peanut butter sandwiches.

I walk along. Because it's January and the farmer's market contains nothing but food grown locally, there are no tomatoes and no lettuce. What there is, is a whole lot of cabbage and root vegetables and apples.

I get home. From my cloth bag I empty onto the kitchen counter turnips, some cheese, some eggs, some apples, and some cabbage. Now what do I do? Michelle and Isabella will be home in a few hours, expecting dinner. And so begins the sustainable-eating phase of the project.

I'd thought that sustainable eating would be a gimme. Like it would just be a matter of continuing to traipse over to Integral Yoga. I figured sustainable eating just meant buying organic, which is all Integral stocks anyway. All I had to do in the food phase, I'd imagined, since organic is generally more expensive, was throw money at the problem.

In return I'd get the promise that there were *almost* no pesticides or herbicides on the produce (fifty-seven

> From my cloth bag I empty onto the kitchen counter turnips, some cheese, some eggs, some apples, and some cabbage. Now what do I do?

different agricultural chemicals may be used, according to the USDA organic standard). I'd also be rewarded with less pollution than from conventional farming, the promise that there would be no antibiotics or bovine growth hormones in our milk, and the hope, therefore, that Isabella would not be developing breasts at age ten.

But no.

It turns out that, unlike in the no-trash and no-carbon-producing-transportation phases, I would not be pioneering the sustainable-eating phase. There were lots of folks who had already given this aspect of our lifestyle redesign plenty of thought. And in their set, anyone with any cojones at all who wants to eat sustainably doesn't let himself off the hook by changing labels, even if the new label says "organic."

People who are really into sustainable eating take it a step further and only eat seasonal food produced within a truck ride of their home—the "local food" movement. That is why I had forced myself through the farmer's market ordeal and now had to figure out how to cook something that Michelle and Isabella would actually eat.

I was kidding myself to think I could trust organic to stand up to no-impact standards. With corporations like the cigarette company Philip Morris and the processed-food mega-giants H. J. Heinz and Sara Lee scrambling to buy up as much of the $17.7 billion organic market as they possibly can, what does "organic" even mean? Yes, it does equate with fewer toxins, but to what extent is a citizen supposed to trust real environmental stewardship to these corporate giants, or even to the USDA?

I read that the USDA, in April 2004, at the prompting of large food processors, wanted to allow farms to retain the organic seal even if they used animal growth hormones, fed cattle nonorganic fishmeal, or sprayed certain kinds of pesticides. The USDA backed down only after intense consumer complaints.

That's when I heaved a sigh, admitted that I'd have to do better, and started plugging the phrase "sustainable eating" into Google and scrolling through websites like Locavores.com and Ethicurean.com. My work, I discovered, would be more than cut out for me. I was—darn it—really going to have to learn to cook. And not just pasta. What I'd have to deal with was, yes, fresh food from the farmer's market.

I was all the more horrified when it turned out that there were a couple of real local food hard-asses out there, a pair of authors from Vancouver named Alisa Smith and James McKennan who committed themselves to eating only food produced within a hundred miles of their home for a year. They had achieved Internet cult status. They'd already set what, to me, seemed like a terrifyingly high standard for no-impact eating.

> **Agriculture uses a full 17 percent of the oil in the United States.**

I bit the bullet. I called the publisher of their forthcoming book and got Alisa's e-mail address. We swapped a couple of messages and, finally, we talked on the phone.

The hundred-mile-diet project, Alisa told me, began because of the concerns she and James had about the sustainability of our food system. In North America, she told me, the average distance food travels from farm to plate is roughly 2,000 miles. As one ridiculous example, strawberry imports in California peak just as strawberries are coming into season there—which is ironic to me, since the New York market, in turn, is flooded with California strawberries just as they come into season here. Agriculture, it turns out, uses a full 17 percent of the oil in the United States, which correlates to 17 percent of our oil-related greenhouse-gas emissions.

As I talked with Alisa, I had two feelings. One was the feeling of coming home. I hadn't realized how alone I had felt with this project until now. Talking to Alisa, to someone who shared my concerns and the desire to find both a more satisfying way of life and a way that was kinder to the planet, made me feel like the ugly duckling finally

rejoining the swans. Alisa didn't think I was weird. Plus, as busy as
Alisa and James had become as eco-heroes, they were willing to offer
me a little mentoring.

But my other feeling—fleetingly—was one of competition. Who
had the biggest sustainability balls? Maybe if their food-acquisition
radius was one hundred miles, I should make mine seventy-five . . .

Then Alisa started talking about wheat flour and salt. They couldn't
eat bread for a long time, she told me, because they couldn't find local
flour. They'd spent months looking for a local grower and mill. Suddenly, it all seemed much harder. I hadn't thought of this. It wasn't
just the general category of food that had to be local but all of the ingredients. It wasn't a matter of locally baked bread but bread containing only local flour, too.

Then Alisa told me how they finally got salt. They got in a boat,
rowed out into the middle of the bay, splashed a bucket into the sea
and collected salt water. They rowed back and boiled the water away
on a stove until all they had left was salt.

Where competition was concerned, I felt like Popeye about to arm-
wrestle Bluto—without any locally produced spinach.

"But all we did was worry about food," Alisa said. "We didn't have
to worry about all the other stuff that you're thinking about, too.
You'll have to figure out your own standards."

Alisa was telling me to be kind to myself. She was letting me off
the hook. Maybe with the no trash, the no carbon-producing transportation, and the fact that there would later be ever more daunting
phases of the No Impact project, I could forgive myself for not quite
achieving the same standards for local eating that she and James had
achieved. Happily, I admitted defeat in my self-proclaimed competition, just plain gave up when it came to chutzpah. The fact is, I was
so glad to have found some allies. Alisa and James would henceforth
be my local-food gods.

•

Alisa and James didn't choose 100 miles arbitrarily, to prove their mettle. They chose it because local agricultural land extended only as far as the Cascade Mountains to the east, the Coast Mountains to the north, and Boundary Bay to the south. For Alisa and James, in Vancouver, because of these geographical boundaries, food came either from within 100 miles or from farmland more than 300 miles away.

Faced with figuring out my own standards for local and sustainable eating, I make a couple of bike trips to have more local conversations. My first is with Paula Lukats and Cara Fraver of Just Food, a pioneering organization established in the early 1990s to promote sustainable eating by encouraging urban farming, and by forging direct relationships between rural farmers and New York City residents. In other words, Cara and Paula worked to help establish farmers' markets and CSAs, or "community-supported agriculture groups," which club together to buy directly from farmers.

We sit down in the Just Food boardroom and Paula and Cara proceed to tell me the good news that the fertile farmlands of the Hudson River Valley and parts of New Jersey and Connecticut will provide food enough to ensure that my family and I won't be starving. And, unlike in James and Alisa's Vancouver, there are no geographical boundaries here that can easily define food as local or faraway.

Paula tells me, "We work with any farmer that can drive into the city, drop off or sell their produce, and drive back to the farm in one day."

"How far is that?" I ask.

"Two hundred and fifty miles."

That's it: 250. That's going to be my radius, too.

Still hoping I might find the loophole that gets me out of this local-eating thing, I mention that I've read an article in *The Economist* that says that eating local can be a false economy. For example, tomatoes grown outdoors in Spain and transported to Britain use less fossil fuels and cause fewer greenhouse-gas emissions than tomatoes grown in a greenhouse in Britain.

"If your chief concern is greenhouse-gas emissions, then you'll have to eat only what's in season," Paula says. In other words, no hothouse tomatoes from Spain or anywhere else for me.

"What's in season now?" I ask, bearing in mind it is January.

"Ahhh . . . a lot of cabbage, root vegetables, and potatoes."

"People eat like that?"

"It's the way people ate for thousands of years, though people used to preserve out-of-season vegetables. You're too late for that."

"So I'm in for a lot of cabbage soup?"

They laugh.

"And I don't suppose there are too many local coffee plantations?"

They laugh again.

"But you can grow peppermint tea right on your windowsill," Paula says helpfully.

Michelle drinks four iced quad espressos a day from her reusable cup. A switch to peppermint tea seems akin to giving a heroin addict an ice-cream cone and telling him to enjoy the sugar buzz.

While I mentally calculate the risks to my marriage of suggesting that Michelle switch to homemade peppermint tea, Paula and Cara enthusiastically explain to me that the benefits to the culture of supporting local food production extend far beyond the minimization of transportation-related greenhouse-gas emissions. Small farmers, they insist, have a vested interest in taking good care of family land and are more likely to provide good overall environmental stewardship and efficient use of resources.

In fact, according to Bill McKibben's *Deep Economy*, small, local farms produce more food per acre than industrial farms and use land, water, and fossil fuels more efficiently. As it stands, agriculture is the United States's leading source of water pollution, its biggest water consumer, and the main cause of soil erosion and the loss of grasslands and wetlands.

Corn Belt fertilizer washing off the land into the Mississippi River, meanwhile, ends up in the Gulf of Mexico. It turns out that when you

fertilize the ocean you get a massive
bloom of oxygen-hogging algae. The
result is a 7,900-square-mile dead zone

> **Small, local farms produce more food per acre than industrial farms.**

in the Gulf that is so depleted of oxygen that it suffocates fish, shrimp,
crabs, and all manner of marine life. The EPA estimates that 210 million pounds of fertilizer end up in the Gulf every year.

Not only that, but centralization of our agriculture on huge factory
farms exposes us to tremendous food-security risks. In the last year,
thanks to our undiversified food system, we have seen a salmonella outbreak that sickened some 160 Americans and sparked a nationwide
tomato recall; the recall of *E. coli*–tainted spinach that sickened nearly
200 and killed 3; and a recall by a California company of 143 million
pounds of beef, the largest in history.

Local-food advocates argue that diversification of food production
over many thousands of farms located close to the people they feed
would provide a measure of protection from such disasters. A regional-
ized food web would ensure that local problems do not affect national
food supplies, such as occurred when floods in the Midwest, where corn
farming is concentrated, affected the entire world's corn market.

The list of environmental, health, and community benefits of putting responsibility for food production in the hands of small farmers—
people, instead of massive farms and corporations—goes on. Around
New York City, for example, farming upstate and in New Jersey and
Connecticut provides one of the few buffers against increased loss of
land to real estate development and suburban sprawl. By impeding development, preserving the farming economy in upstate New York also
has the effect of protecting New York City's drinking water supply.

Local farmers in the United States are also stewards of agricultural biodiversity and access to nutritional food. In the year 2000,
85 percent of the country's farmland produced only four crops: corn,
soybeans, wheat, and hay. This output goes on to become America's
processed food or to feed the cows for its fast-food hamburgers, which,
in turn, fuel America's obesity epidemic. Local farmers, through their

green markets and produce co-ops, on the other hand, often bring fresh fruit and vegetables to neighborhoods that might otherwise be serviced only by McDonald's, KFC, and the corner bodega.

The goals of environmental stewardship, access to good food, fair treatment of animals, and regional food webs dominated the thinking of the original, truly dedicated organic food producers when their movement first arose in the mid-twentieth century. Activist farmers began experimenting with organic food-production systems largely in response to their concerns about the effects on environmental and human health of the post–World War II concentration of agricultural production on huge, single-crop farms.

Scientists had discovered that nitrogen-rich chemicals used to make wartime explosives could be repurposed as synthetic agricultural fertilizer. Likewise, compounds used to make wartime poisonous gases killed plants and bugs—as well as people—and could be repackaged as herbicides and pesticides. This kept the wartime factories running and helped to form the basis for a new industrialized type of farming that didn't require seemingly antiquated, but ecologically sound, practices like crop rotation, letting fields go fallow, and the collection and use of animal manure.

The victory of modern, conventional, industrial-scale farming meant that organic farming, with its refusal to adopt "modern" methods and its concentration on small local farms, remained a fringe philosophy—at least until the publication in the 1960s of Rachel Carson's *Silent Spring*, which called attention to the hazards of exposure to pesticides.

Suddenly, consumers began to agitate for chemical-free food. The farmer-activist-philosophers who had developed organic farming began to codify a set of standards that could be adopted nationally. Meanwhile, as the organic food sector grew, industrial farmers began to look upon organic farming techniques not as a balanced, ecologically, and socially sound philosophy of farming but merely as a form of food production that attracted a consumer base willing to pay more.

By the time the USDA established a national organic standard, in 2002, the original farmer-activist-philosophers had lost a protracted battle with larger farming interests—though, to be fair, some of the original organic growers felt that the goal of a "perfect" standard was the enemy of the "good" standard. They wanted an organic standard that they felt could be realistically adopted by the entire American food system.

Either way, the USDA's organic standard failed to embrace many of the fundamental tenets of social, ethical, and environmental responsibility upon which the organic farming movement had been founded. An organic dairy cow was no longer required to graze on pasture. Organic chickens and pigs could now be denied outdoor privileges. Food additives and synthetic chemicals could be used in organic processed food. A whole host of synthetic agricultural chemicals could be used with impunity.

Perhaps worst of all, a factory farm could be certified organic. The organic standard was stretched to include some of the industrial practices the avoidance of which was the original purpose of the organic movement.

This is why, as Paula and Cara told me back in the boardroom of Just Food, many of the local farmers I'd find in the farmers' markets considered themselves "more organic than organic." Even without regulations to adhere to, most local farmers I would buy from considered it vital to, for example, give their animals access to pasture, use integrated pest management, rotate their crops, plant heirloom varieties, and offer access to fresh produce to underserved neighborhoods.

"So all the local farms are organic, right?" I ask.

"Most of them are part of the old-fashioned organic movement, though they may not have the USDA certification. The certification process is too expensive and labor-intensive for many small farms." Even the USDA's certification requirements are biased toward larger farms.

"But without the certification, how can you tell?"

"You look them in the eyes and you ask them. This is the thing about local food. You get to talk to your farmers and ask them what their priorities are, and if those priorities line up with yours, they're the ones you buy from."

To be sure, we'd be better off if the factory farms adopted even the watered-down USDA organic farming standards and saved us and our water and land from the perils of conventional chemicals. But as Michael Pollan puts it in *The Omnivore's Dilemma*: "In precisely what sense can that [plastic] box of salad on sale at Whole Foods three thousand miles and five days away from [where it was grown] truly be said to be organic?"

If that well-traveled plastic box of salad qualifies for the USDA's organic label, then, for the purposes of the No Impact experiment, I want something better.

I stumble across a 2006 UN Food and Agriculture Organization report, "Livestock's Long Shadow," that spends 390 pages enumerating the environmental effects of our planet's supporting 1.5 billion cows. Cattle raising turns out to be one of the top two or three contributors to the worst environmental problems around the planet at every level—from global to local.

Global deforestation to create pastureland and—believe it or not—the methane-filled burps arising from cows' ruminative digestive systems account for 18 percent of the world's greenhouse gases, more than the world's entire transportation sector. The list of other problems to which livestock farming contributes substantially—from water pollution to acid rain—goes on and on.

Then there's fish.

I read a number of reports that spoke of the severe degradation of the world's fisheries, but an article in the November 2006 issue of *Science* said that the oceans would essentially be barren with no chance of recovery by 2048, if current trends continued. There would still be fish. But in a vast, nearly empty ocean, Mr. Fish would have a hard time finding Mrs. Fish in order to make baby fish and the fisheries would be unable to bounce back. Of the world's fisheries, the report said, 29 percent had already collapsed.

The good news is that the trend is still reversible. The oceans can still recover if the fisheries are managed responsibly, which means, largely, taking fewer fish out of those parts of the oceans that are depleted. One approach is to eat only seafood certified by the Marine Stewardship Council, but that approach is not so well adhered to by, for example, New York City's sushi joints.

So the finalized No Impact eating plan looked pretty much like this:

Only seasonal food grown or made with ingredients grown within 250

> **In a vast, nearly empty ocean, Mr. Fish would have a hard time finding Mrs. Fish in order to make baby fish.**

miles. No greenhouse-grown food. No beef. No seafood. The problems of raising cattle notwithstanding, the doctor wants the young Isabella to drink milk—it's in. Since she's allergic to soy, and since I can't find a local source of other beans for protein, we'll also have cheese.

Time to tell Michelle.

"Simple and healthy, the way we've always said we should eat," Michelle says when I tell her about the local produce and the probable lack of pasta made from wheat grown far away or anything else even vaguely processed.

"So nothing that wiggles or has a face," she says cheerily when I mention the beef and seafood ban. "We should really be vegetarian anyway. It's more in line with our values."

"There's just one more thing," I tell Michelle.

"What?"

"Coffee."

"You mean we have to buy it locally?"

"I mean it can't be grown locally."

"What do we drink instead?"

I don't answer her directly. Instead, I tell her about another foodie I'd met, Loren Talbot, an independent local eating expert who'd done her master's thesis on New York City food policy.

"Loren tells me that she gets a wonderful feeling of connection from eating local. She says she finds herself saying a little prayer of thanks to each of the farmers who grew the food on her plate. Like, 'Thanks, Jim, for the peas.' Thanks, John, for the eggs.' "

"Uh-huh," Michelle says. "What are we going to do about coffee?"

I shift for a second. I point to the kitchen windowsill. "I'm going to grow a peppermint plant for you right there and make you tea every morning."

I give her my best aren't-I-a-great-husband smile. Michelle just stares.

One prayer of thanks never once heard in our household: "Thanks, Colin, for the peppermint tea."

And so, in those first cold January and February weeks, I work my way over and over again from one end of the farmer's market to the other, slowly learning how it goes. At first I don't know what is where. And the paradigm is entirely different from normal cooking and food shopping. You can't go to the cookbook, choose a recipe, and then go out and get the ingredients. Instead, you work your way through the market, see what there is, and when you get home, you figure out what you can make from the ingredients you've been blessed with.

"You'll be forced to experiment with vegetables you've never cooked with before," Cara and Paula had said, excited, as if that was a good thing.

I discover a Korean farmer who grows his own soybeans on Long Island and makes his own tofu. Cool (but not for allergic Isabella). I ask at a baker's stand whether the flour they use comes from within 250 miles, but no. Not so cool. On the other hand, I discover the Blew Farm, which has wheat and oat flour grown well within my limit in Pennsylvania. I can make bread. Whether that will be cool or not, I've yet to discover.

I buy what looks good and what I think I might be able to use. I feel my way along. This is the adventure part that excites culinary experts about local eating.

Before the local-eating phase, I hadn't been able to find acceptable cheese because it all came wrapped in plastic. Not here. They cut the cheese from hunks and wrap it in paper. To do them one better, in front of a cheese-maker who keeps pasture-fed cows, I self-consciously pull out my own muslin cloth, to avoid the paper. "That's what we all used to do," the vendor says appreciatively.

I'm starting to relax and joke around. I even ask farmers about their use of chemicals. One farmer tells me, "I'll use a bug spray if I really have to, but you can see from the produce that I haven't used it this season." He means that his vegetables are not blemish-free like in a grocery store.

Over these lean winter months, my larder tends to contain eggs and oats (which will serve for breakfasts), potatoes, leeks, cabbage, carrots, turnips, parsnips, several types of cheese, homemade bread, milk, onions, butter, and, of course, the rutabaga.

I sauté up the leeks, scramble in some eggs, throw the pan under the grill with some cheese on top, and before long we have a frittata. I shred up some cabbage, too, for a salad. In the morning I make us oatmeal. I send Michelle to work with a big jar that has frittata in it and leftover salad. That night I make us some leek-and-potato soup.

A new family routine emerges.

While I cook, Michelle sits at the table and chats with me. Isabella stands on a chair in the kitchen and pretends to help. We can't resist, even after only a few days of local eating, contrasting this with the old life of shoveling in greasy takeout while we sat in front of the television. Now we're talking. Instead of the TV being the center of our life, the kitchen table is. We spend more time talking to Isabella than we used to.

The soup is ready. I put it down on the table. "It's delicious," Michelle says.

"You don't have to say that."

"I mean it. I want us to eat this way for the rest of our lives. What were we thinking all this time?"

The hard part for me about no coffee is not having a place to hang out. I mean, the coffee is not so much about the coffee sometimes as it is about having a place to pretend to read the newspaper while really looking at other people pretending to read the newspaper.

The good news is that we've decided on what we call the "social exception." It's a clause within our local-eating contract with ourselves that says we are allowed an out if the point of the out is to spend time with friends. If someone asks us to dinner, we don't wave our fingers and say, "Oh no, we're environmentalists." We go and have fun. By the same token, it means that I can, as long as I'm with a friend, drink a coffee or go to a restaurant.

The genius of this rule is that it forces me not to eat or drink coffee alone. It forces me to socialize more. Restaurants and coffee places are no longer a Band-Aid for the fact that we are just too busy and harried to sort out our own food. It's all about using food and coffee and resources not for convenience, because I'm too strapped to make it myself, but to forge social bonds—the way it probably ought to be used.

I sometimes wonder if our lack of social connection and community is at the root of our environmental problems. I wonder, at least in my case, if that lack has meant that I don't feel responsible or accountable to anything beyond myself. Without real community, where is the visceral sense of connection to something larger, to something to which I owe my care? Maybe one reason I felt like I couldn't make a difference when the project started was because I wasn't firmly connected to anything to which I could make a difference.

But about the not drinking coffee, what's hard for Michelle is sheer physical addiction. In anticipation of the local-food rules, rather than easing herself off, she has been ramping up her coffee drinking. Like an addict faced with a dry spell. Somebody gave her a $25 Starbucks gift card. She used it in one day. Five times in one day, my poor wife went into Starbucks and ordered four shots of espresso over ice—and then asked them to put it in her reusable cup.

I'm getting the hang of this! Blew Farm has dried hot chillies that are putting some punch in the cabbage. I made a really tasty apple crumble, replacing the sugar in the recipe with local honey. And I've come upon a way to make a light, tangy vinegar, having found none that is local and unpackaged.

What you do, you get your scraps of fruit—apple cores, dregs of berries (though no berries for us because they're not in season), whatever—and chop them up coarsely. Dissolve a quarter cup of honey (the recipe calls for sugar, but I had to modify that to fit the project rules) in one quart of water. Throw the scraps in and cover with a cloth. Let the mixture ferment for two or three weeks, stirring occasionally.

Adds great flavor to—you got it—cabbage.

What do you get when you combine no throwaway packaging with local food only? Not too many tasty treats, I can tell you, at least not until you get the hang of things. Every time I find something new, I want to do a dance.

I trundle along to a party and I bump into a friend who happens to tell me that her mother, who emigrated from Greece, makes yogurt nearly every day. Hearing this, I jumped with joy. Why? Because on this regimen, I haven't been able to find yogurt or, really, any other snack food that comes unpackaged and thus won't break the no-trash rule.

So my friend e-mailed me her mom's recipe, and I made it for the first time that night. It's the best. I'd thought you needed some sort of machine to make yogurt, but no way. You boil a quart of milk, wait till it cools enough to stick your finger in, mix in a tablespoon of yogurt culture, transfer it to a container and cover with a blanket, then wait till morning and—yippee—you've got yogurt. Mix with honey. Delicious.

But where do you find the time to cook and shop and make yogurt and bread and sauerkraut and family meals? people want to know.

Well, for starters, by not watching TV. Since the average American watches four and a half hours of TV a day, that means that between us, Michelle and I have an extra nine hours a day to, well, take care of ourselves by preparing food that is actually good for us.

Besides, according to Alisa and James's book *Plenty* (or, *The 100-Mile Diet*, its title in Canada), a study in the United Kingdom showed that the amount of time people now spend driving to the supermarket, looking for parking, wandering the aisles in search of frozen pizza or premixed salad nearly equals the time people spent preparing food from scratch just twenty years ago. And what of the time spent making the money to pay for take-out food and restaurants and packaged meals?

Where do I find the time to make bread?

The longer this project goes on, the more backward things seem to me. How come for so long I put up with the doughy stuff called "bread" that comes from the grocery store in a plastic bag? How come I didn't ask for better? Did I even know that there *was* better to be had?

> But where do you find the time to cook and shop and make yogurt and bread and sauerkraut and family meals? people want to know.

In thinking about my life, and what I want from it, I'm just not sure that the question is supposed to be, Where do I find time to make bread? Certainly, it's not supposed to be, as it has sometimes been, How do I find the time to spend time with my child? How did I let my life get set up that way?

Is this the way I wanted my pre–No Impact life to be?

Is this the way that, once the project is over, I want my post—No Impact life to be again?

One thing I realize about this year of no impact: it's a luxury to be able to make all these adaptations. I'm lucky to have the time. My job, in a way, is to bake the bread and ride my bike and let my life slow down as I refuse so many of the modern culture's so-called efficiencies and conveniences. It won't be too long, though, till the year is over. I'll have to get back to some other kind of work. What will happen then? What kind of life will I have?

A frigid February day, and we are out in the East Village, a half-hour walk from our house. It is Isabella's birthday, and we go to Jane's Exchange, a children's secondhand clothing store, to let Isabella choose her present. We let her pick anything she wants. Anything. She chooses a pair of shiny gold slippers and nothing else.

"Are you sure, honey? You can have anything."

"I want the gold slippers."

There are toys, and all sorts of clothes. "But you can have anything."

"I want the gold slippers."

They cost two dollars.

We come out and it's freezing and, really, we have no choice but to duck into a café to warm up. They don't let you just sit at their tables, rubbing your hands together and not eating during brunch on Sunday. I get tense. This is not local food.

Michelle says, "Relax, honey, it's Isabella's birthday."

I relent. We order eggs and potatoes and have just a dandy time, but afterward I feel guilty. To confess, I e-mail Alisa.

She writes me back, "Oh, the perils of a warm café on a cold day. . . . According to the rules we gave ourselves, the occasional meal out was allowed, and I daresay helped preserve our sanity." But, she added: "Only through strictness do you have a conversion."

•

Speaking of cheats, in a departure from the project's travel moratorium, for the sake of a little research, I climb on a train out of Grand Central Terminal and make my way about two hours north along the Hudson River. There has been a whole long discussion on the phone with Ronny Osofsky about whether I would be able to ride my bike to his dairy farm from the train station, but, finally, I see that I am beginning to look like a nut, so I let the bike go and he meets me in his pickup truck.

His farm, he tells me, was started by his mother and father in 1941. We drive over rolling hills into beautiful countryside. We hop out of the truck at the farm. It is a bitterly cold February day. There is the requisite silo and the barn, but what's missing is the cows. "We have to keep them inside today," he says, "to keep the barn from freezing."

The milking and piping system would apparently freeze solid if it weren't for the body heat of the seventy-or-so-strong herd keeping the barn warm.

Ronny shows me around the farm's bottling plant and yogurt and ice-cream making facilities, which are a tangle of stainless-steel pipes and vats. We turn a corner and enter the cow barn. I stop.

It is like another world. The windows are very dusty and the sunlight coming in has a resulting brownish-red tinge to it. The sturdy animals stand in their stalls in two long rows. There is the rhythmic crunch of their chewing the corn strewn on the ground before them. Because of the cold, their breath steams out of their nostrils and curls into vaporous whirlpools in the air. The steam makes them seem like dragons.

I recently saw a video recorded secretly by a Humane Society investigator. It is the video that sparked the country's largest-ever beef recall. The investigator spent a few weeks at a confined-animal feeding operation (CAFO) in California and focused on "downed cows." Apparently, as part of the USDA inspection process, cows must be able to walk under their own steam to slaughter as a precaution against their having, for example, mad cow disease and thus introducing tainted meat into the food stream.

The Humane Society video showed slaughterhouse workers doing anything they could to get downed cows to walk. They sprayed hoses of water into their nostrils to try to get them to stand. They tied chains to their legs and dragged them through the mud with trucks. They used bulldozers to try to force the cows to their feet. And throughout the video, you can hear the sounds of the cows—they are screaming.

> A dairy cow, bred over the centuries to produce large quantities of milk, would die without people to withdraw the surfeit that a calf couldn't consume from its udders.

The relationship between man and animal at this farm is entirely different.

Ronny is on the move: he walks through the barn, talking to the cows and looking at them and touching them. He addresses each by name. He likes them. I can tell he likes these animals. They are not his possessions. They are his partners. Ronny explains to me that a dairy cow, bred over the centuries to produce large quantities of milk, would die without people to withdraw the surfeit that a calf couldn't consume from its udders.

Despite everything I've read about the environmental impact of keeping cattle, I can't help thinking and feeling that there is something important about the symbiotic relationship. I am not speaking of the role that man plays in CAFO operations, where the cow is a commodity whose juice must be squeezed from it; here there seems to be a wholly different understanding of that relationship.

"You know which cows have always been my favorite?" Ronny says. "The naughty ones. The ones with a little devil in them. The ones that won't go through the gate when you tell them to. The ones with personality."

He goes on to explain that his cows get to spend most of their time outdoors, grazing on grass. They eat corn that Ronny grows on his own farm when they come in to be milked. He has to buy about 10 percent of his corn from elsewhere. In other words, his cows live a good life. I feel proud that I've been drinking his glass-bottled milk.

"But I have to ask," I say. "Why aren't you certified organic?"

"Because we use antibiotics."

"You put antibiotics in your feed?" I ask, momentarily horrified.

"No, no. But if a cow is sick or has an infected udder and the vet comes and says that the only way to cure the cow is with antibiotics, we treat the cow. On an organic farm, you'd have to send the cow to slaughter. We treat the cow, keep it off the milking machine until the antibiotics are clear from the milk. I think killing a cow because it has an infection is cruel." Ronny is proud that his cows live to be fifteen and twenty years old. No more than 25 percent of dairy cows in typical cattle farms live to be over seven years old.

Ronny takes me into the farm office for a coffee before he drives me back to the station. I meet his brother. I ask his brother what criteria he thinks a person should apply when deciding where to buy milk. "There's only one," he says. "You have to go see how the cows are treated."

We climb back into Ronny's truck for what will be about a tenth of my total car riding for the year. "It seems like hard work for not much pay," I say. "What makes you stay in the game?"

Ronny looks at me like I've missed the whole point of the afternoon. "I love cows," he says.

I'm walking down the street, and I bump into our friend Michelle, who sometimes babysits Isabella. She comes up to the apartment and I give her soup.

I know what's it's like to run around New York City in search of a meal. And I've often felt it wasn't good food I was looking for. What is it that I really want at dinnertime? Is it cheese or meat or the feeling that I can put my feet up and be with people that I like? I felt good to be providing that right now for my friend Michelle.

My wife and I have started telling people to drop by at dinnertime, even if they have plans for later in the evening. They come. I offer them some frittata or scrambled eggs or sometimes just grilled cheese and homemade sauerkraut. Our food is not complicated.

Friends come and we eat and we talk, and then they might cancel their plans and sit. We play Scrabble. Even better, we've rediscovered charades. Teams of four face off in our living room and we laugh, I swear, till tears are just pouring down our cheeks. The rhythm of our lives is changing.

It's not based on electronic entertainment. It's based on home-cooked food, and not especially good home-cooked food, either. It's based on the fact that the kitchen table, not the TV, has become the center of our lives. It's based on the fact that our house has become a home.

It's true that we sometimes miss the strawberries we can't have and the nonlocal balsamic vinegar we used before the project started. And we dread that our stock of nonlocal salt is soon to run out, too. But, still, I enjoy feeling a little like a grandmother, feeding all my friends. There is something wonderful about it, and wonderful about playing host and everybody just being able to kick their shoes off and relax.

This rush we're in—I don't think people like it. At least for this year, my family has opted out of it. Is that why people flock to us lately?

I ride with Isabella across the Brooklyn Bridge. She makes us stop. She just stares. At the buildings. At the river. At the boats. The next day she says, "Can we go on a bike ride to the bridge again, Daddy?"

It's night and I hang up the phone with my best friend, Tanner, and Michelle is on top of me immediately about his wife. Is he mad that she started smoking again? Does he worry about her? What are they going to do? Friends and meals and charades are great, but Michelle needs some scandal, some excitement. I overhear her phone calls to her own friends. She questions them about their marriages, tries to get the dirt on the drama in their lives.

Something else weird: Michelle comes walking up to me carrying a handful of colored markers. She says, "I want to write on the walls."

"What?"

She repeats herself.

"What for?"

"I just want to," she says. "I feel like it."

"I don't think so," I say.

"That's not fair. How come you decide everything about this project?"

"The project is about environmental living, not drawing on the walls."

"No," Michelle says. "The project is about figuring out how we want to live. It's about lifestyle redesign, and I want to try writing on the walls."

I think for a minute. "Would you consider, at first, limiting yourself to the bathroom walls?"

"Yes," she says.

She goes in and writes, "Sunlight is the best disinfectant." It's a quote from U.S. Superior Court Justice Louis Brandeis. Michelle writes it in reference to the spuriousness of the lawsuit against her by one of her story sources. She means when the truth comes out, the stink will go away. She writes a bunch more stuff in different colors.

Sooner or later we're lying on the couch and I ask her, What is going on with you? The conversations you've been having? The markers?

"Without TV I have to get my entertainment somehow," Michelle quips. It's like she's trying to create her own home-movie version of *Temptation Island* to keep herself amused. But that's not it, Michelle says.

"It's scary to have a real fantasy life of your own," she tells me. "You get worried it will affect your real life and destroy everything. So you turn yourself off and get your thrills from TV, which poses no risks, and live your whole life on the couch. It's as though I was asleep to my own life. I'm waking up to my life. We're never watching TV again."

A few days later my dad visits and asks about the writing on the bathroom wall. I explain. He wants to know if he can write something. "There is nothing so powerful as an idea whose time has come," he writes, referring to the No Impact project.

Is everyone going nuts?

An update on the Great Diaper Experiment:

Michelle has begun taking part.

She had started thinking about the potential toxicity to Isabella of the plastic diapers lying against her skin twenty-four hours a day. As Lori Taylor from the Real Diaper Association put it to me, who knows what potential effect molded petrochemical goop might have on your child? That might sound paranoically wacky, but by way of reasonable comparison, look at the dangers baby bottles made with bisphenol-A have been shown to pose. Meanwhile, nobody's worrying about the dangers of putting organic cotton next to their baby's skin.

Scientific analysis and parental anxiety aside, Isabella added her own two cents one day when I thought it would be easier to reach for a plastic diaper, still lurking at the back of the closet, instead of hunting around for a clean cotton one. Isabella struggled and cried and wouldn't let me put the plastic diaper on.

> **Who knows what potential effect molded petrochemical goop might have on your child?**

"I want Bella's new diapers," she cried.

If I spent a day with some form of plastic wrapped around my butt, I'd probably understand why.

•

And now for perhaps the most important discovery of the entire No Impact project. I'm talking here about the effects of not having TV. It has to do with our realization, one Sunday afternoon, that the TV was taking time away from more than just our cuddling and talking and playing charades.

I'm sitting around, doing not much. The front door opens and Michelle comes in. Isabella is in bed, taking a nap. At first, Michelle and I are at a loss for something to do to amuse ourselves. Then we figure it out. I won't say much else except that we've finally realized the best thing to fill the space in our schedule once occupied by TV.

And now you know why some male friends of mine have ever since been lobbying their wives join in on the no-television part of the No Impact project.

SEVEN

Conspicuous Nonconsumption

The no-trash, no-carbon-producing transportation and sustainable-eating phases are all in place, and what I'm trying to figure out now is how we manage to make no impact while dealing with our purchases of things like clothes and toys and other household items. How do we consume, as it were, inconspicuously?

While I begin to research ideas and options, I keep coming up against the idea that, here in the United States, to be a good citizen is to be an aggressive consumer. To be patriotic is to shop. To bury ourselves in credit-card debt, apparently, is to do our part in keeping the economy going. But here's what I don't get: Why are we supposed to be of service to the economy? I thought the economy was supposed to be of service to us (though lately it's not doing such a good job).

Growth in gross domestic product, the common wisdom says, is a good thing that all of us should work for. A growing GDP is a sign that we're all doing well, it is said, an indicator of the common good. But as I do my research, I read that the more people get cancer, the more the health sector grows. The more people get divorced, the more the legal sector grows. The more Hurricane Katrinas there are, the more the emergency-services sector grows. Should our goal simply be to blindly "grow our economy," or should we find ways to ensure that it grows in ways that both improve quality of life and protect our habitat?

Growth in our economy doesn't necessarily mean that there's more money in the average person's pocket or that the average person is more content. It doesn't necessarily mean we're all going on more holidays or getting more Jet Skis. Growth in the economy could just as easily reflect the average person spending his life savings to deal with some terrible family catastrophe.

It could also mean that we're all working ten hours a day instead of eight, that we're all spending twice as much money on our kids at Christmas because we feel guilty for not spending enough time with them.

Since 1950, the U.S. gross domestic product has grown 550 percent. Want to know how much measures of happiness have increased? Just about zero. So, in the service of a healthy economic system, many of us no longer live near our families but cross the country to be near jobs. Some of us work two jobs, get more stuff, take only two weeks' holiday a year while Europeans take seven. How much satisfaction do we get for all that?

Meanwhile, even if undifferentiated economic growth was a reliable measure of a better life, it turns out that 40 percent of that growth goes straight into the pockets of the richest 1 percent of the population. That means that if you take a hundred people, one of them is getting nearly *half* of the economic cream. So much for the idea that economic growth "trickles down" to the people who need it.

None of this would be relevant to the No Impact project if it weren't for the fact that all this "growth" depends on industry making all the stuff we're supposed to want, and, in the process, sucking resources from a planet too depleted to furnish them. This growth we're supposed to be working for is literally pulling the rug out from under us by destroying the planet's ability to support us.

It's a vicious circle. We work our butts off so we can get the stuff, but the making of the stuff destroys the planet, which makes us more depressed, so we think we need more stuff to cheer us up, so we work even harder.

The question is: Why? Presumably because we like it, right? Except that one survey showed that more than 70 percent of respondents wished Christmas was not so commercial, and yet those same respondents are part of the annual shopping stampede. Remember those psychologists who study the science of well-being? They told us that getting more stuff has only a transient effect on our happiness, while things like community, a sense of working toward a higher purpose, and using our most prized individual talents can give us a lasting happiness boost.

So what do we do? We spend more time working, trying harder to get more stuff, and bemoan the fact that we can't use our creativity or spend time with our friends.

I'm not moralizing. I'm not blaming. Because it's me, too.

While I'm sitting around, researching the "evils of consumption," I find myself completely obsessed with checking my blog's rating on Technorati (an Internet search engine for blogs) to see how it compares in popularity with other blogs. How many people have visited by 11:00 a.m.? I click on the visitor meter. How many at 11:10 a.m.? Click. What about five minutes later, at 11:15?

How pathetic I am in this regard became all the more apparent to me when I mentioned this compulsion to a friend who didn't even know what Technorati was.

Is that why I was born? To achieve a good Technorati rating? Besides, even if I got the number one spot, would I then be satisfied? No.

The danger, for me, is that I get attached to goals like these, find out that I've used up my limited time in this life on something—a Technorati rating, for heaven's sake—that is essentially meaningless, and, meanwhile, in my tunnel vision, manage to hurt myself, the planet, and other creatures by not attending to what is really important. And then I see everyone around me doing the same thing and, quite frankly, I get scared.

Honest to God, if I thought it actually worked for me—or even for everyone else—I would just shut the hell up. But it doesn't work. Every time I put money and stuff and accomplishment first, I can't help thinking that no one lying on his deathbed says, "You know, I

just wish I had managed to get more stuff." It's the endgame that both-
ers me. I can't stop thinking about the endgame.

Is it just me? Do other people feel the way I do? Do I get to thinking so morbidly about it all because my kid brother died in his sleep
and my uncle shot himself? Or is it because the world is off-kilter?

Continuing my research about economics and quality of life, I read
a *New York Times* story about how dissatisfied the Silicon Valley millionaires were with their lot. As the *Times* reported, many of them felt
worried to death that they still didn't have enough and toiled for the
day when they would.

The solution most of these millionaires have come up with for
their unhappiness? Work harder to get even more, because the problem must be still not having enough.

When your blog is ranked number 2,000 in the entire world and
you're still not happy, your brain tells you you'll be happy when you
get to number 1,000. When you're a Silicon Valley millionaire and
you're not happy, your brain tells you it's just a matter of buckling
down and becoming a billionaire.

I once read this story about a Japanese Zen master who founded a
temple in Minneapolis. As I remember it, he was very old and ill and
had ceased teaching, except on special occasions.

At one celebration at the temple, the Zen master was due to talk,
but as the appointed hour approached he was nowhere to be found.
Yet when the time arrived, the door to the dharma room slammed
open and the Zen master hobbled to the center of the room.

When he got there, he cleared his throat, said one sentence, then
turned around and hobbled out of the room and back to his apartment. Here is the one sentence he told the many guests who had
gathered to hear his wisdom:

"Soon," he said, "we will all be dead."

•

The summer before No Impact, in August 2006, Michelle, Isabella, and I are in Tuscany driving toward Siena, when Michelle looks in the back and sees that vomit is erupting volcanically from the then eight-month-old Isabella. We pass through Siena's ancient city walls, park, and pull Isabella out of the car seat.

Suddenly there is a squishing sound from beneath her and she is now erupting liquid from her bottom, too. How do you find a doctor in Italy when you don't know Italian?

Isabella's head suddenly flops forward on her shoulders. She is unconscious. But that doesn't stop the vomiting or the diarrhea. Michelle steps into the road and virtually knocks a young woman from her Vespa scooter. Michelle shouts: "Get an ambulance! My baby!"

Neither Michelle nor I mention it, but the ghost of my baby brother who died at eight months—Isabella's current age—is suddenly haunting us. Superstitiously, we have both been urging the days past until we could happily say Isabella was no longer eight months old. Why isn't the ambulance here yet?

I start shouting Isabella's name. I've got it in my head that she must not be allowed to remain unconscious. I shout again. Nothing. In my panic, I bite her thigh. Hard. Isabella emits a cry, raises her head, but it rolls forward again almost immediately. I bite again. The doctors will ask about the red welts at the hospital.

Amid squeals of sirens, the ambulance arrives. The baby is inside on the stretcher, naked and with her arms outstretched as in the Crucifixion. Out of the corner of my eye, I see an ambulance man helping Michelle into the front seat. They think she is going to faint.

This is it, my mind is saying to me. I'm not losing two babies in one life. If Isabella goes, I'm going, too. My mind is getting ready to jump off a cliff. My mind is telling me that even if my body lives on, *it* will not. This, my mind is telling me, is not worth sticking around for.

Focus. I have to focus.

We're moving. It is hard not to fall over as we speed through the winding ancient streets. I will never be able to hear the two-tone sound of a European ambulance again without getting a knot in my stomach. Now the baby is gray and her normally bulbous stomach has become concave, sunken.

"She's not breathing!" I shout. "Is she breathing?"

"Yes, she is. She is breathing," the pediatrician in the ambulance says. She looks deeply into my eyes and holds my gaze. We arrive at the emergency entrance and about ten doctors and nurses get to work over Isabella's tiny prostrate body.

> I will never be able to hear the two-tone sound of a European ambulance again without getting a knot in my stomach.

"We want to do an MRI," a doctor tells us. "We're worried about a neurological event."

Michelle and I are on the floor on our knees, praying to whatever. While we waited for the ambulance, I held it together and Michelle fell apart and nearly fainted. Here in the MRI waiting room, Michelle is the strong one. She leads the prayer. Months ago, I had had a dream where David, my baby brother who died, said he would always protect Isabella.

"David is taking care of Isabella," Michelle tells me. "David is taking care of her." Then a doctor comes out smiling.

Smiling.

"She has woken up," he says. "We had to sedate her. She kept trying to play with our stethoscopes. And her brain is perfect."

We're in the hospital room now and it's three in the morning and Isabella is awake but dozy from the sedatives. I blow a raspberry in her neck and she laughs, weakly, but all the same, it's a laugh.

It's over. She's fine. Dehydration, maybe, the doctors say, maybe a bug, maybe—and this is the reason we can't give her tofu—an allergic reaction to the soy formula we'd given her earlier. "The good news is that we've run every cardiac and brain test a baby can have. So now you know better than most parents that you have a perfect baby."

But perfect as Isabella remains, I cry every time I tell, write, read, or edit that story. I cannot shake the feeling that—as the Zen master told the Minneapolis assembly—life is tenuous. We're all just "Beloved Visitors." I cannot stop wondering, since life is so precious, whether we all share a tendency to waste our lives—and therefore our planetary resources—on things that just aren't important.

By the way, for all my talk about keeping up with the Joneses and consumption of resources not making us happy, I'm only talking about people who actually have excess resources to consume. There are plenty of people, of course, who have way less than they need and by rights really should be consuming more.

That's one of the issues that makes this whole sustainability thing so complicated. By 2050 there will be 9 billion people on this one planet, but only 1 billion in the developed world. The 1 billion of us from the rich countries can go zero-impact, but if the other 8 billion still can't afford our shiny new solar panels and windmills and they have to burn coal for a better life, we're done for.

Not only do we in the United States and Western Europe have to find a way to reduce our resource consumption, but, paradoxically, we also have to find a way to transfer renewable energy and sustainable product manufacture to the developing world so the planet can withstand it as its inhabitants begin consuming more.

This is not about the old-fashioned, socialistic paradigm of redistribution of wealth. This is about the fact that—as at no other time in our history—we're all in the same boat. If we can't help each other not kick a hole through the bottom, we'll all sink together.

So here's the challenge of the No Impact project as of mid-2007: If the idea is to try to achieve some balance between quality of life and resource consumption, how do we proceed in terms of our purchases?

Is it actually possible to not consume? Can you get by not buying anything? Not using anything? If "consumption is bad," does that make consuming absolutely nothing good? By 2009, we'd be told that our economic crisis was perpetuated, in part, by lack of consumer demand—reduced societal consumpiton. Does that mean consumption is somehow good? Or is our economic well-being falsely pitted against our environmental well-being?

Judith Levine, both the author and subject of her book *Not Buying It*, simply didn't buy anything but absolutely necessary consumables for a year. The thing is, her ability to do that depended upon her use of the accumulated goods she had accrued during all the previous years of her life. And unless she was willing to become a true ascetic or a scavenger, it was not something she could continue once her stored goods ran out.

> **My object in the nonconsumption phase wasn't bare survival. My object was not to waste.**

As much as I appreciate her good work, I wanted a set of practices that would remain relevant to my life moving forward. Plus, as I've suggested, there are plenty of people who already have nothing, so the idea of buying nothing may be less than aspirational for them.

I mean, I eat. I breathe. I use resources to stay alive. My object in the nonconsumption phase wasn't bare survival. My object, when it came down to it, was not to waste. That's what the whole No Impact experiment is about, really. It's about not wasting resources and not wasting life. How can we live good lives without harming the planet?

But if we're saving the planet and we're not living good lives, that is a terrible waste, too.

I find myself intrigued by this question of balance between the attachment to worldly things, on the one hand, and the true elements of the good life, on the other. I wonder what the faiths say about this. What paths do they lay down?

Jesus on asceticism: According to *A Dictionary of Christ and the Gospels* by James Hastings, Jesus preached that a person need not forgo worldly possessions except to the extent that attachment to them comes before pursuit of *summum bonum* (Latin for "the highest good"). Possessing worldly goods was not the issue so much as how they were used, or abused.

Buddha on asceticism: "There are two extremes, Monks, which he who has given up the world ought to avoid. What are these two extremes?" The first is the hedonistic life devoted entirely to pleasures and lusts. The second is a life of worldly denial through the mortifications of asceticism. Between these two extremes, he said, is the Middle Way.

No Impact Man on asceticism: Even if I just tried it, my wife and child would leave me.

Two friends add further thoughts. Rabbi Steve Greenberg wrote to me in an e-mail that he thinks there are two kinds of asceticism: one that is a fundamental rejection of creation, the body, pleasure—in short, a rejection of being human—and one that, used temporarily as a tool, "might just educate some of us well in regard to what is and what is not necessary, needed, or even truly desired." This, in some ways, is a pretty good summary of what the No Impact experiment is all about.

Over coffee, I ask the professor and author Juliet Schor if our problem is that we are too materialistic and not sufficiently spiritual. She replies that this is a false dichotomy—something she discusses in her new book *Plenitude: Economics in an Age of Ecological Decline*. In the Eastern religions, Schor says, the material and the divine are not seen as separate. The material *is* divine, she says, and we should treat it so. Our problem is that we see the material—and the associated planetary resources—as base and trash it, treating it as though it has no divine value.

All of which affords me a good philosophical basis for the sustainable-consumption phase of the project, if little of practical value. Since I was, after all, trying to live up to my No Impact plan, I wanted to find a way of doing things that sucked no new resources out of the ground. Cut no trees down. Excavated no new mountains. Polluted no streams or rivers to make what I used. But how do I go about doing this when our entire economy is predicated on the idea that the more resources we use, the better?

Back in the 1940s and '50s, thanks to further mechanization and other new production practices, people had to work a lot less than in previous decades to achieve the same manufacturing output. People's needs were getting met, yet the economy had all this potential for further production. But once they bought a car, a fridge, a house, and a washing machine, what more did they require? Industrialists began to worry that needs were getting saturated, and that all their factories might soon come to a grinding halt.

Their answer? Designed obsolescence. Manufacturers began looking for ways to deliberately cause their own products to become obsolete so people would have to buy them again and again—repetitive consumption. If your car looked out-of-date you'd buy another one (that's called fashion obsolescence). If your fridge broke down after ten years, you'd get another (that's called built-in obsolescence). Industrialists decided to adapt disposability, formerly reserved for paper plates and razor blades, to all manner of items. Economic problem solved.

This isn't a case of woe is the world and people and business are bad. Quite the contrary. Back then, when the planet's resources seemed limitless, this made a lot of sense. Our culture was then so fascinated with its mastery over nature that it could only imagine technology and stuff bringing us better and better lives. Why not make things obsolete since in ten years we'd have better things to buy, anyway? Repetitive consumption was a way to keep the economy's engine turning to bring us that improvement.

But then population grew and manufacturing grew, and before you know it, virtually all the rivers are getting toxins dumped into them, the atmosphere is getting filled with carbon, and the planet is beginning to wilt. What used to be a perfectly functional way of doing things is now requiring more resources than our habitat can afford. It's an old habit that doesn't work anymore. We need to change it.

We can't afford for our entire economy to be based on the open-ended use of energy and material. We dig resources out of the ground, build something out of them, and then send them back to another hole in the ground—the landfill. What if we could find a way to run our economy without its requiring so much material?

Imagine if cars and washing machines and TVs and computers were actually built to last or built in such a way that they could be repaired and updated. What, for example, if a family had to buy only one washing machine per generation? What if a car typically lasted twenty years or more? What if shoes lasted?

Imagine, too, if what we purchased were the *services* offered by products instead of the products themselves. What if those of us who cut our own grass leased lawn mowers instead of owning them? Since most lawn mowers seem to spend all but about an hour a week in the garage, couldn't someone make a lot of money renting one lawn mower to forty separate homeowners? Same for vacuum cleaners. Same for kids' toys.

First of all, think of the time saved manufacturing everything. Think of the money saved. Think of the planetary resources saved. Maybe we wouldn't have to work so hard. Or maybe our work could be more meaningful. Maybe we could create green jobs producing renewable energy.

> **Imagine if cars and washing machines and TVs and computers were actually built to last.**

Or maybe we could use the extra manpower in our economy to solve problems such as getting drinking water to the billion or so people who don't have it.

Perhaps if we employed our labor force on the provision of vital necessities for all the people—instead of luxury goods for some people—we'd find that demand wouldn't disappear in a downturn.

•

Meanwhile, though, I still searched for a way to make my own family's purchases as sustainable as possible for the sake of the No Impact project. I didn't think that buying "eco" would cut it. Because what's truly eco?

For example, cotton—even organic cotton—takes a huge amount of water to grow. Bamboo fiber has become an attractive alternative. But if the entire world switched from cotton to bamboo while our rate of consumption continued to rise, wouldn't the cultivation of bamboo ultimately burden the planet just as much? I felt convinced that the way forward was not just to use different resources but to use fewer.

That's when I heard of a San Francisco group called the Compact, whose members have decided to make an imperfect attempt at being sustainable by making a commitment—a compact—not to buy anything new. In other words, they weren't ascetic, in the sense that they weren't denying their own needs, but neither were they causing resources to be pulled from the ground.

Bolstering secondhand markets also creates an incentive for people who buy new stuff to take care of it so that it will ultimately have resale value. The Compact was, in its way, providing an economic incentive for the stewardship of resources.

So I e-mail one of the founding Compact members, Rachel Kessel, and she e-mails me back their rules. I adapt them for the No Impact project. All I have to do now is share them with Michelle.

We sit down on the couch, ready to have the conversation, and I look at my wife, whom I've dragged through this project. She sometimes appreciates it, sometimes hates it, usually resists a new rule but often discovers its benefits before long. She loves the local food, loves taking the scooter to work, loves that we spend more time together because of no TV, but she has a constant caffeine headache and is forever falling off and then climbing back on the coffee wagon.

Now, on the couch, I plan to introduce new restrictions. I start by explaining that we are entering the "sustainable consumption" part of the project.

"But I already don't buy anything," Michelle interrupts.

The fact is, Michelle has been making a lot of decisions for herself regarding the project. While I had come up with this whole ecological program, she had simply decided that the entire thing could be her way of cleansing herself of the things she felt she was addicted to and that didn't work well for her.

Hence, she'd given up the TV well in advance of our forthcoming farewell to electricity, gave up McDonald's and other kinds of junk food way before local food kicked in, and had given up shopping from the very beginning. By giving up her own addictions she had found new benefits: she'd lost weight, we had improved, um, marital relations, and we weren't spending money in ways we couldn't afford.

But Michelle's purchasing moratorium was not as complete as the one I had in mind. I proceed.

"Here are No Impact's adapted sustainable consumption rules," I say, and I spell them out, something like this:

1. Don't buy new products.
2. Borrow, rent, or buy used (except underwear and socks).
3. Buy only organic underwear and socks.
4. No movies or other forms of canned mass entertainment (this on Michelle's insistence).
5. Find alternatives for all the throwaway products, or products that come in throwaway packaging left over from before the project started: cosmetics and skin-care products, soap, shampoo, cleaning products, disposable pens, disposable razors.
6. "Also," I say, "we'll need to find replacements for toilet paper and tampons."

On the positive side, I continue, in order to replace all the things I've just mentioned, we can:

1. Have fun with Craigslist, Freecycle, and other secondhand sources.
2. Read all we want online.
3. Putter around antiques stores and flea markets.
4. Go to more live entertainment.
5. Socialize more.

I wait for the blowback but it doesn't come. Michelle says simply, "But my version of No Impact is no shopping at all. So I don't have to buy even used stuff if I don't want to, right?"

"Of course not," I say.

Then she asks, in a surprisingly sanguine way: "Does toilet paper really cause so much harm that we should give it up?"

"I'm just trying to get rid of all disposable products," I say. "And we already know the harm that paper products do."

"Why can't we use recycled toilet paper?"

"Because even the resources used to recycle paper should be used for something better than flushing them down the toilet."

Looking back, I can't help realizing how extreme it must have seemed. But experiencing it, it didn't seem extreme at all. More than half the world believes that washing their nether regions is far more hygienic than using toilet paper, a practice largely confined to our Western culture. What I didn't think about, though, was what the *New York Times* reporter who had lately been following us around would make of this.

Meanwhile, Michelle, still on the couch, thinks for a minute. She says, "What we're really doing is taking apart our whole life. Instead of just living the way of life we've inherited and been told to lead,

> More than half the world believes that washing their nether regions is far more hygienic than using toilet paper.

we're taking it all apart and seeing how we want to put it back together. It's not that we'll never use it again. It's that we're doing this
yearlong experiment in order to decide if we will."

To replace my disposable razors, my dad gives me a straight razor as
a gift, but aside from learning how to avoid cutting my jugular while
at the same time shaving my beard, the sustainable-purchasing stage
leaves me with little new to do.

With no trash and no carbon-producing transportation, and only
sustainable eating, there were many elements of our daily life that had
to change. And, of course, those changes are still in place. But meanwhile, since we've decided that the sustainable-consumption phase
doesn't mean much more than buying secondhand, and we don't need
anything, we feel like we're kind of coasting.

While dropping off some old clothes at the Housing Works Thrift
Shop, we see a rocking horse handmade from wood. Its mane is made
from knitting wool, and it has a name stenciled on it: Miles. The
name is obviously that of the child it had been made for, which gives
us pause, but we just decide that Miles could be the name of the horse
itself and we buy it as a surprise for Isabella.

We take it home and she immediately jumps on it and starts
rocking. She calls for the dog to get on with her. "Come on, Frankie.
Come on." She laughs and rocks.

Instead of feeling, as I might have expected, like the used rocking
horse is somehow grubby, I found myself imagining it to be alive with
history. I find myself imagining that it is the by-product of the love
of some handyman grandfather for a grandchild. I feel more warmth
about this gift for Isabella than I would about something plastic and
anonymous from the toy store.

Later we would find, in a little boutique stall in a flea market on

Twenty-sixth Street, a Louis Vuitton blue-and-white-striped blouse for Michelle. She needed a little lift, she said, a little hark back to the shopping days. At the market, the boutique owner, a man, said to us, "I probably shouldn't tell you this, but the shirt belonged to an old drag queen who died."

I find myself thinking of something Steffen Schneider, head farmer of Hawthorne Valley Farm, told me. Hawthorne Valley is "biodynamic." That is to say, at the center of Steffen's philosophy of farming is an idea, developed by Rudolf Steiner, that the farm is one big living organism. In the case of Hawthorne Valley, the beating heart of that organism is the dairy herd.

The herd grazes all day on sixty acres of grass, and once a day the cows are brought in to be milked. The manure collected in the cowsheds is composted and finally will become the only fertilizer for the fourteen-acre vegetable garden. But, as Steffen explained to me, it wasn't that the manure just fertilized. There was something more mysterious carried by the manure that synthetic chemical fertilizers could never carry. Life.

First of all, the cows ate the living grass, which carried the life force of the earth, the organisms within the earth, the rain, the clouds, the sun, the entire universe, and the grass itself. Then, too, the grass, as the cows chewed it and it worked its way through their digestive tracts, collected the life force of the cows themselves. Putting the manure of the cows on the fourteen-acre vegetable garden concentrated the life force of sixty acres in one place, like focusing the sun with a magnifying glass.

Whether I believe this in a literal way or not, I can't help but wonder if it is something like this carrying of life force that explains my sentimentality about Isabella's rocking horse and Michelle's blouse. The story of the blouse, like the rocking horse, gave me a sense of connection to the people who had owned them before. And I think, perhaps, I like it better than the feeling of owning something new. It has to do with the story.

Because she can buy nothing new, Michelle takes to "shopping in my own closet." Every time she pulls something out, she pulls out a story and puts it on, like the time she and Jen met that guy. Or when her sister Maureen had her kids.

There are cuff links of my grandfather's that make me feel, when I wear them, like maybe I am as important and have as much gravitas as he did. Even my jar, the one I drink my coffee from, has a story now. Or my straight razor, which all my guy friends now find themselves wanting. These

> **Because she can buy nothing new, Michelle takes to "shopping in my own closet."**

types of stories make me want to preserve things and take care of them instead of throwing them out. This, perhaps, is an element of Juliet Schor's spiritual-in-the-material.

About the reasons we consume:

There's this Pepsi commercial in which a man is lying in bed when his alarm clock rings. He hits the snooze button over and over, finally rushes to work all disheveled, arrives at a board meeting late and gets asked to leave. Cut to the same guy, the alarm clock goes off, *he drinks a can of Pepsi* (or some Pepsi product), he springs out of bed, puts on a stellar suit, looks like the handsomest James Bond you've ever seen, gets to the board meeting to give his presentation, and everyone applauds.

What's so interesting about the ad is that, at first glance, you think that it's saying that drinking Pepsi will make you successful. But it's not the success that is the payoff. It's the applause. Drink Pepsi, the story goes, you'll be successful, and *then* you'll be loved.

Annie Leonard's online video *Story of Stuff* makes this point. All the ads say the same thing: You suck, but if you buy this, you won't, and then everyone will love you. What the ads don't say is that the reasons we need the love is because we're working so hard so that we can buy the stuff. We're too busy for love because we're working to get the stuff that the ads say will bring us love.

Now, this is going to sound radical, but it's a conclusion you can't help coming to if you've been doing this project as long as I now have:

If it's love we're after, how about we cut out the middleman—the stuff—and just hang out?

Speaking of stuff with a story, by the way, I need a teapot and a tea strainer. I mean, I'm still growing mint on the windowsill and still hoping against hope that we might give up coffee, and so we need to be able to brew the peppermint tea.

On the one hand, I could just go to Bed, Bath & Beyond and buy a teapot. On the other, I could try the Yahoo group Freecycle. What you do is you either list things you have and that you want to give away or list things you need that you hope someone is looking to give away.

So what I do to try this no-new-stuff economy is, I list that I need a teapot and a strainer and I also list that I have a Sony Walkman radio headphone thingy that I no longer use. Before long, someone e-mails me that she has both a teapot and a strainer I can have and that she lives over on Fourteenth Street near Hudson and I should come over and get it.

I'm getting ready to go and Michelle says, "What does the teapot look like?"

I suddenly realize I have no idea. How interesting. It's just a matter of getting what you get and being satisfied with that. Well, it turns out that the teapot is a standard and perfectly attractive blue ceramic affair. There are actually two tea strainers up for grabs.

I ask the lady, who is covered in paint and appears to be an artist, what she herself has gotten through Freecycle. She tells me she got a trailer home—yes, a trailer home—and a pair of pet rats. Meanwhile, someone has picked up the headphones, and this person e-mails me and says how lucky she feels, and how never in her whole life has she ever gotten anything for free.

I get the blue teapot home and make some tea and I get to tell the story about where the tea came from—my windowsill—and where the teapot came from, and the artist lady and the rats.

I get home one night and there is a big gigantic, tree-stuffed Sunday *New York Times* sitting on the table. The rules of the project don't allow newspapers. Up until now, we've been scavenging papers from the recycling bin.

But Michelle is still jonesing for some form of entertainment. I get it. I completely get it. But that night I got all uptight about how the rules are the rules. I was also freaked out, not least because with movie cameras and *New York Times* reporters following me around, I felt vulnerable and exposed, like we could get "found out"—for being human.

"That's not allowed," I say.

"I know, but . . ."

"Are you taking this project seriously? Are you buying newspapers when I'm not around?"

And I feel the strangest mixture of hurt and ludicrousness. Ludicrousness because I feel about as idiotic as the Pepsi commercial. I feel like I'm trying to save the world by not buying a newspaper, and, worse, forcing my wife not to, either.

"One newspaper isn't going to make a difference," Michelle says.

"Except that if we don't live the extreme experiment, how are we going to know what it's like? What I am supposed to do? Make up a narrative about what it's like not to have a newspaper although we actually *have* one?"

"Do you want me to take it back?"

"Yes."

And she did. But that wasn't really satisfying. It's not satisfying to take something away from your wife. It's not satisfying, either, to embark on a project with rules and then break the rules. Maybe I should have realized that part of the project included understanding what happened when we broke rules and examining the strictness by which we stuck to them.

But that night, I guess I was worrying about the thin edge of the wedge. Like, first we'd get a newspaper and the next thing we knew we'd be taking taxis everywhere. What would I say on the blog? What would they show in the documentary? What if we started with this kind of thing and the dam burst? The fact is, not only was I trying to do the right thing environmentally but I was scared of living in a bubble.

What I've come to face, again and again, throughout this project is my own attachment to accomplishment. There is now no way I'm not going to do this project "right." It's like the Technorati rating. Here I am berating my own and our culture's attachment to stuff, and talking about how that attachment stands in the way of the well-being of the planet and of human happiness, but then I let my own petty attachments cause unhappiness in my partnership with Michelle.

We understand at the deepest levels that the way we live our lives is harming the planet; okay, but if it's not about being part of this great rat race, what *is* it about? If it's not about getting more and more stuff and more and more technology, then what is it for? If we're not supposed to be of service to the economy, then what are we supposed to be of service to? Better to be part of the rat race than no race at all.

It feels better, we think, to go in the wrong direction than to feel we don't understand our true direction. It feels better to be unkind to Michelle in service of this so-called purpose than it does to just respond in the moment to the way things are—a poor, big-hearted, persevering wife who just needs one night off.

Using fewer resources won't fill the empty spaces in my life. It won't stop loved ones from dying. But it is just possible that a world in which we already suffer so much loss could be made a little bit better if husbands were kinder to their wives. This is the truth of saving the world as it exists in this moment, right in front of our eyes.

•

I watched a video of Pema Chödrön, a Buddhist nun, discussing the reaction of New York citizens when the World Trade Center was destroyed. She talked about how the basic human state is what she called "groundlessness." By "groundlessness" she meant the basic human state of not knowing—not knowing, for example, the answers to questions like: What will happen to us when we die? And since we don't know what's happening next, it's hard to know what we should be doing now. So we don't really know what our lives are for. We don't know why we were created, or who created us, or anything.

Now, there are a lot of stories we tell ourselves to try to make sense of what we don't know. We tell ourselves religious stories and family stories and success stories and all sorts of different stories. Lately, I'd attached myself to stories about how everything will be fine if we just consume less. We tell ourselves such stories because we don't trust that we'll do the right thing if we simply accept the groundlessness of not knowing. Another Zen master once told me that this was the entire point of practice: to become comfortable with not knowing.

But Pema's point was that when something like the planes crashing into the World Trade Center happens, the information is just too big for our stories. Everything is just too big and too confusing. And there is no way to understand it and no story big enough to follow and you are again returned to your natural groundlessness—your not knowing.

What happens then? Well, what happened to me on 9/11 was that I didn't want to be sitting in my apartment by myself. I wanted to be with other people, so I went out to the street and just started talking to the first person I could find. We all began trying to get downtown and none of us knew what was going on and we could see that no one else did and we were all in the same boat of not knowing what the hell this all was.

To see that is to suddenly understand what this life is for: it's for grabbing on to the equally confused soul standing next to you and working together to help each other get through it. This is, Pema said in the video, the only thing that makes sense.

I come home and Michelle is lying in bed. Isabella is sleeping in her "big girl bed" nearby. Michelle sits up and her eyes are red and her cheeks are wet.

I sit down next to her. I push her hair out of her face. "What is it, honey?"

"I'm sorry about the newspaper," she says.

"Oh my God, don't be silly."

"I can't stand the thought of something like that ever happening to Isabella again."

She's talking about Italy. My eyes instantly well up, too.

"She's so little," Michelle says.

"She's okay, honey. She's okay," I say, but how do I know?

"I read about a man whose daughter has cancer and the insurance is refusing to pay on the grounds that the treatment is experimental. I started crying at work."

She cries a little more now.

"How do I know that nothing like that won't happen to Isabella? Or to you?"

"It won't," I say, because it is the right thing to say.

"That's the reason," Michelle says.

"For what?" I ask.

"The TV. The books. The newspaper. The shopping," she says. "I don't want to face it sometimes. It's all too much. How do you face it?" she asks.

So I hold her.

EIGHT

Click and the Lights Go Out

We're getting ready to flip the electricity off, when *The New York Times* finally publishes the op-ed they asked me to write. They made it shorter than I had originally hoped, and they published it in the Sunday paper's City Section instead of on the main opinion page, but so what? I'm excited. It's a dream come true to have an op-ed in *The Times*.

I get a few calls from friends. I'm pleased with the piece and pleased, too, to have published what I consider to be my own move beyond the dichotomy between progressive and conservative approaches to societal change. Then the phone rings.

Twice.

The first call comes from New York's local National Public Radio affiliate, WNYC. *The Brian Lehrer Show*, a morning talk program, wants me to come in the following Thursday for half an hour to discuss my op-ed and the experiment. I feel nervous. It's very unusual for an author to be expected to talk about a book he hasn't yet finished researching, let alone writing. I still think of myself as more of an everyman than someone who knows the first thing about our environmental crises and what we should do about them.

The phone rings again.

This call comes from the *New York Times* reporter who has lately been following me around. "The story is coming out on Thursday," she says. "It's going to be on the first page of the Home and Garden Section."

"Is that big?" I ask Michelle later.

"It's big," she says.

Thursday morning comes, and I get a moment to read the *Times* story before I head out to the radio station. It calls the experiment "at best like a scene from an old-fashioned situation comedy and, at worst, an ethically murky exercise in self-promotion." My feelings are, quite frankly, hurt. That's a lie—I am devastated.

All the same, I hop on my bike and ride down to WNYC's studios near city hall. Brian Lehrer greets me and together we walk up the stairs to the twenty-fifth floor. The interview goes well. I ride my bike home, thinking over the part of the *Times* story that really disappoints me: the headline.

I feel that it has trivialized my work. It worries me that I've single-handedly managed to make a mockery of the entire environmental movement. Here's what the headline called the project: "The Year Without Toilet Paper."

I get home and decide to check my e-mail to see what friends and family have to say about all this. Before I do, I check to see if the article has affected my blog traffic. It's eleven in the morning and the site meter says that something like 20,000 people have visited my blog so far today.

> **Generally, I get 10 or 20 e-mails a day. So far today there are some 150 e-mails.**

That can't be right. I click refresh: 21,000. I click refresh again: 22,500. An audience! It's every writer's dream, right? Wrong. I am, shall we say, totally freaked out.

I turn to my e-mail. Generally, I get 10 or 20 e-mails a day. So far today there are some 150 e-mails. The subject lines say things like "Greeting from the Today Show" and "60 Minutes would like to profile you." Then I check the voice mail. There are phone messages from television stations as far away as Japan and Australia.

People all over the world, apparently, want to hear from me. What the hell am I supposed to say to all these people? That we're in the middle of what I think is the biggest crisis to hit humanity? Call me grandiose, but at that moment what scared me to death was the possibility of saying the wrong thing and steering people the wrong way. I felt sheer panic.

Everyone jumps in to help. My publisher. My agent. But as I go from quietly figuring out how to live an ecological life to being caught up in a small media whirlwind, here's what keeps me sane: making my own bread.

No matter how many newspaper reporters or radio shows wanted to talk to me, I still had to feed my family. And so, sooner or later, I'd have to go back to the kitchen, roll up my sleeves, measure out some flour and water, and start kneading. It's like meditation with a survival imperative. Meditate over the kitchen counter, the story goes, or you and your family will go hungry tonight.

Somewhere I read, or was told, that even a rabbi should spend 10 percent of his time gardening and washing dishes and cooking and tending to the basics of daily life. There is something about it that connects you to other people. But also something that gets you out of your head and into the real world in an important concrete way.

Bread-making, this quiet, noncerebral activity, provided much-needed space in my life. It's a break. It's one of those things that takes the rhythm of your day and slows it right down to what it's supposed to be. You can't answer the phone when you're making bread unless you want to get dough all over it. The BlackBerry tempo just disappears, and the No Impact project goes on.

•

As I get ready for the no-household-related-carbon-emissions stage—
and the prospect of no power-plant-generated electricity—I read that
people without artificial lighting often experience a phenomenon
known as "second sleep." They go to sleep when it gets dark, wake up
halfway through the night, light a candle, get up for an hour, and
then go back to bed. They supposedly end up more rested than people
who go to bed later and sleep through the night.

From an op-ed by A. Roger Ekirch in *The New York Times*:

Until the modern age, . . . people would retire between 9 and
10 o'clock only to stir past midnight to smoke a pipe, brew a
tub of ale or even converse with a neighbor.

Others remained in bed to pray or make love . . . Often,
people might simply have lain in bed ruminating on the meaning of a fresh dream, thereby permitting the conscious mind a
window onto the human psyche that remains shuttered for
those in the modern day too quick to awake and arise.

The principal explanation for this enigmatic pattern of
slumber probably lies in the nocturnal darkness that envel-
oped pre-industrial households—in short, the absence of artificial lighting.

What if you don't live like everyone else? What if you try different
things? What if you get off this people-mover of a culture and try a
different direction? What if you unplug? Why do we need what everyone else needs? Why can't we go to sleep when it's dark? Why don't
we question?

For most of my years I've just lived my little old life the way the
people around me wrote it, but now I'm definitely turning a lot of it
upside down. I'm defining my life for myself. And you know what?
It's kind of a blast.

•

Note, please, that I said *kind of* a blast, because—okay, I'll admit it— back when we were about to go off the grid in order not to contribute greenhouse gases through our use of power, I was freaking out. Yes, I greeted with curiosity the prospect of "second sleep." I was also grasp- ing at straws.

When we started, when I first came up with the whole No Impact scheme, I had deliberately not thought the whole thing through. I wanted to fumble along, just as anyone else would. Back then, it was easy to commit to going off the grid while assuming we would find some alternative source of electric light that didn't create carbon dioxide.

After all, the idea was not deprivation for deprivation's sake. I had simply assumed that I could find a better source of electricity. There had to be some renewable alternative to ConEd, right?

Wrong. Not in New York City. Not for apartment dwellers with- out legal access to the roof space for solar panels or wind turbines.

I also investigated bicycle generators—you've got to pedal for a couple of hours for a day's worth of minimal power. I subscribed to ConEd's green electricity option—and discovered that, although the profits help sustain electricity-generating windmills elsewhere in the country, my actual electricity would still come from natural gas plants in New York City.

Worthy though the green power option may be, to be entirely rigorous, it still meant that turning my air conditioner on caused more natural gas to be burned and therefore more CO_2 emissions from New York City's power plants.

In fact, it turns out that living in most American cities without access to significant outdoor space in which to generate your own power, no matter how much money you're willing to throw at a problem, you can't really get 100 percent renewable energy. Here was an area where individual action could not help me at all. If I wanted renewable electricity, I needed power companies to provide it and—at least while fossil fuels stayed cheaper than renewable energy—the government regulation that forced the power companies to do so.

That, in itself, made for a worthwhile discovery. It was interesting to begin bumping up against the limits of individual action, to see that collective action was also completely necessary.

But finding things out wasn't the only point of No Impact Man. Living with the implications of them was. So, given the fossil-fuel-dependent state of our culture, if I was really going to insist on sticking to the no-impact thing—and I was—the best course of action, I discovered, would be to use no electricity at all that comes by plugging into a wall socket.

Great.

For the first time, I found an aspect of the No Impact experiment a little ludicrous. Who on earth was ever going to turn their lights off for the sake of the planet? That represented no sort of path forward. Quality-of-life experts around the world might be prescribing bicycling to combat obesity, or village living to combat suburban loneliness, but they weren't calling for no electricity to bring about a resurgence of the second sleep phenomenon.

The whole no-electricity thing seemed pretty outlandish, but I had committed not to any particular sensibility but to achieving the lowest possible impact, which, as I've said, has a value of its own. Having called for the lowest possible impact, I was forced to come face-to-face with the question of whether the approach was entirely sensible. My mind began to look for more nuanced approaches.

Michelle, meanwhile, was incredibly sanguine about turning the power off.

"It'll be fine. Let's flip the switch today," she said.

"You're not freaking out about this?"

"The TV is gone," she said. "The shopping is gone. What more have I got to lose? Besides, I'll have a great excuse to do nothing but read my books by candlelight."

I couldn't help feeling that she enjoyed the fact that we'd come to a point where the No Impact project seemed harder for me than for her.

When it came to candles, by the way, they would have to be bees-wax. Petroleum-based candles would mean taking carbon that had been sequestered in the ground and releasing it into the atmosphere.

"Just relax," Michelle said. "There's going to be something to learn from this. You'll see. That's the point, right? It's an experiment. An investigation."

"What can we possibly learn by being plunged into darkness?" I said. "It's okay for you. You'll go to the office every day, where you can enjoy the air-conditioning and have a place to plug in your computer. I need to work from home sometimes. How will I power my computer? Besides, what are we supposed to do about the refrigerator, the laundry, and the summer heat?"

"You'll figure it out," she said.

Translation: *You're the one who got us into this mess.*

What I had to figure out was the following:

- A way to keep my little girl's milk from going sour.
- Provision of at least a certain amount of artificial light when the sun went down.
- A method for keeping cool on breezeless, hundred-degree New York days.
- Powering my laptop and Internet connection so I could still run my blog, do my research, and write at home (as opposed to just at the Writers Room).
- Doing laundry without use of a washing machine or dryer.

Not to give too much away, but lest a reader jump to the conclusion that it is ludicrous to think one could learn anything at all from the coming stunt of turning the electricity off, bear in mind that 1.6 billion people—a full quarter of the world's population—still have no access to electricity. Bear in mind, too, that lack of electricity is closely linked to poverty, lack of access to good drinking water, and poor health.

Families around the world without electricity are daily faced with the problems of:

- A way to keep their little girls' milk from going sour.
- Provision of at least a certain amount of artificial light when the sun goes down.
- A method for keeping cool on breezeless, hundred-degree days.
- Powering computers or any other means of communication with the rest of the world.
- Doing laundry without using a washing machine or dryer or, indeed, any sort of labor-saving device.

Think for a moment of farmers who can't get their produce to market without refrigeration. Think of village doctors who can't keep crucial medicines from going bad in the heat. Think of parents whose children can't do homework because they can't see at night.

> **1.6 billion people—a full quarter of the world's population—still have no access to electricity.**

This is one of the reasons why, justifiably, as I've mentioned, the 1.6 billion people who face these problems daily will choose, as their economies develop, coal-fired electricity, just as we in the developed world have chosen, even when it means more global warming. When you take the "use less" philosophy to scale, you have to question its worldwide applicability. Because how on earth can someone who has no access to electricity possibly use less?

Here are the ways greenhouse gases got emitted in the operation of my pre–No Impact Man home:

Heating oil got burned in a boiler in my building's basement to push steam through my radiators and hot water through my faucet. Natural gas flamed below my pots and pans to cook my food. And, as we've mentioned, more natural gas got burned in power plants across the city to create my electricity.

That's pretty much it for how residences contribute to global warming: heating, electricity, and cooking. Of course, we have to remember that residences use only 37 percent of our electricity production. The rest is accounted for by industry (27 percent) and business (36 percent).

According to an article by Eric Roston, author of *The Carbon Age*, the story of how these fossil-fuel-burning activities contribute to global warming begins 359–299 million years ago in planet Earth's Carboniferous period, so named because 90 percent of atmospheric carbon dioxide was sequestered in the earth at that time. As the story goes—or at least part of it—woody plants populated bogs all over the earth's then-supercontinent.

The plants would grow, die, then fall into and bury themselves in the bogs in a seemingly endless cycle. Through the process of photosynthesis, every one of these billions upon billions of woody plants extracted carbon dioxide from the atmosphere, which then ended up buried in the mud. Over a couple of hundred million years, those carbon-sequestering plants petrified to become coal.

Jump forward to the period that begins with the Industrial Revolution and we find ourselves digging those petrified woody plants out of the ground and burning them in our machines and power plants. Burning coal produces heat, which turns water into jets of pressurized steam, which cause turbines to spin, which generates the electricity that powers our air conditioners.

The problem is that every shovelful of coal thrown into the power plant's fire reverses the process of photosynthesis and sequestration of carbon dioxide that occurred so many million years ago. As we burn those now-petrified woody plants, we release back into the atmosphere the carbon that they once took out of it. And at the rate we've been burning fossil fuels, we are putting it back much faster than they took it out.

Two pieces of good news:

Although we generate 42 percent of our electricity by burning those petrified woody plants, we already have many alternative methods of creating electricity, such as solar, wind, hydroelectric, and geothermal. Also, energy experts estimate that we could increase our society's energy efficiency by as much as 50 percent—think insulating buildings so the energy of heating and air-conditioning is not lost, for starters. We would burn 50 percent less fossil fuel and create 50 percent less greenhouse gas for every unit of electricity produced.

Two pieces of bad news:

Partly because of the planet's growing population, world energy demands are expected to rise by 45 percent in the coming twenty years. That means that just about every shovelful of coal we take out of the fire through efficiency we'll have to put back in to satisfy new customers. On top of that, as long as fossil fuel remains so much cheaper than solar and wind, businesses and power companies won't have the financial incentive to switch to renewable energy on the required scale.

Another ripple: The fact of the matter is that fossil fuels are *not* less costly than renewable energy. Fossil fuels cost us and our planet much more to use. The problem is that the *true costs* of the use of coal and oil are not immediately apparent in the price.

Consider, for example, the damages to a mountainside community when the mountaintop is removed to extract the coal. Consider the costs of the resulting water pollution, the health costs of the people who live downstream, and, of course, the costs of damage to the atmosphere caused by the resulting emissions when the coal is burned. None of these costs are contained in the actual market price of the coal.

Economists call costs like these "externalities," because the price of a product does not include them. The fact that the true cost of fossil fuels to our society and our planet is much higher than what is reflected in the price is known as a "market failure." The market failure causes business and industry to continue to use the more costly resource. We need to correct this market failure before it causes the temperature of the planet to skyrocket and we all, not so metaphorically speaking, fry.

By way of solutions, two current streams of thought exist, and they both require government intervention. One is to account for externalities by making the price of fossil fuels match their true costs by forcing industry to pay for the permission to emit greenhouse gases, the idea being that this would make renewable energy relatively cheaper. The other approach is to invest huge amounts

> **If we do nothing about climate change, then we will have to spend a full fifth of our planet's economic energy on dealing with the floods, hurricanes, droughts, food shortages, and epidemics that will result.**

of government money into subsidization of the deployment of existing renewable-energy technologies and into research for future technologies. Again, this would bring the relative price down while also creating millions of jobs.

As I write, however, in the year and half since I began the No Impact project, no measures to do either have been taken by the U.S. government. Special interests of every description have managed to stymie all meaningful action. Meanwhile, climate scientists tell us that in order to avoid the worst effects of climate change, we must completely stop using coal within ten years.

What would it cost the world economy to do this? Well, let's look at the scenario in reverse. Let's take the question, first, of what it would cost to do nothing.

The senior British economic thinker on climate, Sir Nicholas Stern, has estimated that if we don't reverse climate change, the costs of dealing with the resulting catastrophe could be as much as 20 percent of the world's gross domestic product. He's saying that if we do nothing about climate change, then we will have to spend a full fifth of our planet's economic energy on dealing with the floods, hurricanes, droughts, food shortages, and epidemics that will result.

On the other hand, Stern estimates, we could avoid the most dire consequences if today we began to spend 1 percent of the world's GDP on efficiency measures and renewable energy investment. That would mean spending one penny of every dollar in our economy on dealing with climate. Pretty cheap, especially when compared to twenty pennies on every dollar.

Now let's take a look at how, as of the end of 2008, this information feeds into the collective wisdom of the one American president, the one vice president, the 435 American congressional representatives, and the 100 U.S. senators who do us the kind service of looking out for our interests in Washington, D.C. Together, these 537 men and women have compared Stern's 1 percent now or 20 percent later figures. They've digested the information that any number of economists and scientists have given them about climate change.

Together, with all their law degrees and other advanced degrees and thousands of years of collective experience in public service and government, they've cogitated and discussed and meditated and argued. Using all their resources and smarts and power—and also a couple of pollsters—they have come to one collective conclusion:

That what is scientifically necessary to avert climate change is not politically possible. Therefore, as of this writing, at the end of 2008, over the course of the nearly two years since I first started the No Impact project, the politicians of the executive and legislative branches of the U.S. government have stayed the course on a strategy they seem to feel deals most effectively with our climate crisis:

Do nothing.

It's enough to make you want to turn your electricity off, no?

There is another story I love, about the Korean monk who founded the school of Zen where I meditate. Dae Soen Sa Nim decided that world peace would come if all the religious leaders of the world got together and had a good, human conversation. The way to do that, Dae Soen Sa Nim decided, was to have all the world's religious leaders get into a hot tub together.

In order to get all the religious leaders into the same hot tub, Dae Soen Sa Nim thought it was important that the invitation come from the Pope. He wanted the Pope to send out a letter that said, essentially, "Dear Religious Leader, How about we get into a hot tub and figure out how to attain world peace? Yours truly, the Pope."

So, without invitation, Dae Soen Sa Nim got on a plane, traveled to Rome, marched up to the gates of the Vatican, and asked to see the Pope. No, he told the guard, he did not have an appointment. The guard sent Dae Soen Sa Nim to see one of the priests. A day or two later, the priest sent him to see a bishop. A couple of days after that, the bishop got him an appointment to see a cardinal.

As the story goes, the cardinal in question did not see the value in Dae Soen Sa Nim's hot-tub approach, and there the effort died.

But why this story gets told again and again in the Zen school is because of the sheer "just try" energy of Dae Soen Sa Nim's approach. It suggests that instead of trying to save the world by sitting around figuring out the best course of action, we should just start trying to save the world. If we all just start trying from where we are, even if some of us fail, one of us or a couple of thousand of us will cross the finish line and get the job done.

And if we don't, we will inspire other thousands to start from where they are, just as the story of Dae Soen Sa Nim and the Pope has inspired many hundreds of his students to just try. If one of those students succeeds, then Dae Soen Sa Nim's stunt will have worked.

Okay, Dae Soen Sa Nim's attempt was a little crazy, and so is mine. I mean, the idea of turning off the electricity. But I'd rather be the kind of nut who tries something than the kind of nut who, knowing what could happen in the world, doesn't.

And, besides, sometimes doing crazy things attracts much-needed attention.

The interview requests keep pouring in, and what I want more than anything is to make sure that I somehow use this fifteen minutes of fame to help change people's minds. I call a number of well-seasoned environmentalists to ask for advice. What should I say? I ask them.

One of them says, "Well, if everybody did what you're doing, then the environmental problem would be solved tomorrow. But they won't, so tell them that now that they've changed their lightbulbs, they need to change their senator."

And so I am faced with going on TV and talking to journalists and I worry that I have no authority because I've barely been doing this project for any length of time, so I think I should just say what the guy with twenty years of experience told me to say. But here's the problem: I don't agree with him.

I simply don't believe that changing senators is anywhere near enough. Yes, we need the politicians to get the message, but what is required here is for the United States to reduce its carbon emissions by something like 95 percent. That's huge. Laws alone are not going to do it. Changing our senators—while that is part of the equation— is not going to do it.

We have to change the culture. Not just the government. I don't want business as usual. I want better. I want a way of life that makes both the people and the planet happier.

I surprise myself. I start to tell the journalists what I believe instead of what I've been told to say. I'm finding my voice. Each of us as individuals needs to take responsibility for this world we live in. We need to stop outsourcing our political power to politicians. We all need to believe that we can make a difference.

•

Michelle comes home from work upset. A male friend of hers, having read the *New York Times* article, told Michelle that his wife said he must never shake Michelle's hand. People are disgusted by us, Michelle says. She cries a little. She grabs a marker and goes into our bathroom. She writes on the wall, "I never asked you to shake my hand."

I'm still struggling, meanwhile, with what to do about my non-electric household sources of carbon emissions—the cooking, heating, and hot water. Here's what I was able to do about them: pretty much nothing.

When it came to cooking, I researched the possibility of what's called an anaerobic digester, essentially a sealed vessel that collects methane from rotting food scraps and, often, farm animal feces. But the anaerobic digester turns out not to be a particularly accessible technology for urban apartment dwellers. You can't exactly buy one at Home Depot, and even with Frankie we were a little short on animal feces.

Next, I researched the possibility of buying canisters of cooking gas that had been extracted from someone else's anaerobic digester. Let's just say that the few phone calls I made that contained the question "Do you know how I can buy cooking gas extracted from rotting animal feces?" didn't go that well.

What about a raw food diet, some may ask? Well, I have nothing against proponents of such a regimen, but, on top of the fact that we were already eating only food from within 250 miles, well, let's just say my response, when friends suggested it, was simply, "Thanks for sharing."

Had we a realistic alternative energy source, an electric stove might have been an option, but, mea culpa, we stuck with our gas stove.

As for hot water use, someone treated me to a long explanation of how showering in cold water increases the blood supply to some part of the body or other. I told them I'd forward their e-mail to Michelle

for her consideration. But otherwise we would simply content ourselves with looking for ways to use less.

When it came to heat, I researched the possibility of asking my
building to switch to biodiesel made from used restaurant cooking oil,
but it turns out that no heating oil company was yet supplying biodiesel. So all we could do was turn off our radiators, which we did, and
still found, through the winter, that we sometimes had to open our
windows.

What was happening in the No Impact project is that we had cut
our consumption of resources down to our basic needs. We were no
longer wasting. But as long as we still intended to fill our basic needs,
we relied on the culture. Note to self: the culture, it turns out, is not
offering too many sustainable options.

A quick word about nuclear power as an option:

The insurance industry considers the nuclear industry an unsafe
bet. As a result, the nuclear industry must self-insure, with help from
the government. My view on nuclear is that when it becomes safe
enough for commercial insurers, I'll seriously consider it. But even
then, only if the shareholders, investors, and executives who stand
to benefit are confident enough in the safety that they are willing
to keep the spent nuclear waste from the plants in their own
basements.

A quick word, too, on India and China:

People point their fingers at India and China and say that they're
the real problem now when it comes to climate change. And it's true
that the world does have to find the
answer to providing renewable energy
to developing economies. But to be
clear, although China may emit the

> The United States and much of
> Western Europe still emit five times
> as much carbon per person as China.

same amount of greenhouse gas as the United States, it also has five times as many people.

Whatever else we've heard, the United States and much of Western Europe still emit five times as much carbon per person as China. So, what do I want to say about India and China? Let's get back to worrying about whether our own side of the street is clean.

My strategy for keeping Isabella's milk from going sour came from an intriguing device developed for use in northern Nigeria, where, without electric refrigeration, food spoils quickly in the heat. Developed by a teacher named Mohammed Bah Abba, the "pot in the pot" consists of one earthenware pot placed in a second, slightly larger pot, with a layer of wet sand between the two. The inner pot holds milk and vegetables and is covered with a lid.

As I read in Alex Steffen's *World Changing*, the pot in the pot works because the evaporation of water from the moist sand causes a temperature drop. As a result, the inner pot and the goods inside it are kept cool. Used in Nigeria, the pot in the pot meant eggplants lasted twenty-seven days instead of three. African spinach could be kept for twelve days instead of spoiling after one. Food hygiene standards and overall health improved.

So, back in America, faced with the heat of the New York summer, I started hoofing it around New York, looking for a huge pot to buy. Then I remembered that I vowed not to buy anything new. Luckily, I found two huge plant pots in the basement of my building, along with a bag of sand left behind by some construction workers. I lugged them all up to my apartment, and set the whole thing up. Milk problem solved. Kind of.

Meanwhile, at my request, readers of my blog sent me a variety of suggestions for ways to do the laundry once the lights went out. A woman named Allie e-mailed me about how she did her laundry while working at a boarding school in South Africa. She advised me to put everything in the bathtub and soak the clothes for a couple of hours and then to put on shorts and step into the tub and stomp through the clothes until everything had been agitated enough to be clean.

People sent me about a dozen other methods, including using a toilet plunger to agitate the clothes in a big bucket. You know the logic about why you shouldn't let a dog lick your face because you don't know where its tongue has been? That's the way I feel about using a plunger to clean my clothes. Besides, Allie's method seemed like a lot more fun.

> A suitcase-sized power pack was pumping juice into my laptop and Internet modem, along with charging a couple of large batteries hooked to LED lamps.

I wasn't the only one who thought so, either. During my initial attempt—I was giving everything a try before actually turning the lights out—Isabella joined right in. Then she starting shouting, "Come on, Mommy," until Michelle got in on the act, too. We all jumped up and down on the clothes and had a riot and decided, in the future, to refer to this chore as grape-stompers' laundry day.

Last on the list of preparations for the no-electricity stage, my friend Elizabeth got in touch with a company named Solar One that made, and was willing to loan me, a portable solar power system based on a single panel that was only the size of the average window. We snuck the panel up to the roof and dropped a wire down the side of the building and into our window.

Before you knew it, a suitcase-sized power pack was pumping juice into my laptop and Internet modem, along with charging a couple of large batteries hooked to LED lamps. The apartment wouldn't exactly be lit up like Times Square, but there would be enough light to keep me from melting down as we approached no-electricity day.

My only problems were: for reasons I could never quite figure out, I could not actually get the dumb old pot in the pot to work; also, Isabella and Michelle would soon lose interest in doing the laundry, grape-stomping style or no; and I would find there's a limit to the amount of power you can squeeze out of a single solar panel, once the winter came and it got dark at four-thirty in the afternoon.

•

I'm down at LaGuardia Community Gardens, planting carrots, and my friend Mayer, whose plot I work on as part of the local eating component, is giving it to me about the ridiculousness of turning off my electricity.

"It's not about my turning off the power, Mayer; it's about perpetuating the idea that we should all question our consumption."

"I know that, Colin, and that's what worries me."

"And not only that, but I've been getting press coverage, so even if it's a little stupid, I still get the chance to say the right things."

I might be whining a little. Mayer is a veteran political and antiwar activist and I respect his views. But then he says something that really makes my head spin.

"Of course the corporate media love you. You're out there telling us all that individually we should use less electricity and distracting everyone from the fact that industry is killing us. You're out there worrying us about littering while they get away with killing the world."

Another day we are planting beans. Mayer is in a better mood and more disposed to charity. He says, "You never know who will start the chain reaction. We all have to try in our own ways. Who knows, maybe it will be you."

Another day we're weeding. I ask Mayer why, after thirty-five years of antiwar activism, he hasn't given up.

"I don't know if you've noticed, but there's still war," I say. Maybe I'm making a little dig at the protest approach to civic change that he seems to favor. Maybe I'm still a little hurt.

Mayer says, "I gave up thinking the world was going to change a long time ago. I've accepted the fact that I just have to keep on trying to change it because it's in my nature. I'm just the type of guy who has to try."

Here, then, is what you think when you're faced with the ludicrous prospect of turning off your electricity:

You worry a lot about whether it makes the slightest bit of difference, or whether in fact it might be counterproductive. Eventually you realize that there is no real way of knowing if you can make a difference to this world. And, finally, you are left with the simple question inherent in Mayer's response.

Do you want to be the type of person whose nature it is to try, or do you not?

It's a party.

We've had a few at various stages of No Impact. We had a local-eating potluck where everyone could only bring food from within 250 miles. We had a hundred games of charades and Scrabble. Dinner at our house has been an open affair. And now it's a party to celebrate the beginning of the no-electricity phase. The plan, at the end of the night, is to throw the circuit breaker.

We laugh. We joke. We play charades. Everybody gets into it. Our friends, for the most part, support our project. *I* don't want to do it, they often tease, but I'm glad *you're* doing it.

At the local-food party we had a few weeks earlier, my friend Sean showed up with applesauce that he made during the fall harvest season. He picked the apples. "It's all local except for the cinnamon," he said guiltily. Someone else brought frittatas made from local eggs. Others brought locally grown micro-greens. Whole conversations revolved around who got what where and how they adapted the recipes according to what they could find.

Conversations about the No Impact project itself always broke out at the parties, too. Michelle's boss, Robin, told us that when he told a friend that he was coming to the local-food party, his friend said, "Oh, that's ridiculous. Is their furniture local, too?"

Then Sean said, "Honestly, I love this project, but my first reaction to it was irritation, too. But I like to think I have the self-awareness to probe the irritation a little further and see what's underneath it."

He added: "We're all in a fragile state of denial. We all know on some level that people elsewhere are starving to death and don't know where dinner is coming from. Meanwhile, we go and spend ten dollars on a CD that we will listen to maybe three times. That same ten dollars could have saved someone's life.

"We all know this and we don't know what to do about it and then this dumb No Impact project comes along and shakes us up and makes us remember, and then our fragile denial comes tumbling down and we feel guilty and our first reaction is to feel angry and irritated with the person who has made us feel that way."

And now, we're at this next party where we'll turn the lights out, but first we're playing games and laughing till we wet our pants, and all these New Yorkers who rush around are having fun. This is a gift of the project. We get rid of the TV and a bunch of stuff and get the friends in return. You allow one channel to weaken and the others strengthen. You pull the weeds from your garden and the sustenance-giving plants have room to grow.

> Self-consciously, I hand out one beeswax candle to each person. I throw the circuit breaker and darkness descends.

But at the same time, I feel weird and ashamed. The no-electricity thing still seems so extreme. Self-consciously, I hand out one beeswax candle to each person. We count backward from ten. Everyone shouts like it's New Year's Eve. I throw the circuit breaker and darkness descends. Sparks fly through the air as I light my one match. I touch it to the candle in the hands of the person next to me, who in turn lights the candle next to him, until everyone holds a lit candle. It's a romantic moment.

But then I look at the expression on people's faces. *Now what?* they all seem to say. In the candlelight, people naturally begin to whisper and speak in low tones. People start to yawn. In the dim light, the only thing that makes sense is to go to bed. Fifteen minutes after I threw the circuit breaker, everyone was gone.

I felt awful.

The only thing I could do was remember what Sean had said about the project making people think, even if it made them uncomfortable. The point of no electricity is not to try living without power at all. It's to inspire ourselves and our friends and whoever is paying attention to begin looking for a better way of life, a more satisfying way of life that does not cost the earth.

It's about, in short, trying to get the Pope into a hot tub.

What's hardest? everyone wants to know.

Is it the no packaging or the biking everywhere or the scootering or the living without a fridge or what?

Actually, it's none of those things. What's hardest is habit change. Plain old forcing yourself out of a rut and learning to live differently. Everything about yourself wants to fall back into the rut, at least for a while. By "for a while," by the way, I mean a month. That's how long they say it takes to change a habit.

So if you're used to taking a taxi to work or an elevator to the ninth floor or blowing your nose on a paper towel or putting your little girl in plastic diapers, and then you decide to change, for the first month or so it's going to suck. It's not going to suck because the new way of doing things is inherently difficult. It's going to suck because your whole life is structured around the old way of doing things.

Growing pains. But what's the alternative? Not growing?

Indeed, if our culture ever decides it is really going to do something about climate change and the other crises in the habitat that we depend upon for our health, happiness, and security, we are going to have growing pains. What will we do to help the communities that earn their livings mining coal? What would we do with the auto industry if instead of building highways we built train lines? What if we put the brakes on the resource-intensive consumer economy?

That is why we're dragging our feet so much. It's why many of the politicians act as though doing anything about our climate emergency is politically impossible.

Because they don't think any of us want to face the discomfort of habit change as we move from a way of life our planet can't sustain to one that it can. They don't think we want to face the growing pains. But what they're failing to do, these politicians, is see that on the other side of the growing pains is, well, growth. Not necessarily economic growth—we've determined that may not be the most important parameter, right?—but human growth. Way-of-life growth. Quality-of-life growth.

Of course, as with all the other phases, that's what we faced now with the electricity phase. Growing pains at first. Then human growth.

The pot in the pot, as I mentioned, plain didn't work. Not for me, anyway. The milk went sour. The veggies rotted. On a couple of occasions, the fact that the food went rancid meant we had to break the local eating rules and go to a restaurant. Then I learned to buy less food and go to the market more often. I went to the farmer's market three times a week instead of once. I switched Isabella from milk to preserved milk—otherwise known as cheese. I kept the stalks of my vegetables in bowls of water, like cut flowers, to keep them fresh. It took a while to figure out, but in the end it all worked fine.

The other big problem—for me more than for Michelle—was insufficient power to keep my laptop running all night long. I adapted in this way: I did my work during the day. What a concept, right? To do work during the day instead of letting it leech into my nighttime hours? To actually say, perforce, the work can have my time by day but by night my time belongs to me and my family?

We all think that the stuff and the energy and the accoutrements of modern life make us free, but until I took some time to do without them, I never got the chance to see the extent to which they also trapped me. Having electricity trapped me into the "freedom" of working at night, when I might have been playing with Isabella.

After we started the no-electricity phase I got a number of e-mails from people who asked me, in all earnestness, how I would continue to make bread without the electricity to power my bread machine? My bread machine? When did we start thinking that we couldn't make bread without a machine? Is that freedom or enforced reliance on machines?

What's wonderful about the human race is that we move forward together. We like to be part of the flock. We go where the flock is going, and this is wonderful, because to be part of the flock is to feel the love of community, while to move outside the flock is in some ways a rejection of love. The problem is, while we all move together with the flock, none of us takes charge of where the flock is going.

We need to figure this out and we need to figure it out fast: Where should this flock now go?

One thing I discovered: When you go around turning your electricity off, you put yourself in peril of being called anti-progress. I mean, there I am with no juice flowing through my wires and the next thing I'm talking about how I never needed my food processor or my blender or my electric dishwasher or my microwave or my freezer or even, really, my fridge.

Please note: I did *not* say I don't need a washing machine. Try washing a clumsy, white-clothes-loving, food-spilling wife's and a toddler's clothes by hand for a month or two and you'll see why. People ask, what is the hard part? Here it is: washing your family's clothes by hand, as do so many people across the world, is the hard part.

So people start labeling me antiprogress. Sometimes angrily. "Are you suggesting we go back and live with tuberculosis?" they might add.

"No," I'd say. "I just wonder sometimes whether the big hunk of metal and plastic that we call a bread machine is necessarily worth the financial and environmental cost."

"Yeah, well, before they had bread machines, they also had tuberculosis."

After the Industrial Revolution's two hundred years of inventing more and better products, we may have come to a point where certain products have reached their zenith. We may have come to the point of diminishing returns. We may have reached perfection. We may have reached the point where using more resources may actually make us less happy—where there may not be any more progress to be had.

> **Maybe we could turn the great minds to getting fresh water to the 1 billion people on our planet who don't have it.**

Continuing to do what we've done for the past two hundred years is not progress. It's more of the same. Staying on the same path is not the definition of progress.

I simply feel that now that we've so utterly perfected the walkie-talkie to the point where it has become the iPhone, maybe we could turn the great minds that brought us the Nintendo Wii to, say, getting fresh water to the 1 billion people on our planet who don't have it.

Speaking of progress, in February 2007, UNICEF evaluated the overall well-being of children in the twenty-one countries of the industrialized world, reviewing a variety of factors including health, education, and family relationships. Of those twenty-one countries, the United States came in twentieth. The United Kingdom came in twenty-first.

But, hell, at least we have bread machines.

•

Michelle says that having no electricity in the apartment is like a nonstop vacation. Every summer night we search for things to do outside—play in the fountain with Isabella's friends in Washington Square Park, make a trip to the river. Then we come home in the dark, put Isabella to bed, and sit up, talking in quiet tones by candlelight.

We go, one night, to the community garden with a jar because fireflies are in season. We catch the tiny lightning flashes, Isabella stares at them through the glass of the jar, we let them go. "Daddy, this is so much fun," she tells me. We stay in the park till after dark, since there is no point going home to an unlit apartment, and we listen to a group of Japanese music students play Bach.

The world of techno cannot intrude. It's like we're taking a break. Summer is here and all sorts of fruits are bursting into our lives courtesy of the farmer's market. I spend lots of time with Isabella because there's no light to work by anyway.

"Daddy," Isabella says when we come in to the dark apartment the first night after the electricity is turned off, "turn on the lights."

"We don't have lights anymore, honey, we only have candles," I say.

Next night, when we come in, Isabella, without blinking, says, "Daddy, turn on the candles."

We eat blueberries and strawberries and plums around the table by candlelight. Then Isabella goes to bed and Michelle and I talk. We are asleep most nights by ten. People keep telling us how good we look.

Michelle and I are at the farmer's market early on a Saturday morning and a very grand and elegant woman glides by pedaling a three-wheeled rickshaw contraption that contains not only her bounty of local food but also her little boy in a sort of a bench at the back and her cairn terrier in a cubbyhole behind that.

"That's the woman," Michelle whispers to me.

Michelle has been spotting this woman around town. We had bought Michelle a secondhand Schwinn two-wheeler from a flea market, but she didn't feel comfortable with Isabella on it. She had told me that, if she could have a bike as cool and as safe-looking as this woman's, she might consider it.

"C'mon," I say to Michelle, and I run off after the woman.

I accost her and ask her about her bike and she tells me that she had it custom made by a bike genius named George Bliss, a man apparently famous in New York bicycling circles for having been the first to introduce the pedicab.

"You can get him to build you one," the woman says.

"Actually, I can't," I say. "I can't buy anything new."

I explain to her about the No Impact project and how we're only buying secondhand. "I don't suppose you have another one that isn't new you'd like to sell us?" I joke.

"Actually, I do have another one," she says.

Within a couple of days I'm riding around town on a three-wheeled bike with Isabella having the time of her life in the back. Michelle tries it, and a couple of days after that, my wife—Ms. You'll Never Catch Me Or My Daughter On A Bike In New York—tells me, "You can get your own bike. This one is mine."

But I'm hooked, too. The rickshaw turns out to be a complete replacement for motorized transportation in Manhattan. It's great for carrying groceries home from the farmer's market, and riding around with Isabella is enormous fun for both of us. I go over to George Bliss's bike shop—The Hub Station—near the Hudson River, and I explain my predicament about not buying anything new. "How would you like the challenge of building one of these things without using any new parts?" I ask. Turns out there's nothing he'd like more.

He gets a secondhand utility trike, scavenges some thrown-away plywood from dumpsters, digs out an old can of green paint, and a couple of weeks later I'm Rudolf to Isabella and a bunch of her friends who think the new/used rickshaw looks like a green Santa's sleigh.

All of a sudden, Manhattan has become, well, an island to me and my little family. We're more mobile than we've ever been. We find ourselves almost every evening lolling on the grass of the Hudson River Park, a place we never would have walked to and would've felt too foolish to take a taxi to.

Isabella wakes up late in the night and barfs all over her sheets. We worry. It scares us. But it isn't now that we have the repeat of Italy. It isn't now that we fear again that our little girl is dying. That is yet to come.

What does happen is that after she pukes all over her bed and we change her sheets, she pukes again, and now two sets of sheets and pajamas are done for. And I simply can't bring myself to wash this mountain of laundry by hand. I feel like a failure, but I use the machine down in the basement of our building.

It is at this moment, when it comes to washing our laundry by hand, that I give up.

This is perhaps the main learning experience from the no-electricity part of this project. That there is a level of non–resource use below which things just get miserable. That there is a level of resource use below which people cannot and will not voluntarily go or stay in order to save the planet.

It is at this point that using less does not feel like life redesign. It does not feel like finally striking out on our own and choosing a new way. Instead, it feels like deprivation. For all my talk of happiness coming as we use less, there is a point at which the trend reverses.

A family will not voluntarily stay away from a washing machine when their kids soil the sheets. A dad will not keep his school-age child away from reading light.

This needs to be part of the equation. Because while we are figuring out how certain Americans and Western Europeans can make do with less, we need also to figure out how people in the Southern Hemisphere can have much more. Having no electricity has driven home to me that there are two parts to the equation: one is figuring out what is the good life—how many and what kind of resources we need to make us happy. The other is figuring out how to deliver that same level of (reduced) resources, by Western standards, to everyone in a sustainable way.

In addition to caving in on the laundry issue, we've given up on not drinking coffee. Michelle could not take the withdrawal. I could not take sitting in a coffee shop with her not having coffee while she got to drink it. And, I admit, we've weakened when it comes to olive oil and balsamic vinegar, too.

But small weaknesses aside, everything is pretty much in place. We don't make trash. Except for once or twice, we don't create carbon when we travel. We have our rickshaws. We eat only local—except for coffee and salad dressing. We don't buy anything new. We use no electricity from the grid, except for the washing machine. Seven months of the project has passed.

We still have to make some adaptations on water use. And I have to figure out how to make a positive impact to balance out the negatives.

But for the most part, all we have to do is continue to live this way for five more months.

NINE

Trying to Do Enough Good to Outweigh the Harm

There was one stage before the giving-back phase. Water. Problems with water, in my book, are not complicated to understand, at least not like global warming. There are no invisible gases and no fancy physics concepts. In figuring out what steps my family needed to take to understand the little-heralded water crisis, I needed to know only two basic concepts:

1. If we use it all up, there won't be any left to drink.
2. If we keep pouring toxins and pollutants into it, even if we haven't used it all up, we won't be able to drink it.

Pretty simple. What I needed to know next was how long until we've used it all up, how much of it is already undrinkable, and how do I avoid adding to the problems?

So I start with these figures: By 2025, just over fifteen years from now, two-thirds of the world's population will face water scarcity. By 2050, after another 3 billion people have been added to the population, we will need an 80 percent increase in water supplies just to grow our food and feed ourselves. We have no idea where this water will come from. Yet we are dangerously depleting our supply of fresh water through pollution and overuse.

In the United States, for example, the average single-family household uses some seventy gallons of water every day. A full quarter of that we use to flush our toilets. In other words, while 1 billion people in the world don't have access to clean drinking water, Americans are flushing 2.5 trillion gallons a year down the toilet.

Until I started reading about it, I thought this was someone else's problem. You know, like the Southern Hemisphere's. But Arizona is already out of water—it has to import it. California has only twenty years of drinking water left. New Mexico has only ten. The EPA estimates that in the next five years, if water use continues unchecked, thirty-six American states will suffer water shortages.

Meanwhile, a person like me, who lives in New York, where Adirondack lakes still provide plenty of good water, could become complacent, thinking he is safe from the problem. Except that some of the parts of the world that are running out of potable water—northern China, large areas of Asia and Africa, the Middle East, Australia, the midwestern United States, and sections of South America and Mexico—are where my food is grown.

> While 1 billion people in the world don't have access to clean drinking water, Americans are flushing 2.5 trillion gallons a year down the toilet.

No water for them, no food for me.

Already, around the world, people with preventable waterborne diseases occupy half the hospital beds. More children have died from diarrhea than people have been killed in war and conflict since World War II. A child dies every eight seconds from drinking dirty water.

But never Isabella, right? Never Isabella. Except for one thing: that time in Italy, the time I was on my knees begging God not to take her from me, the doctors never got to the root of it. It could have been dehydration, they said, lack of water. Or it could have been something she drank.

How did we get here? Consider this: 90 percent of wastewater produced in the Third World is discharged, untreated, into local rivers, streams, and coastal waters. Oh, those naughty Third Worlders, right?

Except that, for example, here in New York City, our sewer system overflows when it rains, thanks to storm-water runoff, some fifty times a year, spilling in excess of 27 billion gallons of raw sewage into our rivers. Nationally, sewer systems dump some 850 billion gallons of overflow into our waterways. And that's not even counting the waste-water discharged into our waterways by industry and agriculture.

Even if our sewage goes where it is supposed to, once it's treated, processed, and dried, the remaining solids end up back in the land— either in landfills or, some of it, on farmland, as fertilizer.

Guess what happens to the toxins then? They leach, ultimately, back into our water supply.

In 2002, for example, a nationwide study of man-made chemicals and hormones revealed that 80 percent of streams were contaminated with them. Of the chemicals found, several have been proven to disrupt, and others are suspected of disrupting, hormone systems in animals and people. With increasing frequency around the United States, researchers are discovering male fish with immature eggs—yes, eggs—in their testes.

In 2008, the United States Geologic Survey released study results showing that earthworms in soybean fields fertilized with "bio-solids"—sludge from sewage treatment plants—contained chemicals found in household products. The chemicals we flush down our toilets end up not only in our water but in the fields where we grow our food.

Even in fields that hadn't been treated with sewage in over seven years, researchers found that the earthworms contained phenol (used in disinfectants), tributylphosphate (used as an antifoaming agent and flame retardant), benzophenone (a fixative that binds fragrances in soaps and other products), trimethoprim (an antibiotic), and the synthetic fragrances galaxolide and tonalide.

To top all this off, a 2007 study by the Environmental Working Group showed that our own bodies are typically contaminated with the chemicals that, even at low levels, turn boy fish into girl fish—endocrine disrupters. Such chemicals are contained in everything from nail polish to canned food to antibacterial soaps and cleaning products.

What goes into our sewer and septic systems must come out.

So if we use a lot of chemicals around the home or in our industries or on our farm fields, they end up in the water. Bottled water, by the way, keeps no one safe, since the U.S. government does not require that bottled water be tested for these types of chemicals.

A little bit of good news for me: If I stop using a lot of chemicals in my house as part of the No Impact project, not only will they not end up in the water, but I and my family won't be exposed to them, either.

Where does this leave us? Where are we headed? Well, according to Maude Barlow, water activist and author of *Blue Gold*:

> Desalination plants will ring the world's oceans, many of them run by nuclear power; corporate-controlled nanotechnology will clean up sewage water and sell it to private utilities, which will in turn sell it back to us at a huge profit; the rich will drink only bottled water found in the few remaining uncontaminated parts of the world or sucked from the clouds by corporate-controlled machines, while the poor will die in increasing numbers from a lack of water.
>
> This is not science fiction. This is where the world is headed unless we change course—a moral and ecological imperative.

At the societal and community levels, there are lots of ways to conserve water and prevent, for example, storm-water runoff from carrying sewage into our watershed. Widespread use of green roofs—systems of vegetation placed on top of city buildings that have the effect of providing insulation and lowering heating and cooling costs—would absorb rain and reduce the amount of waste that's washed into rivers.

"Gray water" systems that filter and recycle water from kitchen sinks and washing machines can hugely reduce fresh-water use by making sure we don't flush perfectly good drinking water down our toilets. And, of course, there are many other residential measures—not to mention those that could be taken by industry and agriculture— that would be good for the planet and good for the people.

But dwelling in an apartment, and short of going the collective-action route, there are only limited measures I can take to make my water use no-impact. We do three things: we use less water; we forgo privatized drinking water; and we put no toxins in our wastewater.

To use less water, we put low-flow fixtures on our taps and shower, we share baths, we flush less often, we wear our clothes more than once before we wash them, we let no faucets drip.

To forgo privatized drinking water, we drink tap. It's that simple. We carry our jars and get delis and restaurants to fill them up with water for free. One time, a kind young man said, "I'm going to give you the good stuff" and sweetly filled my jar from his own gallon jug of Poland Spring. I couldn't bring myself to tell him why that wasn't the good stuff.

We're the luckiest country in the world in having good, potable tap water and relatively abundant drinking-water resources, and yet we're putting it in the hands of the corporations through our consump-tion of bottled water from privatized sources. What worries me about the 2008 spike in gas prices is what they say about the coming water prices. If we put our drinking water in the hands of corporations and we don't give our municipalities the money they need to provide us with good tap water, we will one day run out. And when we run out, the price will rise, and that's when the corporations will make a mint on the water resources they're currently buying up.

To keep toxins out of the wastewater, around the house we use nothing toxic. Pretty simple. We learn to make our household and personal cleaning products from a combination of borax, white vine-gar, baking soda, and Dr. Bronner's vegetable-oil-based liquid soap. Baking soda, it turns out, makes the world's best underarm deodorant. A vegetable-oil-and-beeswax moisturizer made by a local person is bet-ter for our skin than anything we've ever used before.

Brushing teeth with baking soda—okay, not so enjoyable. But the point is that with our personal and household products, we both create no packaging trash and add no toxins to the water supply. Anything that goes down the drain quickly and simply biodegrades. No little fishes will have two sets of genitals on account of our cleaning products.

With just about everything in place, a day in the No Impact household goes like this:

1. If I get it together, I wake up before the girls when my wind-up alarm clock goes off (no electricity) and use a little quiet time to meditate. Otherwise, I wake up with Michelle when Isabella makes the short, two-foot trip from her new toddler bed to our bed. How I miss the cage—I mean, crib.

2. Michelle and I contort our bodies to fit into the space allowed us. We sleep on one quarter of the bed; Frankie, during the night, progressively takes over three-quarters. When Isabella arrives and insists that we make room for her, our share reduces by another half.

3. Eventually, after noisily sucking her thumb for a while, Isabella gets up and starts running around after Frankie. The windows are open (no air-conditioning) and Michelle can't bring herself to believe that the window guards, which could stop a gorilla, are strong enough to prevent Isabella from cartwheeling out. We have to get up, too.

4. We brush our teeth (baking soda) using a cup of water (rather than letting the faucet run). We may or may not take a bath—one at a time, in the same water—depending on whether it is bath day. We use homemade unscented beeswax soap to wash our bodies and baking soda for shampoo.

5. Breakfast consists of marvelously fresh cantaloupe and bread, both from the farmer's market. I haven't been able to bake my own bread for the past few weeks because the combination of a 400-degree oven, 90-degree weather, and no air-conditioning could overwhelm my family's ability to live with me.

6. One of us—depending on who wins the "discussion"— walks Frankie down the nine flights of stairs, around the block, and back up the nine flights of stairs (no non-self-propelled transportation, which means no elevator). We scavenge for plastic bags from the corner trash bin to pick up her poo.

7. We all get dressed in clothes that are just this side of fermented (thanks to our attempts to conserve water).

8. We stumble down the stairs, Michelle carrying the bags and bike helmets and Isabella riding on my shoulders.

9. We stop at the Gray Dog with our glass jars. It's not that uncommon that the workers give me coffee for free, because they get a kick out of my jar. We sit outside on a bench and chat

> I haven't been able to bake my own bread for the past few weeks because the combination of a 400-degree oven, 90-degree weather, and no air-conditioning could overwhelm my family's ability to live with me.

with passersby, often about our rickshaws, parked out front, which are something of a neighborhood novelty.

10. One of us delivers Isabella to her new Montessori nursery school—by rickshaw, of course. Sadly, Isabella recently left her child-care provider of two years (we love you and miss you every minute, Peggy). Thankfully, the nursery school is on the ground floor (can't say we exactly miss your six flights of stairs, Pegs).

11. Michelle pedals her rickshaw up the very substandard Sixth Avenue bike lane to work, eliciting smiles and comments

all the way. I ride over to the Writers Room, where I work.

12. Michelle gets a pass and takes the elevator to her office because she works on the forty-third floor. The Writers Room is just on the twelfth floor. I take the stairs to the eleventh and then take the elevator the last flight because there is no reentry on twelve. My brain wonders every time whether that is idiotic (my legs are quite sure it is).

13. After lunch (generally fruit and cheese, which we both bring from home in big Mason jars), I climb up and down what seems to be about a thousand more flights of stairs in order to shop at the farmer's market, take the food home, take Frankie for her walk, and then go back to work at the Writers Room. The farmer's market is bursting with seasonal produce. Going there and joking with the farmers is a fixture of my social life.

14. I write the next day's blog post and work some more.

15. One of us picks up Isabella, again on a bike. If it's me, Isabella and I "see what happens"—which means we ride around, searching for adventure. We go to the Hudson River and watch the sunset, or we stop at George Bliss's bike shop and Isabella plays with his dog, Scout, or we play in the fountain at Washington Square Park.

16. We meet Michelle back at the apartment as it's just getting dark. Dinner consists mostly of salads and eggs or cheese (simple fresh food that makes us happy and thin). We chat around the table. We spark up the one solar-powered lamp and read.

17. Michelle and I flip to see which of us will wrestle Isabella into her bed. Isabella says she's not tired. We ask when she will be tired. She says, "Not today."

18. On my nights, I sit on Isabella's bed and tell her stories: about the day she was born, about the day we got Frankie

from North Shore Animal Rescue, about pretending to go alligator fishing with Uncle Bing when I was a kid. (Isabella doesn't know, of course, that Bing shot himself. She doesn't know that she kills me when she asks me to tell her stories about Bing. She doesn't know that she cleans me out and washes me dry. She doesn't know that I do it all the same because I would do just about anything she asks. "Another story, please . . . Another story, please," Isabella says.)

19. Michelle and I brush our teeth by beeswax candlelight. We talk a bit. One of us takes Frankie out. We talk some more, until around nine-thirty, when our bodies, apparently cued by the darkness, tell us bedtime has arrived.

In the words of Kurt Vonnegut, "And so it goes."

I start the giving-back phase like this:

My friend Morgen and I ride up the West Side Highway to just below the George Washington Bridge, where from the bike path you can climb down to the banks of the Hudson. The idea

> Somehow, the garbage is much dirtier than I imagined.

is to pull trash out of the river before it makes its way into the ocean to choke and kill turtles.

As we ride north, we make guesses about what kind of garbage we're going to find. It's cold and windy but sunny.

We climb over the rail and down the rocks. Somehow, the garbage is much dirtier than I imagined. It's wet. And also it's incredibly dense. From above you can't see how much of it there is, but when we climb down it's all wedged in between the rocks. There are people's clothes and plastic *New York Times* delivery wrappers. There is so much plastic film.

Crazily, I have brought only two large garbage bags. I guess I figured you'd have to walk a long way to fill them both up. In fact, we fill them both up in a stretch of river of probably no more than fifteen feet. In the course of our work we clean up lots of plastic bags, lots of plastic bottles, at least two of which were filled with pee and had obviously been thrown out the window of a passing car.

I wanted, as part of giving back, to plant trees as a method of sequestering carbon. Since you can't just go around planting trees willy-nilly in New York City, I start calling environmental organizations and offering to volunteer. Finally, I reach Sustainable South Bronx and a worker there, Phil Silva, explains to me that planting trees is more complex than it seems but that there is plenty to be done helping trees that have already been planted to survive.

Sustainable South Bronx, it turns out, works with the New York City Parks Department to green the streets. Street trees not only absorb CO_2, but they reduce the urban heat-island effect and so reduce the need for air-conditioning. They also filter diesel particulates out of the air and help reduce storm-water runoff, and their presence, statistical studies show, even correlates with improved school performance of children. Besides, streets with trees are simply more pleasant.

I help clean garbage and dog poo out of tree pits—the holes in the sidewalks in which trees are planted. I work alongside lots of young volunteers, and in some ways this is where the No Impact project really comes to life for me. I volunteer not just with Sustainable South Bronx but also with a bunch of other organizations.

At the River Trust, we measure baby oysters to see whether seeding them on a slightly electrified metal grid helps them to grow faster. Reseeding the waterways around New York with oysters is one way to help clean up the water. I take part in a sponsored swim with the Manhattan Island Trust, which hopes to make the water around New York clean enough to swim in.

It is the workers at the organizations I volunteer for who confirm for me that environmentalism is not about trying to use less but about

trying to be more. It is not about sucking our tummies in but pushing our hearts out. Environmentalism is not about the environment.
It is about people. It is about a vision for a better life—for people.

Paul Steely White, the director of Transportation Alternatives,
leans on a cane after a bike accident on unsafe New York streets broke
his hip. He takes me out to a crowded Sixth Avenue, and he doesn't
talk about fewer cars. He talks about more trees and more kids playing
outside and neighbors on benches and what he calls "livable streets."
His vision is one of more, not less.

Christine Datz-Romero, head of the Lower East Side Ecology Center, challenges me to imagine a way where we build things not to throw
out but to use over and over. She thinks about things like zero waste,
a way of dealing with materials where we don't have to keep building
and buying the same things over and over again, so that we can use
our energies for more.

Like, to take one example, getting good drinking water to thirsty
children.

Kate Zidar, a New York City water activist and cofounder of the
coalition of nonprofits that make up SWIM (Storm Water Infrastructure Matters), invites me to canoe on the filthy Harlem River through
the South Bronx with a bunch of kids from Youth Ministries for Peace
and Justice, which teaches them to become the future leaders of their
communities.

Even in this filth, fish schools pass us, and eighteen-year-old
Xyomyra, who captains my boat, explains to me that it was her parents' dream to get out of the neighborhood but that it's her dream to
make her neighborhood better. What if we could swim in these rivers?
What if we cleaned them up, not just for the fish but for us, too?

Alexie Torres-Flemming, founder and head of Youth Ministries
for Peace and Justice, tells me about lying in her son's bed, crying,
while he has an asthma attack triggered by the fumes in her neighborhood. She challenges me to imagine a world where our children
can breathe.

And what I feel when I meet and talk to all these people is that I've been mistaken. For what purpose have I been using my life? I feel that, until this year, I have been distracted from what's most important. It is from these people who have spent their entire professional lives trying to make the world better for other people that I get an inkling of life's true meaning.

The seasons are changing. The darkness is coming. It's getting much harder to live without the light, the project is nearing its end, and I am confused. Perhaps, unsurprisingly, volunteering at the nonprofits has made me feel more responsible than I felt before. I want to contribute, but I am feeling shame because I'm looking forward to the end of the project.

It's not that I want to make trash or buy new things or eat packaged food from far away. But I'm tired of not traveling. I'm tired of not having electricity. The reduced hours of sunlight means the solar panel is no longer producing enough energy for us to read at night, or for me to get much work done. One week it rains four days in a row and we are completely without power.

I am confused. I feel guilty and ashamed.

Because after all this time I worry that if I am not willing to maintain all elements of this lifestyle, then what does this year of No Impact living end up telling the world? What do my choices tell the world? I've done this all so publicly. I can't just shrink away without getting noticed.

The truth is that we feel we can live comfortably using quite a bit less than we used to. But neither of us feels that we can commit to not flying. One long-haul flight causes the same carbon emissions as an entire year of the average American's driving. And I feel guilty because I will not be an eco-martyr.

But, at the same time, I'm not sure that reducing individual resource use is the entire way forward. At their root, most religious philosophies say do less harm, yes, but they also say do more good. There is a limit to how much less harm I can do. But my potential for good is unlimited. All of our potentials for good are unlimited.

The question becomes not whether we use resources but what we use them for. Do we use them to improve lives? Or do we waste them? My life itself is a resource. How shall I use it?

Strangely, I find myself in the office of Congressman Jerrold Nadler. No Impact Man started with me deciding, essentially, to disengage from the political process, deciding that it had lost its ability to change and act, which is why I struck out on a course of individual action.

Volunteering for the nonprofits has taught me, though, that as much as I value individual lifestyle change, there is also the fact that we can do together what I can't do alone.

An activist organization called 1Sky has sent out an e-mail asking people to visit their elected representatives, to call on them to support a political agenda that does something about climate change. I'm joining in. I'm at my congressman's office and I'm telling him that we need to act aggressively on climate change.

He's listening and he's nodding and he's agreeing, but it doesn't mean that much. Because what he agrees with privately in a meeting with me and what politicians are willing or able to do publicly are two different things.

All the same, a couple of weeks after I visit the congressman, his legislative director e-mails me to say that Nadler has agreed to co-sponsor a House bill calling for a moratorium on building new coal power stations.

I went into this project wondering if I could make a difference. But the question isn't whether or not I make a difference. The question is whether I want to be the type of person who tries. We can all make a difference. We all have the responsibility to make a difference. You might think the responsibility part is oppressive, but I began this experiment, in part, as an expression of my victimhood and powerlessness. To understand that I can make a difference is so freeing.

The job is simply this: to live our lives as though we make a difference. Because, paradoxically, when we imagine we don't make a difference, that is when we do the most harm. The special interests have money on their side, but we have the people.

And while I am grappling with my way forward, trying to understand all that I've learned and to decide the direction of the future project that is my life, that's when it happens.

I'm asleep, but then I'm not. It takes a moment before the noise that woke me comes into focus. It's coming from the corner, where Isabella sleeps. It's like a gurgle. I'm half asleep and still not sure what it is. Then I know.

My body flies out of the bed. Isabella is hot and stiff as a plank, and she's flopping like a fish pulled out of the water and her eyes roll back in her head.

"Michelle!" I shout.

Please, God.

Michelle jumps out of bed and starts to scream: "Help! Help!" She is standing naked in the living room, shouting, "Help!"

But who will help? It's late. We're in our apartment. It's dark. Who will help?

"Call the ambulance," I shout.

Michelle is talking into the phone. Why does she move so damn slow? Why is everything moving so slow? What is happening?

Isabella is in my lap. Her body is jumping up and down, and I know that I should put her on the floor but she screams when I try. There is a demon in my girl but she can still say one word. She says, "Daddy," over and over. My girl is begging me for help.

My girl is begging me for help, but I cannot help her.

I am not too far away to help her. I am right there. But it's as though I'm not right there. A little girl's body is in my lap but it's as though Isabella herself has been forced out of it and she is somewhere far away, and from that distance she keeps asking me for help.

"It's okay, honey, it's okay," I say, but it's not okay at all.

"Daddy . . . Daddy . . . Daddy."

The ghosts surround me. I cannot let them overwhelm me. The ghost of Bing. The ghost of David. The ghost of Italy. A trapdoor has opened in the back of my mind and my whole body just wants to jump through, to give up. How can this be happening again?

There is only one thing that makes sense, Pema Chödrön said. There is nothing to hold on to and no safe place and nothing permanent and there is only one thing that makes sense, Pema said.

The ambulance men arrive and they ask for lights, but there is just the one solar-powered lamp and we are too upset to realize that we could just throw the circuit breaker in the kitchen and have the whole apartment blazing in light. We have forgotten that the electricity is even there, but it doesn't matter because now the oxygen mask is over Isabella's face and I am carrying her and the siren starts and there is no traffic yet the ambulance moves so slow.

At just about the same time, I would soon learn, another ambulance is carrying a little African American girl, just a couple of years older than Isabella. Her name is Sharon. She comes from the South Bronx. She's had an asthma attack. In the Bronx, children suffer from asthma at record levels, studies show, because of the huge number of garbage trucks carrying the rest of New York City's trash into the neighborhood for processing.

•

Swinging doors slam open and we hop out of the ambulance, and there is little Sharon in a blue dress on a stretcher with an oxygen mask on. Her mother sits next to her, and I look into the mom's eyes and I imagine her feeling of helplessness as her little girl's voice calls, "Mommy . . . Mommy . . ."

Then, as quick as it started, it's over.

Whatever happened in Italy, the doctor said, this isn't that.

Isabella's face has no mask on it now. She is running around the pediatric emergency room and there is an ice machine and she says, "Daddy, can I have some ice?"

Isabella is crunching on the ice and the doctor is laughing and he says it was a febrile seizure. She is fine. It's something that happens in certain children when they spike a high fever. Later, my dad would tell me that I had them when I was young.

Isabella stands near Sharon's bed. Sharon's mask is off now, too. Sharon calls everyone "Doctor." "Hi, Doctor," she says to me. She walks around and sees a patient with blood down his shirt and she calls him doctor. "Bye, Doctor," she says when she leaves. Sharon waves at Isabella. Isabella waves back.

Isabella will outgrow febrile seizures, but the scars in Sharon's lungs from the fumes of the garbage trucks will never go away.

It sounds like this story ends well, but it is not over, because Michelle is pregnant. She wanted another child and I did not, but we played Russian roulette and Michelle won and she was pregnant and I was pissed but now I'm not.

How could I be? Another Isabella is coming.

Eight weeks pass and Michelle is pregnant and I'm used to it and friends who've raised two kids in a one-bedroom apartment invite us over and assure us we'll figure it out. I've started talking to Michelle's tummy and, worst of all, I tell Isabella to do it, too. "Hi, Baby, this is your big sister."

But at the doctor's office Michelle laughs because the wand is cold on her tummy and then the doctor says he's having trouble and he needs to do the exam vaginally and then he says just this: The baby's heartbeat is not there.

Your first response is to ask for options. There must be options.

There are no options.

How cruel. I didn't want the child, but then I got used to it, and then I loved it, and now my wife is crying. With her feet in stirrups, she is crying. I hold her. She is wearing a paper hospital gown and it falls open at the back, and she doesn't sob. She just looks at me with eyes that look like fruit that has split open.

My heart is broken by the fragility. My heart is broken by our fragility. In that doctor's office I realize that we all have this. Whole island nations will disappear when the ocean levels rise if we allow climate change to go unabated.

It has taken me all this time to understand that this project is an expression of an understanding I have. It is about something I learned way too early. It is about something I learned through the loss of my brother and uncle. I thought that it was a lesson that applied only to me and came only from my own despair.

But while my wife is crying in a paper gown, I realize it is not about *my* despair. There is no my despair or your despair. There is only our despair. But I forget that. We forget that.

I understand now about Bing and David. Everyone loses Bing and David. Some people lose them at the beginning of their lives and some in the middle and some at the end. Some will lose their children and some their siblings. Michelle lost her unborn child at age thirty-nine. David stopped breathing in his crib when I was four. And you? And you? This is the root of my religious belief: we are not separate.

It's terrible and it's wonderful, but it's true: we're all in the same boat. That's the consolation. It's not just me who's scared and lonely and worried and isn't sure how to help myself. We don't know how to help ourselves, but there is one thing we do know how to do. We know how to help each other.

Michelle is crying and there is only one thing to do and the whole world is crying and there are storms and wars and miscarriages and what should we do, fight about oil? Fight about driving? They feel it like we feel it and just now the pain is everyone's and I still have my little girl Isabella. But for how long?

> Waste fewer resources. Waste less life.

Dae Soen Sa Nim tried to get the Pope in a hot tub. Mayer protested war. I tried not making trash, and I dragged my poor wife along with me. At a child's grave, did you ever wish you had another video game? When I take my last breath, will there be a wish that I had more stuff?

I'll wish for only one thing, I think. That I loved better. That I had been better at loving and not being distracted by stuff or accomplishment. This life is so short and it will soon be over. What will we use it for?

There is nothing to do about the miscarriage, or about Isabella's febrile seizures, but we can stop the water shortage and the kids dying of diarrhea. There is no reason for Sharon to have asthma. All we have to do to cure children like Sharon is make less trash. Waste fewer resources. Waste less life. I only say this because Sharon is your daughter, too.

There is only one thing that makes sense, Pema said.

Can I help? Do I help?

Isabella is fine.

It has now been one year since we started the experiment. It's so strange after all this, after thinking of all these things, it's very confusing, but I go to the circuit breaker and I turn the lights back on.

Epilogue: Life After the Year Without Toilet Paper

Here are the questions I get asked most often about the No Impact project:

1. What was the hardest part?
2. What aspects of the lifestyle did you keep?
3. How did the project change you?
4. What did you use instead of toilet paper?

Here are the questions I still ask myself:

1. With scientists expecting thousands of species to become extinct if the planet warms susbstantially, how do we make sure that we are not one of them?
2. In other words, how do we save the planet?
3. Will I ever—God help me—live down the toilet-paper thing?

We switched the lights back on just before Christmas, 2007. Thanks to the long-distance travel moratorium of the No Impact project, Michelle hadn't been back to Minneapolis to visit her family for more than a year. We planned to go for the holiday, but to avoid the excessive carbon emissions associated with air travel, we figured we'd take the train.

Then we did the research. It would take two days each way (at an average speed of twenty-five miles per hour). We'd have to get a roomette, since we couldn't imagine fellow coach passengers enjoying the energy that would pour out of Isabella during two restless days on a train. And, to top things off, it would cost $2,500 for the three of us. By comparison, the three of us could get from New York to Minneapolis, and back, by air for only about $1,000.

That clinched it. Although Europe boasts high-speed trains that average 120 miles per hour, here in the United States, practical, low-impact travel is not yet available. Michelle and Isabella would take the plane.

An eco-car service took them to the airport by Prius, but not me.

"Do you feel weird getting on a plane?" Michelle had asked me.

"Yes," I said.

"Then you don't have to come."

I just couldn't bring myself to climb on a plane within days of the No Impact project ending.

So I rattle around our apartment in New York by myself for the week. I'm disoriented. I find myself sitting in the living room at night, begrudging myself the use of electric light, even though the bulbs are compact fluorescent. I will only let myself have one lamp on at a time.

I feel dumb for being stingy with the lights. But also I feel like a hypocrite for having lights on that I don't truly need. It's strange. Like turning a light on or off is some sort of a moral quandary.

My problem is that I have been living for a year under the yoke of so many rules. My life ran along in a groove carved out by what I could and could not do. But now there are no rules. Only an attempt to figure out what actually makes sense in our lives when it comes to finding an ecological balance. But without the boundaries provided by the rules, I feel uprooted.

There is something so comforting about living within rules. On my blog, there are many hundreds of people now reporting that they have made eco-rules for their lives, too. My friend Rabbi Steve—referring to the rules of kosher—says that I have evolved a sort of "eco-Kashrut." Sometimes a group of rules and living traditions has the benefit of connecting you to some larger sense of community and meaning. Without the rules of No Impact, who am I?

There is that slice of pizza that so long ago I couldn't have and that I felt bitter about missing, but because it comes on a paper plate, I still can't bring myself to eat it. There is the taxicab that could get me from A to B without my getting wet in the rain, but it still pollutes the air and I can't bring myself to take it. I *do* take the elevator sometimes instead of the stairs, but I feel guilty.

I feel very lonely. Who could possibly understand the strangeness of the transition I am going through? I mean, it is more than just the project that has ended. It is my identity. My entire identity has disappeared. Yesterday, I was No Impact Man. What am I today? Moderate Impact Man?

What I'm describing sounds crazy, even to me, but as Annie Leonard says in her online video *Story of Stuff*, so is the norm:

> We are in this ridiculous situation where we go to work, maybe two jobs even, and we come home and we're exhausted so we plop down on our new couch and watch TV and the commercials tell us "YOU SUCK" so we gotta go to the mall to buy something to feel better, then we gotta go to work more to pay for the stuff we just bought so we come home and we're more tired so you sit down and watch more TV and it tells you to go to the mall again and we're on this crazy work-watch-spend treadmill. And we could just stop.

We could just stop.

•

Somewhere I read a talk of Pema Chödrön's where she says something like, "Most of us in this room are not so rich that we have nothing material to worry about and we're not so poor that we can't think about anything but getting ourselves fed. So let's start by giving thanks for our middle birth."

What Pema means by "middle birth" is to be born neither in abject poverty nor in extreme wealth. We can be so overwhelmed by the suffering of poverty that we don't have the luxury to examine our lives. Or we can be so distant from suffering and so coddled by the material comforts of extreme wealth that we become too complacent to examine our lives. In a middle birth—where we are confronted with only moderate hardship—we have just enough suffering to get our attention but not enough to overwhelm us.

> If the pleasures we seek are not permanent, then how important are they?

Perhaps part of the problem in our response to the planetary crisis—why we don't just stop, as Annie Leonard suggests—is that so many of us in the developed world have such a cushy lifestyle that we are stuck in our complacency.

This is like the story of the Buddha himself. His father, the king, wanted more than anything to protect his son from the knowledge of suffering. As a result, his son was never allowed to see anything that might upset him. Buddha came to believe that life was only about the pursuit of personal pleasure. He never questioned his life, because he never had a reason to. He just lived it as it had been delivered to him— until one day he ventured outside the palace.

For the first time he saw sick people and old people and dead bodies. He saw that these things ultimately happen to all of us. That sooner or later we all suffer. If old age and death are what happen to us, he asked, then what is the meaning of our lives? If the pleasures we seek are not permanent, then how important are they? What is the worth of all the riches and pleasures I've experienced in the palace if one day they will be taken away?

Buddha was shocked out of his complacency and began searching for a better life. The good news is that, at least as the legend goes, he found it.

Maybe this global-warming thing, along with all the environmental crises, along with the economic meltdown, could be for us in the developed world like leaving the palace and seeing the dead bodies and the old people and sick people. Maybe it will wake us up enough to ask: What is this life? What is it for? What is its meaning? How should we live?

Maybe it will wake us up enough to make us search for a better, more meaningful, more purposeful life—for us and for our planet.

Here's the big question I have about progress: If we can have better and better cell phones, but they are not accompanied by better and better understanding of ourselves and our place in this universe, can we really say that we have progressed? If we are born and then spend our lives moving from one toy to the next, without ever answering the big questions, have we progressed or have we simply been distracted?

Perhaps, if we really examined our lives, we'd come to the conclusion that our purpose is to make sure we can all ride around on Jet Skis during vacation and in SUVs the rest of the time. So be it. It's our life. It's our planet. As long as we make the collective decision consciously instead of blindly, then all well and good.

I suppose we could decide to burn hot and short. We could be the Hunter S. Thompson of species. I'm just suggesting that we should at least wake up long enough to make it an active decision. And, yes, it's our decision. It's a decision that belongs to us. Not to the government. Not to big business. It belongs to us.

If we do wake up, though, I rather doubt we'll decide to go out like Hunter Thompson. Mark Vonnegut, Kurt Vonnegut's son, went crazy and ended up in a mental hospital. Metaphorically speaking, he ventured outside the palace. He had to wake up. He had to ask himself some hard questions. This is why when his dad asked him what are we here for, Mark didn't say to ride on Jet Skis and in SUVs. Instead, he said, "We are here to help each other get through this thing, whatever it is." It was about helping each other.

I've had this hammered home to me lately—that if I want to manifest peace in the world, I have to find peace in my own mind.

They say a peaceful mind makes a peaceful man. A peaceful man makes a peaceful family. A peaceful family makes a peaceful village. A peaceful village makes a peaceful country. A peaceful country makes a peaceful world.

What does this mean? That if I want to change the world, I have to change myself.

There is a whole school of modern environmentalists, by the way, who don't much like connecting saving the planet with all this what's-the-meaning-of-life stuff to which I am so naturally inclined. They think it's a counterproductive turnoff that will have the effect of driving people away from, rather than toward, the idea of stewardship. They also worry—as I do—about tainting the environmental movement with thoughts of asceticism and having less.

They believe, as I do, that the human spirit is expansive and aspirational and that anything that reeks of tightening our belts or of being less or making ourselves smaller—part of the old environmentalism of the 1970s—is counter to human nature. They believe, as I do, in rising to the challenge rather than shrinking from the obstacles.

This group of modern environmentalists place its faith in technology—solar panels and electric cars and planet-saving inventions that no one has even heard of yet. New tech is cool and attractive to the young and fashionable and creates jobs for the underprivileged and deprived. Most important, since the tighten-your-belt philosophy cannot apply to the bulk of human population, many of whom don't even have electricity, technology is the way to provide for the development of old and new economies in a sustainable way.

So these new, modern, gung-ho, "forward-looking" environmentalists are right. Aspiration and vision and a view to a better life, rather than a constricted life, is central. Technology is a hugely important part of the answer. But for a few reasons, I suspect it's not the whole answer.

For starters, to accomplish what is scientifically necessary to ameliorate catastrophic climate change, the United States would have to reduce its carbon emissions by at least 95 percent (some scientists are beginning to say 100 percent). In other words, we have to get the same result out of the same energy while causing twenty times less environmental damage. That's like telling the owner of an old juice factory that he needs to get the same juice from one orange that he used to get from twenty. He can get juicier oranges and he can get better juicing machines, but getting twenty oranges' worth of juice from one orange? Better tech may not be sufficient. We may also have to change the way we live.

Second, relying entirely on new tech may mean that we just create a whole new slew of environmental problems, like those created by the initial push for biofuels. The same thing applies if, for example, we choose to go with nuclear energy. What do we do with the waste?

Third, if we rely on technology alone, then we miss the tremendous opportunity for lifestyle improvement that we find in this crisis. If we build electric cars, we will still be stuck in traffic jams. If we keep building suburbs, we will still be isolated and lonely. If we put improving cell phones first, then our best minds will still be distracted from getting clean water to the billion who lack it. If we use technology, in other words, to rebuild the current system so that it can last forever, then we miss the opportunity to ask whether the current system really delivers the good life. We miss the opportunity to have happier people as well as a happier planet.

Working two jobs to get an electric car instead of the gas-guzzling variety is better, but it's still working two jobs. In an economy based on delivering the most stuff to the most people, education and health care are still secondary priorities. What if we redesigned our economy to include the cost of externalities like car exhaust and toxic garbage? What if we replaced GDP as our measure of national success with some measure of life quality? What if we designed our economy around the most important elements of the good life instead of around the throughput of material and energy? After all, if the environmental and economic crises we currently face are any indicators, things the way they are aren't working.

> **What is the purpose of our lives?**
> **What makes us happy and fulfilled?**

The new environmentalists are right—we need to be expansive and aspirational. We also need huge investment in the rapid deployment of renewable energy production and sustainable technology. But conflating technology with progress is a two-hundred-year-old idea. It's not really aspirational. And it's not really progress. No, we need to figure out what the good life really is and then design our social and technical systems to facilitate it. Some people call this socio-technical design.

Which brings me back to the meaning-of-life questions. If we are to have good socio-technical design, we have to ask those questions. Why are we here? What is the purpose of our lives? What makes us happy and fulfilled? What, in short, is the good life? Because it is upon the definition of the good life that our socio-technical designs must be based.

Who, by the way, gets to decide what the good life is?

We do.

And who is *responsible* for deciding?

We are.

There has also been a debate raging within the environmental movement about the relative merits of individual versus collective action.

Back in 2007, on the subject of individual action, the *New York Times* columnist Tom Friedman wrote, "You can change lights. You can change cars. But if you don't change leaders, your actions are nothing more than an expression of, as Dick Cheney would say, 'personal virtue.'"

Meanwhile, *Newsweek* reported that during the presidential campaign, Barack Obama remarked in frustration about having to answer a question by Brian Williams about his personal green choices: "What I'm thinking in my head is, 'Well, the truth is, Brian, we can't solve global warming because I f——ing changed lightbulbs in my house. It's because of something collective.'"

I'd hear criticisms like this constantly throughout the No Impact project. What difference can one person make? Well, absolutely none if that one person doesn't try to make a difference. But who among us knows how much we will influence the people around us? Which one of us knows which of us, by applying their talents and efforts to what they believe in, may not become a Martin Luther King, Jr., or a Bobby Kennedy or a Betty Friedan or a Nelson Mandela?

Not that great names are necessarily the most important aspects of movements. They are like the proverbial straw that breaks the camel's back. Thousands and thousands of straws must weigh the camel down before the final one breaks its back. No one of these straws is more important than the other, not even the last one. It's just the one that happens to get remembered. Just because our individual actions are not remembered does not mean they're not crucial. The straw that breaks the back requires all of the rest of us straws. The domino that begins the domino effect requires each of us to be in line for the chain reaction to take place.

Of course, both Friedman and Obama are correct to suggest we need collective action on climate change. We need gigantic investment in green infrastructure. We need regulations to curb industry excesses. These things cannot be done be individuals. Those of us who are concerned about our environmental crisis must get involved in the political arena and find ways to keep pressure on our politicians in this regard.

But to suggest that collective and individual action are mutually exclusive, or even different, is wrongheaded and dangerous. It ignores the way cultures change, the responsibilities of citizens, and our potential as agents of change. Collective action is nothing more than the aggregation of individual actions. And individual action does not preclude involvement in collective action. In fact, it absolutely demands it. The two work together.

Think about this: How much more convincing is an advocate for urban bike lanes who rides his bike every day? Who is more convincing—an advocate for climate-change mitigation who takes the subway or one who drives alone in an SUV? Living our values across all areas of our individual lives—from the private to the public—demonstrates an integrity and conviction that can help persuade the skeptics. Instead of fruitlessly debating the utility of individual versus collective action, why not promote them both under an all-encompassing term like "engaged citizenship"?

The climate crisis has revealed a second crisis: the inability of our culture to effect rapid and crucial change. Through what channels do we exercise our concern to get something done about the climate crisis? The federal government has a record of making itself too cumbersome and too beholden to institutional interests to lead radical change. It tends to yoyo between more tax and more government and less tax and less government. Back and forth. It is not good at leading larger cultural change.

This climate problem is so big that we need a change in the culture. We need to look at the way we live. We need to find a good life that does not depend so much on energy and material throughput. And government should not be in the business of telling us how to live. Government should be in the business of facilitating the way of life the people have chosen. If we want to ensure that the planet maintains its ability to support us, we have to choose differently. This is a battle not just for votes but for hearts and minds. And hearts and minds are captured by individuals, not by governments.

We know we have to change the system, but we must also remember that the system is only a collection of individuals. What the system does is just the aggregation of all of our individual actions as citizens, as shareholders, as CEOs, as product designers, as customers, as friends, as family members, and as voters. We have to stop waiting for the system to change and remember that every decision we make in our homes and in our workplaces amounts to "the system."

> **We cannot wait for the system to change. We individuals are the system.**

On the street, people tell jokes. They say excuse me if they bump into each other. They help each other. But we go to work and make decisions that are "not personal but business." Our institutions don't reflect our human kindness. We allow our corporations to focus only on profits. We allow political institutions to focus mostly on reelection. We must insist that our institutions reflect the full truth of the humanity they are supposed to serve. We must, in our roles within those institutions, act the same way we would act when we find an old person having trouble crossing the street.

As individuals—as product designers and accountants and CEOs, for example—we all make crucial decisions that affect the world. We cannot wait for the system to change. We individuals are the system.

We need to pick up a new model of engaged citizenship and realize that the way we live affects everyone around us. We need to develop new ways to take up and assert our responsibility. We need to take "participatory democracy" to a new level, where we don't just vote for the leaders who will bring us the culture we want, but where we take responsibility for making the culture ourselves.

And what we get in return is the feeling of a life fully lived, in a world where we are not victims of the system but leaders of it. Where we choose instead of inherit. Where we stride purposefully instead of sleepwalk. Where we are true masters of our destiny.

•

So. About these questions regarding what I did about toilet paper and what parts of the project I kept:

I was in a radio studio in midtown Manhattan doing a live interview with a presenter from the BBC World Service. He asked me about the toilet paper. By then, I had been asked about this by journalists from Montreal to Tel Aviv, and I was sick of it. I would always deflect the question by saying that this was no trivial issue.

Why, when the world is in peril, would you waste all of our time discussing my toilet habits? I would say. How crazy is it, I would ask, that we chop down the trees we need to absorb carbon dioxide and then flush them down our toilets? There are better systems, I would say.

But this one particular BBC journalist would not let it go. "Yes," he said, "but our listeners would like to know what you did instead of toilet paper."

Finally, I snapped. I said, "I clearly do not want to discuss my toilet habits on the radio, and I'm sure your listeners are embarrassed for you that you keep pressing me on this issue. Would your mother be proud of you for asking such a personal and embarrassing question within the hearing of millions? Because I'm sure my mother would not be proud of me for answering you."

That put it to bed.

As for what we kept, well, let me say first that I am over the strange confusion and shame that infected me in the first week.

The refrigerator is back on but the freezer, which is separate, is not. After a year of disuse, the dishwasher would not come back to life, and we did not replace it. We gave our air conditioners away and sweated through the summer and plan to keep doing so. The radiators are still turned off. There is no TV, though we park Isabella in front of a movie on the computer once in a while. I carry my jar everywhere for coffee and water and, mostly, ride my bike. I have been in perhaps ten taxis in the year since the project ended, and I take the subway when it rains.

I still wash my hair with baking soda, and use it for deodorant. I use homemade moisturizer and soap with no toxins. We still don't eat meat. Sadly, for me, Isabella, who is now three and half, got angry and said she did not want to be a vegetarian anymore. She said the other kids get to eat meat and she wants to, too.

"Do you know that meat is animals?" I asked.

"Yes."

"So if you eat meat, you're eating animals. You get it?"

"Yes. I want to eat animals," Isabella said.

So this Thanksgiving, Michelle and I decided that she could have turkey at her friend Ruby's house. The turkey came, Isabella tasted it, but she didn't like it. She asked for cheese.

As for those questions I'm still left with after the No Impact experiment, let's start with this one: How do we save the world? How do we keep ourselves from going extinct? I say this starkly, because if you read the scientific literature, you'll find this climate emergency is much worse than the press is making out.

The answer to my question is that I don't think anybody fully knows yet. This is why it is not a problem that can be outsourced to government alone. We all have to turn our minds to it. But before we turn our minds to it, we have to actually believe we can make a difference. That, by the way, is one of the most important results of the project: that I've come to believe that I can make a difference.

Paradoxically, it may not have been the creating less trash and other measures per se that made the greatest difference. Instead, what made the difference was publicly letting people know that I was trying, and trying hard, and having them see the efforts. Going to extremes for a year changed the way I think about these things—another result of the experiment. Changing the people around me—the unforeseen consequence of individual action—is still one more result. By continuing to think about these issues and doing my best, even if it's not as extreme as during the project proper, I continue to change the people around me. We can all change the people around us by changing ourselves.

I still sometimes flounder. I'm far from perfect. I'm cruel sometimes and insensitive. I get all caught up in my petty concerns. Indeed, people close to me have called me a hypocrite at times for my callousness. "How can you call yourself No Impact Man?" they've said. They're right, of course.

But what wouldn't be right is if I didn't at least in some small way keep trying to do something.

I can choose how I live. I can be involved politically. I can give talks and try to change other people's minds. I can participate in the local community garden and see if the idea of urban agriculture catches fire. I can carry my jar around. I can take planes less. I can blog. I can talk to people. I can look for new ways to participate in our cultural response to our environmental crises.

I'm not going to make myself a martyr. But I am going to keep trying to live my life deliberately. For most of my forty-five years I didn't try hard enough. I got too paralyzed by this question of whether I was the type of person who could make a difference. Finally, during the year of the project, I realized that's the wrong question. The real question is whether I'm the type of person who wants to try.

Throughout this book I've tried to show how saving the world is up to me. I've tried hard not to lecture. Yes, it's up to me. But after living for a year without toilet paper, I've earned the right to say one thing: It's also up to you.

So, what are you going to do?

no impact project

The Book Is Just the Beginning

The No Impact Project is an international, environmental, nonprofit project inspired by the *No Impact Man* book, film, and blog. Our goal is to help communities discover a way of life that is better for people and the planet.

We achieve this by promoting lifestyle change, enabling people to experience their own version of Colin's No Impact Experiment, and helping those who don't see themselves as tree-hugging eco-geeks to find a way into the environmental movement.

If you would like to:

- register for our next No Impact Experience
- download our free secondary-school curriculum
- host a community screening of *No Impact Man,* the film
- or find out about our other programs

Please visit us at http://noimpactproject.org/.

To invite Colin to speak or to find out about Colin's speaking engagements, visit www.ColinBeavan.com.

Note on Production

It's no easy feat pushing the envelope on sustainable book production. At first, the thought was to print this book on paper made from alternative materials—materials other than wood, that is. Everything from coconut fiber to bamboo was considered. But it turned out that some of those materials couldn't easily be printed on, and others couldn't be gotten in sufficient quantities. So the no-wood idea had to be dropped.

The decision to print the book on paper raised the question of whether to use virgin paper made from trees grown in sustainably managed forests or recycled paper that was made from other paper but would have to be brought a very long distance, by gas-guzzling tractor trailer, from the paper mill to the printer. Which would be better?

The point here, as I've mentioned, is that acting, living, and producing sustainably, which should be as easy as falling off a log, is in fact complicated and nonstandard and hard. This is what has to change. This is what *we* have to change.

Having said all that, I am very proud to say that this book is made from 100 percent postconsumer recycled paper, processed without chlorine. Additionally, the paper was manufactured using energy generated from biogas.

I like to think this means that we are one book closer to publishers manufacturing their books sustainably as a matter of common practice.

Appendix: You Can Make a Difference!

For tips on environmental lifestyle redesign, engaged citizenship, and my own continued journey, please look at NoImpactMan.com.

For ways to participate in our cultural response to the crises in our habitat, go to NoImpactCommunity.org.

If you get nothing else from what I've written, I hope I've made clear that we need to go way beyond recycling, hybrid cars, compact fluorescent bulbs, and using "green" products. Nor can we simply vote in the right politicians. We need massive citizen participation in our cultural response to the evolving crises in our planet's ability to support human and nonhuman life. It is time for people to take up the reins of government and business and to force the change we want and need. We cannot wait for leaders. We are the leaders.

Each of us has a role to play according to our circumstances and talents. Some of us will be excellent at making our lives function according to the ability of the planet to support us, and at leading others to initiate the same lifestyle redesign. Others of us are great communicators and visionaries with the ability to change people's minds about the way our culture needs to function. Still others have the capacity for organizing their fellows into productive action that gets the attention of local, regional, and national government. Together, we can change.

As yet, no overarching structure for participation exists that we can all easily plug ourselves into. There is no one place to sign up, no one person or organization that can tell us what to do. Indeed, I had great difficulty finding organizations to volunteer with during the giving-back stage of my project. Please, if you work for an environmental organization, find ways to accommodate people who want to get involved, and quickly. There is nothing that saps people's motivation more than to be told there is no place for them in a movement.

But that doesn't excuse each of us as individuals from finding and making our own place in the movement for change. When I wasn't sure what to do, I called a friend and we went and picked garbage off the banks of the Hudson. It was a first try, a first response. With continued effort, I found organizations to be part of, and more flamboyant and mind-changing measures. But we must all start from where we are. If there is no organization that does what you want to do, make one. Start. Now. Please.

I will give detailed resources throughout this appendix. But if you get no further than this introduction, here are some general resources you may be interested in.

If you think your passion lies in lifestyle change and you want more information than this book or my blog supplies, the following will help. They vary in tone and approach, from easygoing to extreme, but they all have thought-provoking ideas for lifestyle change that go beyond the lightbulb approach:

Depletion and Abundance: Life on the New Homefront, by Sharon Aystk.
The Urban Homestead: Your Guide to Self-Sufficient Living in the Heart of the City, by Kelly Coyne and Erik Knutzen.
Toolbox for Sustainable City Living, by Scott Kellogg and Stacy Pettigrew.
Seven Wonders for a Cool Planet: Everyday Things to Help Stop Global Warming, by Eric Sorensen.

The website of the Center for a New American Dream has excellent resources for people who want to develop more satisfying lifestyles while consuming fewer planetary resources: NewDream.org.

As a starting point, Michael Pollan, in an excellent article about individual action and lifestyle change in *The New York Times Magazine* (www.nytimes.com/2008/04/20/magazine/20wwln-lede-t.thml?partner=permalink&exprod=permalink), suggested finding

> one thing to do in your life that doesn't involve spending or voting, that may or may not virally rock the world but is real and particular (as well as symbolic) and that, come what may, will offer its own rewards. Maybe you decide to give up meat, an act that would reduce your carbon footprint by as much as a quarter. Or you could try this: determine to observe the Sabbath. For one day a week, abstain completely from economic activity: no shopping, no driving, no electronics.

Or, he went on, you could grow some of your own food.

If you don't think you are up to a lifestyle change per se but would like to make an effort to use less damaging resources, Michael Brower and Warren Leon's *Consumer's Guide to Effective Environmental Choices: Practical Advice from the Union of Concerned Scientists* (Three Rivers Press, 1999), though slightly dated, goes beyond simple lists to help you learn to make choices for yourself.

If you dig the celebrity approach, you'll also enjoy Ed Begley, Jr.'s, *Living Like Ed: A Guide to the Eco-Friendly Life* (Clarkson Potter, 2008).

GoodGuide.com provides an excellent guide to good purchasing choices.

If you want to get involved in organized action, you'll find institutions worthy of your support throughout this appendix. But what follows is the list of my favorite environmental organizations, the ones I hope thousands of you will support with your action and your wallets. The list is quirky, but I chose the organizations because I got to know the people involved during the No Impact project. In addition to the fact that they have become friends who have helped inform my thinking. I have come to greatly admire their common approach, which is, for the most part, to get as many citizens involved as possible.

FAVORITE NATIONAL ORGANIZATIONS

350.org is environmentalist Bill McKibben's attempt, along with a group of former students from Middlebury College and across the globe, to create citizen action to focus our political leaders' attention on policies that will bring atmospheric carbon dioxide down to a level the planet can tolerate.

1Sky.org is a Washington-based citizen and lobbying group that aims to harness citizen action and bring U.S. policy into line with climate goals that are scientifically necessary rather than simply politically possible.

The BreakThrough Institute (TheBreakThrough.org), though not a citizen organization, keeps the environmental movement honest. In their work in general and in their book in particular (*Break Through: From the Death of Environmenatlism to the Politics of Possibility*), founders Ted Nordhaus and Michael Shellenberger have insisted that the environmental movement move beyond healing the planet by limiting human aspiration to healing by embracing our ambition. It is Ted and Michael who have helped make mainstream the idea that environmental responses must help people as well as the planet.

The Center for a New American Dream (NewDream.org), also mentioned above, works with individuals, institutions, communities, and business to conserve natural resources, counter the commercialization of our culture, and promote positive changes in the way goods are produced and consumed. It has an online membership of 143,000, who form the backbone of campaigns ranging from reducing bottled water use to eliminating carbon emissions. New Dream's Responsible Purchasing Network is the go-to source for green procurement. We are a member-based network of over 125 purchasing stakeholders, including multinational corporations and state governments, working together to identify, buy, maintain, and dispose of or repurpose socially and environmentally responsible goods and services.

It is the most economically deprived urban neighborhoods that tend to have the worst environmental problems, like childhood asthma and cancer. Similarly, it is these communities that would benefit most from local investment in, for example, the renewable-energy industry. The Ella Baker Center for Human Rights (EllaBaker Center.org) is preeminent in approaching environmentalism as a subset of social justice: "The safest neighborhoods aren't the ones with the most prisons and the most police. They're the ones with the best schools, the cleanest enivronment, and the most opportunities for young people and working people. That's what we want for urban America: justice in the system; opportunity in our cities; and peace on our streets."

Food and Water Watch (FoodandWaterWatch.org) works to ensure clean water and safe food. Through research, public and policy-maker education, media, and lobbying, we advocate policies that guarantee safe, wholesome food produced in a humane and sustainable manner, and public, rather than private, control of water resources, including oceans, rivers, and groundwater. Perhaps of greatest interest to me is FWW's advocacy for a federal trust fund, such as the one we have for the interstate highway system, that would guarantee ongoing public funding for our sewage and drinking-water systems.

Green for All (GreenforAll.org) epitomizes the aspirational, happier-planet, happier-people approach to curing our environmental ills. Instead of a woe-is-me, we-must-buy-less philosophy, Green for All dedicates itself to building an inclusive green economy strong enough to lift people out of poverty. Founded by Van Jones, author of *The Green Collar Economy*, Green for All advocates for local, state, and federal commitment to job creation, job training, and entrepreneurial opportunities in the emerging green economy—especially for people from disadvantaged communities.

In the few years since its establishment, Hazon (Hazon.org) has become perhaps the largest Jewish environmental organization in the United States. Hazon (Hebrew for "vision") makes its goal "to create a healthier and more sustainable Jewish community as a step towards a healthier and more sustainable world for all." Hazon is one of many faith-based environmental organizations; another is the Evangelical Environmental Network (CreationCare.org), which makes the crucial connection between sustainability and religious values.

The Story of Stuff Project (StoryofStuff.org), founded by Annie Leonard, educates and inspires engaged citizens to seek a society in which our industrial models, economic systems, and consumption patterns sustain rather than undermine public health, social justice, community well-being, and the planet itself. The Story of Stuff project is the home of the Internet film of the same name and plans to create additional films and a website to stimulate citizen action in the coming year.

EXCELLENT NEW YORK–BASED MODELS FOR STRUCTURING CITIZEN PARTICIPATION

To change people's values, so the shrinks say, you change their behavior. You don't barrage them with ideas and cause information overload. You don't tell them their existing values are wrong and get their backs up.

What you do is get them to change their behavior, and once you've done that, you let their ideas and values change all by themselves. "What a great idea we've come up with," they'll say.

So don't convince people to save the world. Just get them started on saving it. Once they realize what they're doing, they'll already be convinced. Remember how Tom Sawyer convinced Huck Finn to paint the fence? The following are my favorites among New York organizations because they epitomize this approach.

By using food as the common element linking diverse organizations and individuals, Just Food (JustFood.org) works to improve the quality of life in New York City and the region. It has the dual goal of getting good food to underserved neighborhoods and getting local, sustainable food to the entire city. Just Food's participatory approach includes organizing community-supported agriculture groups, promoting urban farming, advocating for bee- and chicken-keeping, and food education. Food, like no other commodity, connects people to the environment, and promoting participation in this crucial area can be the thin end of the wedge.

The Lower East Side Ecology Center (LESEcologyCenter.org) provides community-based recycling and composting programs to supplement existing city curbside programs, develops local stewardship of public open space, and increases community awareness, involvement, and youth development through environmental education programs. Especially through its drop-off compost programs, LESEC structures a citizen response to our environmental crises that, often, leads to further involvement and value change, a hugely important approach.

The River Project's (RiverProject.org) programs and interactive exhibits expand public understanding of the Hudson River estuary and inspire people to appreciate the ecosystem they live in. An intimate view of what is at the waterfront and beneath the surface contributes to a sense of well-being for urban residents and to the perception of New York City as a viable place in which to live and work. But most important, to me, is the River Project's oyster restoration project, which gets hundreds of people involved in trying to clean up the waterways, an important approach to structuring citizen participation.

According to the Web page of the Southold Project in Aquaculture Training (counties.cce.cornell.edu/suffolk/spat/home.html), the program "was created to encourage community members to become stewards of their environment and to restore shellfish to the bays." In other words, as it was explained to me by the head of the SPAT program, Kim Tetrault, the volunteers are not there to restore the shellfish so much as the shellfish-restoration program is there to convince volunteers to become stewards of the enivronment.

The mission of Transportation Alternatives (TransAlt.org) is to reclaim New York City's streets from the automobile, and to advocate for bicycling, walking, and public transit as the best means of transportation. From my perspective, this equates with providing a more livable, more vibrant, healthier, happier, and more sustainable city in which the public space, specifically the streetscape, is dedicated to the people who live in it, not to the machines that travel through it. TA has helped win numerous improvements for cyclists and pedestrians and has been the leading voice for reducing car use in the city. Creating a cycling-friendly city means changing the overall transportation stystem, which, even in mass transit–centered New York City, is still dominated by the private automobile.

Youth Ministries for Peace and Justice (YMPJ.org), founded in 1994, has the mission of rebuilding the environmentally and fiscally impoverished neighborhoods of Bronx River and Soundview/Bruckner in the South Bronx by preparing young people to become prophetic voices for peace and justice. They accomplish this through political education, spiritual formation, and youth and community development and organizing. One youth leader from YMPJ said to me, "All my parents want to do is get out of our neighborhood, but I want to stay and make it better."

The organizations discussed above (and the others below) are a pretty diverse sampling, yet it may well turn out that they don't address your specific environmental concern or area—in which case, it's up to you!

Gather together a group of your friends and neighbors. Start a blog that concerns itself with action rather than talk. We need the blogosphere to move from being a chat-o-sphere to an act-o-sphere. Offer to give talks at schools. Write an op-ed for your local paper. Remember to be loving and kind to those who at first disagree with your ideas.

Here are some resources you may find helpful if you want to learn to effect change on your own:

NetAction's self-guided training course, an introduction to Internet outreach and advocacy: www.netaction.org/training/index.html.

The Student Environmental Action Coalition Organizing Guide (good for nonstudents, too): seac.org/sog/index.shtml.

Rules for Radicals, by Saul Alinsky.

Grassroots: A Field Guide for Feminist Activism, by Jennifer Baumgardner and Amy Richards.

Building Powerful Community Organizations: A Personal Guide to Creating Groups That Can Solve Problems and Change the World, by Michael Jacoby Brown.

Momentum: Igniting Social Change in the Connected Age, by Allison Fine.

Generation Change: Roll Up Your Sleeves and Change the World, by Zach Hunter.

Building Communities from the Inside Out: A Path Toward Finding and Mobilizing a Community's Assets, by John P. Kretzmann and John L. McKnight.

The One-Hour Activist: The 15 Most Powerful Actions You Can Take to Fight for the Issues and Candidates You Care About, by Christopher Kush.

Against the Stream: A Buddhist Manual for Spiritual Revolutionaries, by Noah Levine.

The Impossible Will Take a Little While: A Citizen's Guide to Hope in a Time of Fear, by Paul Loeb.

How to Save the World in Your Spare Time, by Elizabeth May.
The Lifelong Activist: How to Change the World Without Losing Your Way, by Hillary Rettig.
Taking On the System: Rules for Radical Change in a Digital Era, by Markios Moulitsas Zúniga.

Below are resources providing background and suggestions for lifestyle change and collective action more specific to the issues raised in each chapter of the book.

CHAPTERS 1 AND 2 (BACKGROUND TO OUR ENVIRONMENTAL CRISES)

Perhaps the most important document you can read to understand climate change is the "Fourth Assessment Report of the Intergovernmental Panel on Climate Change." The entire report runs into the thousands of pages, but you can find a short summary for policy makers at www.ipcc.ch/pdf/assessment-report/ar4/syr/ar4_syr_spm.pdf.

You can also read reports and papers by the United States's most senior climate scientist, Jim Hansen, at www.columbia.edu/~jeh1.

Excellent environmental blogs and Web pages for background on climate change and other environmental issues include:

> Worldchanging.com, which inspires "readers around the world with stories of the most important and innovative new tools, models and ideas for building a bright green future."
> Grist's environmental news and commentary, at gristmill.grist.org.
> The blog of former acting assistant secretary of energy for energy efficiency and renewable energy in the Clinton administration, Joseph Romm, at climateprogress.org.
> The website of the Worldwatch Institute, an independent research organization recognized by opinion leaders around the world for its accessible, fact-based analysis of critical global issues, www.worldwatch.org.

You can find information on the websites of the big-tent environmental organizations, such as:

Natural Resources Defense Council, www.nrdc.org.
The Union of Concerned Scientists, www.ucsusa.org.
Environmental Defense Fund, www.edf.org.

BOOKS

From Apocalypse to Way of Life: Environmental Crisis in the American Century, by Frederick Buell.

Collapse: How Societies Choose to Fail or Succeed, by Jared Diamond.

An Inconvenient Truth: The Planetary Emergency of Global Warming and What We Can Do About It, by Al Gore.

Peak Everything: Waking Up to the Century of Declines, by Richard Heinberg.

Field Notes from a Catastrophe: Man, Nature, and Climate Change, by Elizabeth Kolbert.

Earth: The Sequel: The Race to Reinvent Energy and Stop Global Warming, by Fred Krupp and Miriam Horn.

The Long Emergency: Surviving the End of Oil, Climate Change, and Other Converging Catastrophies of the Twenty-first Century, by James Howard Kunstler.

The Revenge of Gaia: Earth's Climate Crisis and the Fate of Humanity, by James Lovelock.

Six Degrees: Our Future on a Hotter Planet, by Mark Lynas.

The End of Nature, by Bill McKibben.

The End of the Wild, by Stephen M. Meyer.

With Speed and Violence: Why Scientists Fear Tipping Points in Climate Change, by Fred Pearce.

The Song of the Dodo: Island Biogeography in an Age of Extinction, by David Quammen.

Hell and High Water: Global Warming—the Solution and the Politics—and What We Should Do, by Joseph Romm.

Break Through: From the Death of Environmentalism to the Politics of Possibility by Michael Shellenberger and Ted Nordhaus.

The World Without Us, by Alan Weisman.

The Future of Life, by E. O. Wilson.

State of the World 2008: Toward a Sustainable Global Economy, by the WorldWatch Institute.

CHAPTERS 3 AND 4 (NOT TRASHING RESOURCES)

Disposability is the main culprit when it comes to trashing our resources. We've seen that 80 percent of our products are designed to be used once. Meanwhile, 40 percent of our trash is some form of packaging. The energy and resources used to support a throwaway-product-based economy is simply not sustainable. We have to find better ways.

To see all the things I did to reduce trash, go to noimpactman.typepad.com/blog/2008/04/lv-grn-42-ways.html.

To read about getting rid of junk mail, go to noimpactman.typepad.com/blog/2007/05/stoppoing_thejuhtml.

To read about using a glass jar as a replacement for plastic water bottles and coffee cups, go to noimpactman.typepad.com/blog/2007/07/my-ultra-cool-r.html.

Since food waste rotting in landfills is the second-largest source of methane emissions, we can make a big difference by composting. Learn how to compost at noimpactman.typepad.com/blog/2007/03/wake_up_and_sme.html and noimpactman .typepad.com/blog/2007/07/slimy-pets-to-e.html.

If you want to get involved in eliminating one kind of paper trash, consider what Greenpeace has to say on the subject:

> Kleenex, one of the most popular brands of tissue products in the world, contributes to the destruction of ancient forests. Its manufacturer, the Kimberly-Clark corporation, has been unwilling to improve its practices, continuing to rely on paper and pulp made from clearcut ancient forest including North America's Boreal forest. Kimberly-Clark clears these ancient forests, essential in fighting climate change and providing home to wildlife like caribou, wolves, eagles and bears, into products that are flushed down the toilet or thrown away.

Greenpeace runs a campaign against the clearing of ancient forests to make facial tissue; get involved at kleercut.net/en.

GAIA (www.no-burn.org), the Global Anti-Incineration Alliance, is a worldwide alliance of nonprofit organizations and individuals who recognize that our planet's finite resources, fragile biosphere, and the health of people and other living beings are endangered by polluting and inefficient production practices and health-threatening disposal methods.

Sierra Club's National Zero Waste Committee (www.sierraclub.org/committees/zerowaste) aims to lead the transition from traditional end-of-pipe waste "diversion" programs provided by local governments to "cradle to cradle" recycling systems that are designed, financed, and managed by producers. Their goal is to drive improvements in product design, stimulate local economics, and reduce climate-change impacts of transportation- and energy-intensive product chains.

Zero Waste International Alliance (www.zwia.org) works toward a world without waste through public education and practical application of Zero Waste principles.

The Grassroots Recycling Network (www.grrn.org) is comprised of educators on and proponents of the Zero Waste philosophy.

The Algalita Marine Research Foundation (www.algalita.org) studies the effects of plastic pollution and debris in the world's oceans.

Beth Terry's excellent blog about plastics in the waste stream: www.fakeplasticfish.com.

BOOKS

Good Stuff? A Behind-the-Scenes Guide to the Things We Buy, by Brian Halweil.
Gone Tomorrow: The Hidden Life of Garbage, by Heather Rogers.

Garbage Land: On the Secret Trail of Trash, by Elizabeth Royte.
Waste and Want: A Social History of Trash, by Susan Strasser.

CHAPTER 5 (TRANSPORTATION, LIVABLE CITIES, AND LAND USE)

Simple, if not easy: live near your work or work near where you live. For your own health and the health of the planet, walk. If you can't walk, bike. If you can't bike, use public transit. If you can't use public transit, carpool. If you can't carpool, get a more energy-efficient car. Also, fly less. Like I said: simple. Maybe not easy.

The National Center for Bicycling and Walking: www.bikewalk.org.

League of American Bicyclists: www.bikeleague.org.

How not to get hit by cars, and other important lessons on bicycle safety: bicyclesafe.com.

The National Alliance of Public Transportation Advocates (www.napta .net) represents local transit coalitions that support increasing federal investment in public transportation.

The Environmental Protection Agency's Green Car Guide: www.epa .gov/greenvehicles.

GreenCar.com provides car enthusiasts, environmentalists, and everyday consumers with information about green vehicles, energy, and technologies.

Carpooling matchmakers: www.rideamigos.com and www.erideshare.com.

The Livable Streets Network (www.livablestreets.com) seeks to reenvision our cities, reversing decades of automobile-dominated planning and policy to create healthier, more sustainable urban environments. Their blog serves as daily news source, online community, and political mobilizer.

Join Transporation for America's call on Congress to boost our economy and invest in the future with smart transportation investments: t4america.org.

BOOKS

Divorce Your Car! Ending the Love Afffair with the Automobile, by Katie Alvord.
How to Live Well Without Owning a Car: Save Money, Breathe Easier, and Get More Mileage Out of Life, by Chris Balish.
Farewell, My Subaru: An Epic Adventure in Local Living, by Doug Fine.
Asphalt Nation: How the Automobile Took Over America and How We Can Take It Back, by Jane Holtz Kay.
The Geography of Nowhere, by James Howard Kuntsler.
Biking to Work, by Rory McMullan.

CHAPTER 6 (EATING SUSTAINABLY)

The No Impact version of the sustainable eating plan: a diet that is local, unfrozen and unprocessed, seasonal, organic or near-organic, has no packaging, and is based on mostly grain and vegetables, including little or no beef, dairy, or fish (read the rationale at noimpactman.typepad.com/blog/2007/07/the-no-impact-s.html).

For guidance on becoming a vegetarian: the Vegetarian Resource Group (www.vrg.org) and Go Veg! (www.goveg.com).

To learn to eat local: the Eat Local Challenge (www.eatlocalchallenge.com).

To find farmers' markets, family farms, and other sources of sustainably grown food in your area, where you can buy produce, grass-fed meats, and many other goodies: Local Harvest (www.localharvest.org).

To grow your own organic produce: Vegetable Garden Guru (www.vegetable gardeningguru.com) and Grow Better Veggies (loveapplefarm.typepad.com/growbetterveggies).

Eat locally in the winter by learning methods for preserving the summer's bounty, such as canning, drying, and freezing: www.preservefood.com.

The Center for Food Safety (www.centerfoodsafety.org) is a nonprofit public interest and environmental advocacy membership organization using multifaceted strategies, including legal actions, grassroots organizing, submission of policy comments, and public education to accomplish its goals of challenging harmful food-production technologies and promoting sustainable alternatives.

Community Food Security Coalition (www.foodsecurity.org) advocates for all community residents' ability to obtain a safe, culturally acceptable, nutritionally adequate diet through a sustainable food system that maximizes community self-reliance and social justice.

BOOKS

Uncertain Peril: Genetic Engineering and the Future of Seeds, by Claire Hope Cummings.

Food Not Lawns: How to Turn Your Yard into a Garden and Your Neighborhood into a Community, by Heather Coburn Flores.

Sharing the Harvest: A Citizen's Guide to Community Supported Agriculture, by Elizabeth Henderson and Robyn Van En.

Food Fight: The Citizen's Guide to a Food and Farm Bill, by Daniel Imhoff.

The Revolution Will Not Be Microwaved: Inside America's Underground Food Movements, by Sandor Ellix Katz.

Animal, Vegetable, Miracle: A Year of Food Life, by Barbara Kingsolver.

Grub: Ideas for an Urban Organic Kitchen, by Anna Lappé.

Getting a Grip, Clarity, Creativity, and Courage in a World Gone Mad, by Frances Moore Lappé.

Hope's Edge: The Next Diet for a Small Planet, by Frances Moore Lappé and Anna Blythe Lappé.

The Meat You Eat: How Corporate Farming Has Endangered America's Food Supply, by Ken Midkiff.

Food Politics: How the Food Industry Influences Nutrition and Health, by Marion Nestle.

What to Eat, by Marion Nestle.

In Defense of Food, by Michael Pollan.

The Omnivore's Dilemma, by Michael Pollan.

Second Nature, by Michael Pollan.

The End of Food, by Paul Roberts.

Appetite for Profit: How the Food Industry Undermines Our Health and How to Fight Back, by Michele Simon.

The 100-Mile Diet: A Year of Local Eating, by Alisa Smith and J. B. Mackinnon.

Closing the Food Gap: Resetting the Table in the Land of Plenty, by Mark Winne.

CHAPTER 7 (CONSUMING INCONSPICUOUSLY)

The No Impact approach to sustainable consumption? Don't buy anything new except for socks and underwear (see rules at noimpactman.typepad.com/blog/2007/03/if_im_dead_tomo.html). On the other hand, I could have all the fun I wanted at flea markets and thrift stores and other sources of secondhand goods.

Sign the Compact (sfcompact.blogspot.com), a nonconsumer pledge to: (1) go beyond recycling in trying to counteract the negative global, environmental, and socioeconomic impacts of U.S. consumer culture, resist global corporatism, and support local businesses, farms, etc.; (2) reduce clutter and waste in our homes; and (3) simplify our lives.

Freecycle (www.freecycle.org) is an online free-stuff network, the mission of which is to "build a worldwide gifting movement that reduces waste, saves precious resources and eases the burden on our landfills while enabling our members to benefit from the strength of a larger community."

Find a clothing swap near you: www.swaporamarama.org.

Freegans (freegan.info) engage in "a total boycott of an economic system where the profit motive has eclipsed ethical considerations and where massively complex systems of production ensure that all the products we buy will have detrimental impacts most of which we may never even consider. Thus, instead of avoiding the purchase of products from one bad company only to support another, we avoid buying anything to the greatest degree we are able." Dumpster diving features high on their list of strategies.

According to the Simple Living Network (www.simpleliving.net), "voluntary simplicity" is about living an examined life, one in which you have determined what is important, or "enough," for you, and discarding the rest. The network provides resources, tools, examples, and contacts for conscious, simple, healthy, and restorative living.

The Church of Stop Shopping (www.revbilly.com) is a cheeky, exuberant advocacy group spreading the Stop Shopping Gospel. Headed by the charismatic Reverend Billy, they conduct street actions, organize retail interventions, and have even been known to conduct cash-register exorcisms.

For the best guide to organizations that deal with consumption-based issues, go to the resource page on Annie Leonard's Story of Stuff site: www.storyofstuff.com/resources.html.

BOOKS

The Circle of Simplicity: Return to the Good Life, by Cecile Andrews.

Slow Is Beautiful: New Visions of Community, Leisure, and Joie de Vivre, by Cecile Andrews.

Consumed: How Markets Corrupt Children, Infantilize Adults, and Swallow Citizens Whole, by Benjamin R. Barber.

Biomimiery: Innovation Inspired by Nature, by Janine Benyus.

The Consumer's Guide to Effective Environmental Choices: Practical Advice from the Union of Concerned Scientists, by Michael Brower.

Affluenza: The All-Consuming Epidemic, by John de Graaf.

Take Back Your Time: Fighting Overwork and Time Poverty in America, by John de Graaf.

How Much Is Enough? The Consumer Society and the Future of the Earth, by Alan Durning.

Voluntary Simplicity: Toward a Way of Life That Is Outwardly Simple, Inwardly Rich, by Duane Elgin.

Un-Jobbing: The Adult Liberation Handbook, by Michael Fogler.

Manufacturing Consent: The Political Economy of the Mass Media, by Edward S. Herman and Noam Chomsky.

We Know What You Want: How They Change Your Mind, by Martin Howard.

The High Price of Materialism, by Tim Kasser.

Psychology and Consumer Culture: The Struggle for a Good Life in a Materialistic World, edited by Tim Kasser and Allen D. Kanner.

No Logo: No Space, No Choice, No Jobs, by Naomi Klein.

Culture Jam: How to Reverse America's Suicidal Consumer Binge—And Why We Must, by Kalle Lasn.

Not Buying It: My Year Without Shopping, by Judith Levine.

Cradle to Cradle: Remaking the Way We Make Things, by William McDonough and Michael Braugart.

Deep Economy: The Wealth of Communities and the Durable Future, by Bill McKibben.

Radical Simplicity: Small Footprints on a Finite Earth, by Jim Merkel.

Born to Buy: The Commercialized Child and the New Consumer Culture, by Juliet B. Schor.

The Overspent American, by Juliet B. Schor.

The Overworked American, by Juliet B. Schor.

Made to Break: Technology and Obsolescence in America, by Giles Slade.

The Not So Big Life: Making Room for What Really Matters, by Sarah Susanka.

CHAPTER 8 (REDUCING HOUSEHOLD ENERGY USE)

Off the Grid (www.offthegrid.com) provides resources for energy independence using solar, wind, and micro-hydroelectricity.

If you can't go off the grid, you may still be able to choose a Green-e (www.green-e.org) certified electricity provider that generates at least half its power from wind, solar, and other clean energy sources. Even if you don't have the option to select a supplier, you may still be able to support renewable energy through an option on your electricity bill.

Or go to the Natural Resource Defense Council's (NRDC) guide to buying clean energy: www.nrdc.org/air/energy/gcleanen.asp.

The U.S. Department of Energy also provides information on green power providers, product offerings, consumer protection issues, and policies affecting green power markets: apps3.eerc.energy.gov/greenpower.

You can find tips for making your home and lifestyle more energy efficient and less carbon intense from the NRDC (www.nrdc.org/greenliving/toolkit.asp) and from the U.S. Environmental Protection Agency (www.energystar.gov/homeimprovement).

BOOKS

The Homeowner's Guide to Renewable Energy: Achieving Energy Independence Through Solar, Wind, Biomass, and Hydropower, by Dan Chiras.

The Complete Guide to Reducing Energy Costs, edited by Consumer Reports.

Big Coal: The Dirty Secret Behind America's Energy Future, by Jeff Goodell.

Powerdown: Options and Actions for a Post-Carbon World, by Richard Heinberg.

The Carbon-Free Home: 36 Remodeling Projects to Help Kick the Fossil-Fuel Habit, by Stephen and Rebekah Hren.

The Renewable Energy Handbook: A Guide to Rural Energy Independence, Off-Grid and Sustainable Living, by William H. Kemp.

The Home Energy Diet: How to Save Money by Making Your House Energy-Smart, by Paul Scheckel.

Power to the People: How the Coming Energy Revolution Will Transform an Industry, Change Our Lives, and Maybe Even Save the Planet, by Vijay V. Vaitheeswaran.

The Homeowner's Guide to Energy Independence: Alternative Power Sources for the Average American, by Christine Woodside.

CHAPTER 9 (GIVING BACK)

In the No Impact project, giving back was about trying to create positive environmental impact. This can be as simple as committing to picking up garbage once a week on your local riverbank or seashore or getting involved with and helping one of the organizations metioned above.

Tithing is also an excellent way of giving back. Read about how charitable giving has a positive effect on the person doing the giving at noimpactman.typepad.com/ blog/2007/11/it-pays-to-be-c.html. Read Pete Singer's excellent article on how we could solve world poverty if we each tithed just 10 percent of our incomes: www .utilitarian.net/singer/by/20061217.htm.

Last, here is a forty-step list, compiled by readers of my blog, of things you can do to become an environmentally engaged citizen: noimpactman.typepad.com/ blog/2008/08/50-ways-to-go-g.html.

Notes

I: HOW A SCHLUB LIKE ME GETS MIXED UP IN A STUNT LIKE THIS

6 *Kyoto Protocol*: United Nations, "Kyoto Protocol to the United Nations Framework Convention on Climate Change," 1998; unfccc.int/resource/docs/convkp/kpeng.pdf (accessed December 8, 2008).

8 *polar bears*: Will Iredale, "Polar Bears Drown as Ice Shelf Melts," *Times Online*, December 18, 2005; www.timesonline.co.uk/tol/news/uk/article767459.ece (accessed December 8, 2008).

10 *reduce greenhouse gas emissions by 80 percent . . . by 2050*: Intergovernmental Panel on Climate Change, "Climate Change 2007: Synthesis Report," November 2007; www.ipce.ch/pdf/assessment-report/ar4/syr/ar4_syr.pdf (accessed December 8, 2008).

10 *"reposition global warming as a theory, rather than fact"*: Al Gore, perf., *An Inconvenient Truth*, dir. Davis Guggenheim (Lawrence Bender Productions, 2006).

11 *patch of floating plastic garbage*: Algalita Marine Research Foundation; www.algalita.org.

11 *14,000 Canadian lakes*: Lester R. Brown, *Eco-Economy: Building on Economy for the Earth* (New York: W. W. Norton, 2001).

11 *32 million acres of woodland we chop down*: Food & Agriculture Organization of the United Nations, "Deforestation Continues at an Alarming Rate," FAO Newsroom, November 14, 2005; www.fao.org/newsroom/en/news/2005/1000127/index.html (accessed December 8, 2008).

11 *one in four kids who live in the South Bronx*: New York University School of Medicine and Robert F. Wagner Graduate School of Public Service, "South Bronx Environmental Health and Polity Study"; www.med.nyu.edu/SBEHPS (accessed December 8, 2008).

11 *an array of health problems*: Collaborative on Health and the Environment, "CHE Toxicant and Disease Database"; database.healthandenvironment.org (accessed December 8, 2008).

2: DAY ONE AND THE WHOLE THING IS A BIG MISTAKE

23 *4,000 plastic diapers*: Joyce A. Smith and Norma Pitts, "The Diaper Decision: Not a Clear Issue," Ohio State University, July 2, 2001; www.mindfully.org/ Plastic/Diaper-Not-Clear.htm (accessed December 8, 2008).

26 *"hedonic treadmill"*: Michael W. Eysenck, *Happiness: Facts and Myths* (New York: Psychology Press, 1994).

26 *Menominee tribe of Wisconsin*: William McDonough and Michael Braungart, *Cradle to Cradle: Remaking the Way We Make Things* (New York: North Point Press, 2002).

28 *180,000 more people move into urban centers every day*: Anna Tibaijuka, "Urban Millennium," United Nations Human Settlements Programme, June 8, 2001; www.unhabitat.org/istanbul+5/booklet3.pdf (accessed December 8, 2008).

28 *in New York, the average citizen's per capita carbon emissions*: Jonathan Dickinson, "Inventory of New York City Greenhouse Gas Emissions," New York City Mayor's Office of Long-Term Planning and Sustainability, April 2007; www.nyc.gov/ html/om/pdf/ccp_report041007.pdf (accessed December 8, 2008).

28 *80 percent of Manhattan's air pollution*: Environmental Defense Fund, "New York City Faces a Transit Crisis," November 20, 2008; www.edf.org/page/cfm? tagID=19899 (accessed December 8, 2008).

28 *highest risk in the country*: U.S. PIRG Education Fund, "Dangers of Diesel: How Diesel Soot and Other Air Toxins Increase Americans' Risk of Cancer," October 2002; static.uspirg.org/usp.asp?id2=8122&id3=USPIRG& (accessed December 8, 2008).

28 *9 billion pounds of garbage*: New York City Police Department, "Chapter 10: Solid Waste and Sanitation Services," *Public Safety Answering Center II*, August 18, 2008; www.nyc.gov/html/nypd/downloads/pdf/public_information/10_ chapter_10_solid_waste.pdf (accessed December 8, 2008).

28 *27 billion gallons of raw sewage*: Natural Resources Defense Council, "New York City to Clean Up Waterways by Greening Roadways and Roofs," January 30, 2008; www.nrdc.org/media/2008/080130.asp (accessed December 8, 2008).

28 *an entire 1 percent*: Dickinson, "Inventory of New York City Greenhouse Gas Emissions."

30 *Diapers . . . make up 4 percent of our trash*: Real Diaper Association, "Diaper Facts"; www.realdiaperassociation.org/diaperfacts.php (accessed December 8, 2008).

3: WHAT YOU THINK WHEN YOU FIND YOUR LIFE IN THE TRASH

36 *4.6 pounds of trash per day*: U.S. Environmental Protection Agency, "Municipal Solid Waste Generation, Recycling, and Disposal in the United States: Facts and

Figures for 2006"; www.epa.gov/epawaste/nonhaz/municipal/pubs/msw06.pdf (accessed December 8, 2008).

39 *food packaging makes up 20 percent of our solid waste*: Kenneth Marsh and Betty Bugusu, "Food Packaging: Roles, Materials, and Environmental Issues," *Journal of Food Science*, April 2007; members.ift.org/NR/rdonlyres/C3FC4F7C-BE99 -4124-BA67-A5C3A77D1B05/0/FoodPkgEnviron.pdf (accessed December 8, 2008).

48 *80 percent of our products*: Heather Rogers, *Gone Tomorrow: The Hidden Life of Garbage* (New York: New Press, 2005).

48 *4.8 million tons—nearly 10 billion pounds*: U.S. Environmental Protection Agency, "Municipal Solid Waste in the United States: 2007 Facts and Figures"; www .epa.gov/epawaste/nonhaz/municipal/pubs/msw07-rpt.pdf (accessed December 8, 2008).

48 *Kimberly-Clark, just one of the many companies*: Natural Resources Defense Council, "Paper Industry Laying Waste to North American Rainforests," December 2, 2007; www.nrdc.org/land/forests/tissue.asp (accessed December 8, 2008).

49 *827 million tons of carbon dioxide*: U.S. Department of Agriculture (Northern Institute of Applied Carbon Science), "Forests Absorb Carbon Dioxide," May 23, 2008; nrs.fs.fed.us/niacs/forests (accessed December 8, 2008).

4: IF ONLY PIZZA DIDN'T COME ON PAPER PLATES

53 *taxed or restricted plastic bags*: Brian Halweil, "Good Stuff? A Behind-the-Scenes Guide to Things We Buy," Worldwatch Institute, 2004; www.worldwatch.org/ system/files/GS000.pdf (accessed December 8, 2008). See also Lisa McLaughlin, "Paper, Plastic or Prada?" *Time*, August 2, 2007; www.time.com/time/magazine/ article/0,9171,1649301,00.html (accessed December 8, 2008); and BBC News, "Irish Bag Tax Hailed Success," August 20, 2002; www.bbc.co.uk/1/hi/world/ europe/2205419.stm (accessed December 8, 2008).

53 *4 to 5 trillion plastic bags*: Alana Herro, "New Bans on Plastic Bags May Help Protect Marine Life," Worldwatch Institute, January 9, 2008; www.worldwatch .org/node/5565 (accessed December 8, 2008).

53 *less than 1 percent*: Halweil, "Good Stuff?"

53 *4 million tons*: U.S. Environmental Protection Agency, "Municipal Solid Waste in the United States: 2007 Facts and Figures"; www.epa.gov/epawaste/nohaz/ municipal/pubs/msw07-rpt.pdf (accessed December 8, 2008).

54 *wind carries an estimated 1 percent*: The Allen Consulting Group, "Phasing Out Light-Weight Plastic Bags: Costs and Benefits of Alternative Approaches," Environment Protection and Heritage Council of Australia, May 2006; www.ephc .gov.au/sites/default/files/PS_PBag_Rpt__ACG_Phasing_out_light_weight_ plastic_bags_CBA_200605.pdf (accessed December 8, 2008).

54 *the beaches of Long Island*: Edward Laws, *Aquatic Pollution: An Introductory Text* (New York: Wiley, 2000).

54 *46,000 pieces of plastic*: United Nations Environmental Programme, "Action Urged to Avoid Deep Trouble in the Deep Seas," June 16, 2006; www.unep.org/ Documents.Multilingual/Default.asp?DocumentID=480&ArticleID=5300&l=en (accessed December 8, 2008).

54 *"garbage patch"*: Charles Moore, "Great Pacific Garbage Patch: Plastic Turning Vast Area of Ocean into Ecological Nightmare," *Santa Barbara News*, October 27, 2002; www.mindfully.org/Plastic/Ocean/Pacific-Garbage-Patch27oct02.htm (accessed December 8, 2008).

54 *97 percent of Laysan albatross chicks*: Heidi J. Auman et al., "Plastic Ingestion by Laysan Albatross Chicks on Sand Island, Midway Atoll, in 1994 and 1995," in *Albatross Biology and Conservation*, ed. G. Robinson and R. Gates (Chipping Norton: Surrey Beatty & Sons, 1997); www.mindfully.org/Plastic/Ocean/ Albatross-Plastic-Ingestion1997.htm (accessed December 9, 2008).

55 *one hundred industrial chemicals*: U.S. Centers for Disease Control, *Third National Report on Human Exposure to Environmental Chemicals*, 2005; www.cdc.gov/ exposurereport/pdf/thirdreport_summary.pdf (accessed December 8, 2008).

57 *Intregal Yoga Natural Foods*: www.integralyoganaturalfoods.com (accessed December 8, 2008).

66 *"the notorious 'litterbug'"*: Heather Rogers, *Gone Tomorrow: The Hidden Life of Garbage* (New York: New Press, 2005).

5: HOW TO REDUCE YOUR CARBON FOOTPRINT AND ANGER YOUR MOM AT THE SAME TIME

73 *airline flights account for only 3 percent*: United Nations Environment Programme, "World's First Carbon Neutral Airline Gets on Board UNEP's Climate Initiative," November 20, 2008; www.unep.org/Documents.Multilingual/Default .asp?DocumentID=550&ArticleID=5991&l=en (accessed December 9, 2008).

73 *a single long-haul round-trip billows three tons*: BBC Green, "60 Second Guide to . . . Transport Emissions"; www.bbcgreen.com/Travel/Green-Transport/Sixty -Second-Guide-to-transport-emissions (accessed December 9, 2008).

76 *even riding the subway*: Transportation Alternatives, "Rolling Carbon: Greenhouse Gas Emissions from Commuting in New York City," October 2008; www .transalt.org/files/newsroom/reports/rolling_carbon.pdf (accessed December 9, 2008).

80 *"postitive-feedback loop"*: James Hansen et al., "Target Atmospheric CO_2: Where Should Humanity Aim?" *The Open Atmospheric Science Journal*, vol. 2 (Oak Park, Ill.: Bentham Science Publishers, 2008); www.columbia.edu/~jeh1/2008/ TargetCO2_20080407.pdf (accessed December 9, 2008).

81 *5 percent of the world's population*: United Nations Department of Economic and So-

cial Affairs, Population Division, "Population Database," in *World Population Prospects: The 2006 Revision*, 2007; esa.un.org/unpp/ (accessed December 9, 2008).

81 *largest producer of greenhouse gases*: Jane A. Leggett and Jeffrey Logan, *CRS Report for Congress: China's Greenhouse Gas Emissions and Mitigation Policies*, Federation of American Scientists, Congressional Research Service, September 10, 2008; www.fas.org/sgp/crs/row/FL34659.pdf (accessed December 9, 2008).

81 *25 percent of these emissions*: Lila Buckley, "Carbon Emissions Reach Record High," Earth Policy Institute, 2004; www.earthpolicy.org/Indicators/CO2/2004.htm (accessed December 9, 2008).

81 *one-third of our carbon footprint*: U.S. Department of Energy, Energy Information Administration, *Emissions of Greenhouse Gases in the United States, 2007* (Washington, D.C.: GPO, 2008); ftp://ftp.cia.doe.gov/pub/oiaf/1605/cdrom/pdf/ggrpt/057307.pdf (accessed December 9, 2008).

81 *our driving produces* nearly a full half: John DeCicco and Freda Fung, "Global Warming on the Road: The Climate Impact of America's Automobiles," Environmental Defense Fund, 2006; www.edf.org.documents/5301_Globalwarming ontheroad.pdf (accessed December 9, 2008).

90 *Vonnegut*: Mark Vonnegut on Kurt Vonnegut. Clowes Hall, Butler University, Indianapolis, Indiana, April 2007.

90 *" 'Dad, we are here to help each other' "*: Kurt Vonnegut, "Cold Turkey," *In These Times*, May 10, 2004.

91 *Thanksgiving travel*: American Automobile Association, "AAA Projects Slight Decline in Thanksgiving Travel for First Time Since 2002," November 18, 2008; www.aaanewsroom.net/main/Default.asp?PageSearchEnginePageSize=&Loosen Search=&FileSearchEnginePageSize=10000&ArticleSearchEnginePageSize=& CategoryID=8&ArticleID=649 (accessed December 9, 2008).

91 *243.3 billion vehicle miles*: U.S. Department of Transportation, Federal Highway Administration, "Traffic Volume Trends—November 2007"; www.fhwa.dot .gov/ohim/tvtw/07novtvt/page2.htm (accessed December 9, 2008).

91 *Finland and Ireland combined*: U.S. Environmental Protectoin Agency, "Emission Facts: Greenhouse Gas Emissions from a Typical Passenger Vehicle," February 2005; www.epa.gov/otaq/climate/420f05004.htm (accessed December 9, 2008).

92 *seventy-two minutes a day*: Brian Halweil, "Good Stuff? A Behind-the-Scenes Guide to the Things We Buy," Worldwatch Institute, 2004; www.worldwatch .org/system/files/GS0000.pdf (accessed December 8, 2008).

92 *the average American father spends with his kids*: U.S. Bureau of Labor Statistics, "American Time Use Survey—2006 Results," June 28, 2007; www.bls.gov/news .release/archives/atus_06032008.htm (accessed December 9, 2008).

92 *17 percent of the average American's income*: U.S. Department of Labor, Bureau of Labor Statistics, *Consumer Expenditures in 2005* (Report 998) (Washington, D.C.: GPO, February 2007); mobility.tamu.edu/ums (accessed December 9, 2008).

92 *105 million weeks of vacation time*: David Schrank, and Tim Lomax, "The 2007 Urban Mobility Report," Texas Transportation Institute, September 2007; tti.tamu.edu/documents/mobility_report_2007_wappx.pdf (accessed December 9, 2008).

92 *Every ten minutes we spend commuting*: Robert Putnam, *Bowling Alone: The Collapse and Revival of American Community* (New York: Simon & Schuster, 2001).

92 *the more vehicular traffic . . . the fewer friends*: Joshua Hart, "Driven to Excess: Impacts of Motor Vehicle Traffifc on Residential Quality of Life in Bristol, UK," University of the West of England, April 2008; www.livingstreets.org.uk/cms/downloads/0-driven_to_excess_full_report.pdf (accessed December 9, 2008).

92 *70–80 percent of air pollution*: Jane Holtz Kay, *Asphalt Nation: How the Automobile Took Over America and How We Can Take It Back* (Berkeley: University of California Press, 1998).

93 *the less obese they are*: Mohseni M. Lindstrom, "Means of Transportation to Work and Overweight and Obesity: A Population-Based Study in Southern Sweden," *PubMed* (United States National Library of Medicine), July 17, 2007; www.ncbi.nlm.nih.gov.pubmed/17706273 (accessed December 9, 2008).

93 *24 percent more likely to be happy*: Martin Turcotte, "Like Commuting? Workers' Perceptions of Their Daily Commute," *Statistics Canada*, Cat. No. 11-008, July 11, 2007; www.statcan.gc.ca/pub/11-008-x/2006004/pdf/9516-eng.pdf (accessed December 9, 2008).

94 *"years of happy life"*: Nic Marks et al., "The (Un)Happy Planet Index: An Index of Human Well-Being and Environmental Impact," New Economics Foundation, 2006; www.neweconomics.org/gen/uploads/dl44k145g5scuy453044gqbu 11072006194758.pdf (accessed December 9, 2008).

95 *a coalition led by General Motors*: Bill Bryson, *Made in America* (New York: Harper Perennial, 1996).

6: THE CABBAGE DIET SAVES THE WORLD

107 *I turned for advice*: Real Diaper Association; www.realdiaperassociation.org.

116 *"The Human Route"*: Kwan Um School of Zen, 99 Pound Road, Cumberland, R.I., 02864-2726; www.kwanumzen.org.

117 *fifty-seven different agricultural chemicals*: U.S. Department of Agriculture, Agricultural Marketing Service, *Rules and Regulations*, 7 Code of Federal Regulations Part 205, Vol. 72. No. 199 (October 16, 2007), 58469=59470; www.ams.usda.gov/AMSv1.0/getfile?dDocName=STELPRDC5066629&acct=nosb (accessed December 2, 2008).

118 *the USDA . . . wanted to allow*: Organic Trade Association, "OTA's 2007 Manufacturer Survey: Executive Summary," 2007; www.ota.com/pics/documents/2007ExecutiveSummary.pdf (accessed December 2, 2008).

119 *a couple of real local food hard-asses*: Alisa Smith and J. B. Mackinnon, *Plenty: Eating Locally on the 100-Mile Diet* (New York: Three Rivers Press, 2008). See also their blog: 100milediet.org/category/the-latest.

119 *the average distance food travels from farm to plate*: Brian Halweil, "Home Grown: The Case for Local Food in a Global Market," Worldwatch Paper 163, November 2002, Worldwatch Institute; www.worldwatch.org/system/files/EWP163 .pdf (accessed December 2, 2008).

119 *17 percent of the oil*: Dale Allen Pfeiffer, "Eating Fossil Fuels," Wilderness Publications, October 2004; www.fromthewilderness.com/free/ww3/100303_eating_ oil.html (accessed December 2, 2008). See also U.S. Department of Agriculture, "2007 Farm Bill Theme Paper: Energy and Agriculture 2006," August 8, 2006; www.usda.gov/documents/Farmbill07energy.pdf (accessed December 2, 2008).

121 *Just Food*: justfood.org.

121 *tomatoes grown outdoors in Spain*: AEA Technology Environment, "The Validity of Food Miles as an Indicator of Sustainable Development: Final Report," Department for Environment, Food & Rural Affairs, July 2005; statistics.defra .gov.uk/esg/reports/foodmiles/final.pdf (accessed December 2, 2008).

122 *small, local farms produce more food per acre*: Bill McKibben, *Deep Economy: The Wealth of Communties and the Durable Future* (New York: Times Books, 2007). See also Jan Cottingham, "Small Farms Sustaining Agriculture," *Heifer International World Ark*, September 2004: 6; www.heifer.org/arf/cf/%7BE384D2DB -8638-47F3-A6DB-68BE45A16EDC%7D/04%20SEPT-OCT%20WA.PDF (accessed December 2, 2008).

122 *biggest water consumer*: U.S. Environmental Protection Agency, Nonpoint Source Control Branch, Office of Watersheds, "Nonpoint Pointers: Pointer Number 6: Managing Nonpoint Source Pollution from Agriculture," March 1996; www .epa.gov/nps/facts/point6.htm (accessed December 2, 2008).

122 *the main cause of soil erosion*: U.S. Department of Agriculture, Economic Research Service. "Briefing Rooms: Irrigation and Water Use"; www.ers.usda.gov/Briefing/ WaterUse (accessed December 2, 2008). See also U.S. Fish and Wildlife Service, "Finding Solutions to Habitat Loss," January 2002; www.fws.gov/birds/ documents/HabitatLoss.pdf (accessed December 2, 2008); and U.S. Environmental Protection Agency, "Ag 101: Soil Preparation," September 11, 2007; www.epa.gov/oecaagct/ag101/cropsoil.html (accessed December 2, 2008).

123 *7,900-square-mile dead zone*: Michelle Perez, "Trouble Downstream: Upgrading Conservation Compliance," September 2007: Environmental Working Group; www.ewg.org/files/EWG_Compliance_wholereport.pdf (accessed December 2, 2008).

123 *210 million pounds of fertilizer*: Henry Jackson, "U.S. Corn Boom Has Downside for Gulf," Associated Press, December 17, 2007, Environmental Working Group; www.ewg.org/node/25804 (accessed December 2, 2008).

123 *salmonella outbreak*: "FDA Closing In on Source of Tomato Scare," Associated Press, MSNBC, June 11, 2008; www.msnbc.msn.com/id/25075424 (accessed December 2, 2008).

123 *recall of* E. coli–*tainted spinach*: California Certified Organic Farmers; www.ccof .org.

123 *143 million pounds of beef*: Andrew Martin, "Largest Recall of Ground Beef Is Ordered," *New York Times*, February 18, 2008; www.nytimes.com/2008/02/18/business/18recall.html?ref-us%22 (accessed December 2, 2008).

123 *85 percent of the country's farmland*: U.S. Department of Agriculture, National Agricultural Statistics Service, "Agricultural Statistics 2006"; www.nass.usda.gov/Publications/Ag_Statistics/2006/index.asp (accessed December 2, 2008).

125 *USDA established a national organic standard*: International Food Information Council, "USDA Launches Organic Standards: New Rules Welcomed, But Are Organics Better?" *Food Insight*, May 2003; www.ific.org/foodinsight/upload/May-June-2003-PDF.pdf (accessed December 2, 2008). See also U.S. Department of Agriculture, Food Safety and Inspection Service, "Labeling and Consumer Protection: FSIS Responses to Questions from the National Organic Standards Board (NOSB) Regarding Organic Meat and Poultry Products Labeling," May 2002; www.fsis.usda.gov/oppde/larc/Organic/FSISRespons.htm (accessed December 2, 2008).

126 *as Michael Pollan puts it*: Michael Pollan, *The Omnivore's Dilemma: A Natural History of Four Meals* (New York: Penguin Press, 2007).

126 *environmental effects of . . . 1.5 billion cows*: "Food and Agriculture Organization of the United Nations," in *Livestock's Long Shadow: Environmental Issues and Options* (Rome: FAO, 2006); ftp://ftp.fao.org/docrep/fao/010/A0701E/A0701E00.pdf (accessed December 2, 2008).

126 *oceans would essentially be barren*: Marine Stewardship Council. www.msc.org.

132 *the average American watches four and a half hours of TV a day*: Gary Holmes, "Nielsen Media Research Reports Television's Popularity Is Still Growing," *Nielsen Media Research*, September 21, 2006; www.nielsenmedia.com/nc/portal/site/Public/menuitem.55dc65b4a7d5adff3f65936147a062a0/?vgnextoid=4156527aacccd010VgnVCM100000ac0a260aRCRD (accessed December 2, 2008).

7: CONSPICIOUS NONCONSUMPTION

142 *U.S. gross domestic product has grown 550 percent*: Auggie Tantillo, "New Trade Policy Needed to Restore Health of U.S. Manufacturing," American Manufacturing Trade Action Coalition, April 10, 2008; www.amtacdc.org/SiteCollection Documents/Amtac/Director/New%20Trade%20Policy%20Needed%20to%20Restore%20Health%20of%20US%20Manufacturing%2004%2010%2008.pdf (accessed December 10, 2008).

142 *Just about zero*: Richard Layard, *Happiness: Lessons from a New Science* (London: Penguin, 2006).

142 *40 percent of that growth*: World Institute for Development Economics Research, Income Distribution Database, United Nations University, 2006; www.wider/ unu.edu/research/Database/en_GB/wiid (accessed December 10, 2008).

143 *lasting happiness boost*: Gordon Dickson, "Kinesiology, Happiness and Positive Psychology," Australian Kinesiology Association, 2006; www.akakinesiology.org .au/DesktopModules/ViewDocumentacec.pdf?Club=kinesiology&DocumentID -8F2B8BE1-A198-44E9-B7AE-C9DE31B59B37 (accessed December 10, 2008).

144 *Silicon Valley millionaires*: Gary Rivlin, "In Silicon Valley, Millionaires Who Don't Feel Rich," *New York Times*, August 5, 2007; www.nytimes.com/2007/08/05/ technology/05rich.html?_r=1&fta=y (accessed December 10, 2008).

147 *By 2050 there will be 9 billion people*: United Nations Department of Public Information, News and Media Division, "World Population Will Increase by 2.5 Billion by 2050," Press Release, March 13, 2007; www.un.org/News/Press/ docs/2007/pop952.doc.htm (accessed December 10, 2008).

148 *didn't buy anything . . . for a year*: Judith Levine, *Not Buying It: My Year Without Shopping* (New York: Free Press, 2006).

149 *pursuit of* summum bonum: James Hastings, ed., *A Dictionary of Christ and the Gospels* (Honolulu: University Press of the Pacific, 2004).

149 *"There are two extremes"*: E. H. Brewster, *The Life of Gotama the Buddha* (London: Trubner & Co., 1926).

152 *group called the Compact*: Rachel Kesel, *The Compact*; sfcompact.blogspot.com (accessed December 19, 2008).

158 *the Yahoo group Freecycle*: The Freecycle Network; www.freecycle.org.

8: CLICK AND THE LIGHTS GO OUT

166 *a phenomenon known as "second sleep"*: A. Roger Ekirch, "Dreams Deferred," *New York Times*, February 19, 2006; www.nytimes.com/2006/02/19/opinion/19 ekirch.html?ex=1298005200&en=7a2362011318c171&ei=5090&partner =rssuserland&emc=rss (accessed December 14, 2008).

169 *1.6 billion people . . . still have no access to electricity*: International Energy Agency, "The Developing World and the Electricity Challenge: Investment Needs, Barriers and Prospects," IEA Electricity and Development Workshop, January 17, 2005; www .iea.org/Textbase/work/2005/poverty/blurb.pdf (accessed December 14, 2008).

169 *lack of electricity is closely linked to poverty*: "Électricité de France/Direction de la Prospective et des Relations Internationales," *Electricity for All: Targets, Timetables, Instruments*, Global Energy Network Institute, October 2002; www.geni.org/ globalenergy/library/media_coverage/electricite-de-france/electricity-for-all-- targets-timetables-instuments.shtml (accessed December 14, 2008).

171 *residences use only 37 percent*: U.S. Department of Energy, Energy Information Administration, *Annual Energy Review 2007*, June 2008.

171 *planet Earth's Carboniferous period*: Eric Roston, *The Carbon Age: How Life's Core Element Has Become Civilization's Greatest Threat* (New York: Walker & Company, 2008).

171 *90 percent of atmospheric carbon dioxide*: Jennifer C. McElwain, "Plants as a Force of Nature," *American Scientist* 96, no. 3 (May 2008).

172 *increase our society's energy efficiency*: Robert Socolow et al., "Solving the Climate Problem: Technologies Available to Curb CO_2 Emissions," *Environment* 46, no. 10 (December 2004).

172 *world energy demands are expected to rise by 45 percent*: International Energy Agency, *World Energy Outlook 2008* (Paris: Électricité de France/Direction de la Prospective et des Relations Internationales, November 2008).

173 *we must completely stop using coal within ten years*: Victoria Johnson, "100 Months," New Economics Foundation, July 2008; www.onehundredmonths.org.

173 *20 percent of the world's gross domestic product*: Nicholas Stern, "Stern Review on the Economics of Climate Change," UK Office of Climate Change, January 2007.

179 *the "pot in the pot"*: Alex Steffen, *Worldchanging: A User's Guide for the 21st Century* (New York: Abrams, 2006).

187 *overall well-being of children*: UNICEF, "Child Poverty in Perspective: An Overview of Child Well-being in Rich Countries," in *Innocenti Report Card* 7 (Florence: UNICEF Innocenti Research Centre, 2007).

9: TRYING TO DO ENOUGH GOOD TO OUTWEIGH THE HARM

193 *two-thirds of the world's population will face water scarcity*: Maude Barlow, *Blue Covenant: The Global Water Crisis and the Coming Battle for the Right to Water* (New York: New Press, 2007).

193 *seventy gallons of water every day*: American Water Works Association, "Water Use Statistics"; www.drinktap.org/consumerdnn/Default.aspx?tabid=85 (accessed December 12, 2008).

193 *A full quarter . . . we use to flush our toilets*: U.S. Environmental Protection Agency, "Indoor Water Use in the United States," *WaterSense*; www.epa.gov/WaterSense/pubs/indoor.htm (accessed December 11, 2008).

194 *2.5 trillion gallons a year down the toilet*: U.S. National Wild and Scenic Rivers System, "River and Water Facts," January 1, 2007; www.rivers.gov/waterfacts.html (accessed December 12, 2008).

194 *thirty-six American states will suffer water shortages*: U.S. General Accounting Office, "Freshwater Supply: States' Views of How Federal Agencies Could Help Them Meet the Challenges of Expected Shortages," in *Report to Congressional Requesters* (Washington, D.C.: GPO, July 2003).

194 *people with preventable waterborne diseases*: Maude Barlow, "Where Has All the Water Gone?" *American Prospect*, June 21, 2008; www.prospect.org/cs/articles?article= where_has_all_the_water_gone (accessed December 12, 2008).

194 *More children have died from diarrhea*: Michael Specter, "The Last Drop: Confronting the Possibility of a Global Catastrophe," *The New Yorker*, October 23, 2006.

195 *here in New York City*: Mike Plumb, "Sustainable Raindrops: Cleaning the New York Harbor by Greening the Urban Landscape," Riverkeeper, 2006; www .riverkeeper.org/special/Sustainable_Raindrops_FINAL_2008-01-08.pdf (accessed December 12, 2008).

195 *850 billion gallons of overflow*: Rebecca Sutton, "Down the Drain: Sources of Hormone-Disrupting Chemicals in San Francisco Bay," Environmental Working Group, July 11, 2007; www.ewg.org.book/export/html/20919 (accessed December 12, 2008).

195 *earthworms contained phenol*: Chad A. Kinney et al., "Bioaccumulation of Pharmaceuticals and Other Anthropogenic Waste Indicators in Earthworms from Agricultural Soil Amended with Biosolid or Swine Manure," *Environmental Science and Technology* 42, no. 6 (2008); pubs.acs.org/doi/abs/10.1021/es702304c (accessed December 12, 2008).

195 *endocrine disrupters*: Environmental Working Group, "A Survey of Bisphenol A in U.S. Canned Foods," March 5, 2007; www.ewg.org/reports/bisphenola (accessed December 12, 2008).

196 *"Desalination plants"*: Barlow, "Where Has All the Water Gone?"

202 *Street trees not only absorb CO_2*: Lynne M. Westphal, "Benefits of Trees in an Urban Setting," USDA Forest Service, North Central Research Station (Evanston, Ilinois); na.fs.fed.us/urban/treespayusback/vol2/default%20no%20links.htm (accessed December 12, 2008).

204 *One long-haul flight*: Clean Air Conservancy, "Air Travel CO_2 Emissions"; www .cleanairconservancy.org/calculator_air_info.prp (accessed December 12, 2008).

EPILOGUE: LIFE AFTER THE YEAR WITHOUT TOILET PAPER

213 *"We are in this ridiculous situation"*: Annie Leonard, *Story of Stuff*, dir. Louis Fox, Tides Foundation and Funders Workgroup for Sustainable Production and Consumption, 2007.

219 *"You can change lights"*: Thomas L. Friedman, "Save the Planet: Vote Smart," *New York Times*, October 21, 2007; www.nytimes.com/2007/10/21/opinion/ 21friedman.html.

219 *"What I'm thinking in my head is"*: *Special Election Report: Secrets of the 2008 Campaign*, *Newsweek*, November 2008; www.newsweek.com/id/167581 (accessed December 12, 2008).

Acknowledgments

If there is any one activity that teaches you that we are all intercon-
nected and dependent upon one another, it is the writing of a book
like this one. So many people gave so generously of their time and ex-
pertise in order to make the No Impact project work.

Of course, the first among these people is my wife, Michelle. Neither of us realized just what we'd be getting into. Michelle has been
supportive and enthusiastic all the way. I want to thank Isabella, our
little girl, for choosing us as parents and for teaching us, through the
project and always, about love, openness, adaptability, being in the
moment, and forgiveness. Isabella is forever our teacher. Frankie
the dog needs mention, too, if only because Isabella, at age five, still
calls her "my sister."

Generally, authors tend to give thanks to extended families toward
the end of the acknowledgements. But in the case of *No Impact Man*,
the support of Michelle's and my extended families was more crucial
than in other book projects. Our parents and siblings had to accept our
not traveling to see them, for example, but they have also been more
than generous in their emotional and practical support. Love to Keith
and Beth Beavan, Judy Beavan, and Susan and Todd Oliver. Love also
to Michelle's parents, Eddie and Joan Conlin, and to all Michelle's
brothers and sisters.

I relied heavily on the intellectual, community, and critical-
minded support of the readers of my blog at www.noimpactman.com.
Thank you!

As the writing of this book headed down to the wire, Kate Croft, a recent graduate of New York University, approached me almost out of the blue and said she'd like to help me in whatever way she could. She came into my professional life like an angel. Kate selflessly helped compile and shape this book's appendix and notes. She is the epitome of thoroughness and organization.

There are scores of people who for years have been trying to figure out how we might live more happily and with less environmental impact. Many of them so graciously gave me time, advice, and support. Thanks especially to Bill McKibben, Juliet Schor, Annie Leonard, Betsy Taylor, Michael Shellenberger, Lisa Wise, and Majora Carter. I want to thank Arthur Brooks, now of the American Enterprise Institute, for his intelligent conversation, laughter, and support, and most especially for confirming that the crucial "across the aisle" conversations our country needs are more than possible but also fruitful and meaningful.

My friend Rabbi Steven Greenberg, whom I call "my rabbi" (quotes because I'm not Jewish), offered me numerous philosophical and religious perspectives on the No Impact project. My love and thanks go also to my teachers at the Kwan Um School of Zen: Richard Shrobe, Ken Kessel, Steven Cohen, Bobby Rhodes, and Jane Dobisz. Thank you, too, Elizabeth DiSalvo.

At New York nonprofits and organizations, my gratitude goes to Paul Steely White of Transportation Alternatives, Jacquie Berger of Just Foods, Christine Datz-Romero of the Lower East Side Ecology Center, JT Boehm of the River Trust, Phil Silva of the New School (formerly of Sustainable South Bronx), Alexie Torres-Flemming of Youth Ministries for Peace and Justice, Chris Neidl of Solar One, and Jeremy Friedman and Adam Brock of NYU. Thank you also to the staff of all of the above organizations. And thank you to my friend Kate Zidar.

Laura Gabbert, Justin Schein, and Eden Wurmfeld made a wonderful documentary to complement this book. They became fellow travelers and close friends. To them, adoration. Also, to Impact Partners and the Fledgling Fund, thank you for supporting the film and the outreach effort surrounding the entire project. To Dan Cogan, Diana Barrett, and Emily Verellen, let's change some minds!

Eric Simonoff is quite simply the best, both of agents and of friends. Stephanie Koven, Stephanie Lieberman, Dorothy Vincent, and Eadie Klemm, Eric's colleagues at Janklow & Nesbit, are also the best. Howie Sanders and Thora Leiken of the United Talent Agency, thank you so much, too. For personal support, my gratitude to my best friend of many years, Tanner Freeman, and also to all of Michelle's good friends. Thank you, Helga Grunberg and Hilda Aronson.

And perhaps, most important, my deepest debt of gratitude to those who helped edit and publish the book itself:

Authors Joanna Hershon and Catherine Lloyd Burns for their insightful and helpful comments. FSG editors Denise Oswald and Paul Elie for their wonderful job knocking my words into readability. Jeff Seroy and Sarita Varma for supporting this project from the beginning and making sure this book will, after all, get read. Charlotte Strick for the beautiful cover design and Jonathan Lippincott for the interior. Ed Cohen, my copy editor, for that perfect balance between light hand and smart suggestion. Wah-Ming Chang for overseeing production. And Jessica Ferri and Georgia Cool for keeping all the moving parts greased.

Thank you, everyone!

Index